Serenading the Reluctant Eagle

Serenading the Reluctant Eagle

American Musical Life, 1925-1945

Nicholas E. Tawa

SCHIRMER BOOKS

A Division of Macmillan, Inc.

NEW YORK

Collier Macmillan Publishers

LONDON

85-1680

Schirmer Books
A Division of Macmillan, Inc.
866 Third Avenue, New York, N. Y. 10022

Collier Macmillan Canada, Inc.

Library of Congress Catalog Card Number: 84-5438

Printed in the United States of America

printing number
1   2   3   4   5   6   7   8   9   10

Library of Congress Cataloging in Publication Data

Tawa, Nicholas E.
  Serenading the reluctant eagle.

  Bibliography: p.
  Includes index.
  1. Music—United States—20th century—History and criticism.   2. Music and state—United States.
I. Title.
ML200.5.T38   1984   780′.973   84-5438
ISBN 0-02-871760-0

Contents

Preface

Over the years, music historians have analyzed the lives of the more prominent American composers and the nature of their music. In addition, other writers have supplied us with fascinating accounts of noted conductors, virtuosic instrumentalists, and operatic soloists. Scarcely anybody, however, has paid any attention to the musical public for whom the composers wrote and the musicians performed. The omission has made difficult a true understanding of American culture.

The consequence of this omission from most studies of the years between the two world wars has been especially unfortunate. Incomplete understanding has led to a misinterpretation of this period, a repetition of many of its mistakes, and a deemphasis of its accomplishments.

This book is offered to the reader with the hope that it will abet a fuller comprehension of American musical culture in the twentieth century. It describes how contemporary American art music struggled to exist during the twenties and early thirties, and how the Great Depression seemed poised to wipe it out altogether. But, wonder of wonders, music took a new lease on life. Men and women began to flock to concerts as never before; performing ensembles proliferated; and composers felt they might have a real function to perform in American life. The period of the thirties and early forties has been described as the Golden Age of American music, a time when composers created vital works that audiences greeted with curiosity and which they often learned to enjoy.

How this period of great cultural achievement came about and why it ended is the subject of these pages. First, the composers are allowed to speak of their problems with making a living, with creativity, and with finding performers to play—as well as audiences to listen to—their music. They set forth their artistic attitudes and expectations and reveal the fact that some of them eventually had to accommodate their styles to meet the needs of the American people, while others remained adamantly unyielding in their cultivation of individual expression. Avant-gardist, conservative, and Americanist take equal time to expose their views. Artists like Roger Sessions, Howard Hanson, Aaron Copland, and Virgil Thomson tell what it was like to write music in the years between 1925 and 1945.

The next consideration is the influence of conductors, instrumentalists, singers, managers, and boards of trustees—in short, everybody standing between composer and listener—on the direction music in America has taken. Musicians like Leopold Stokowski, Arturo Toscanini, and Serge Koussevitzky, and managers like Sol Hurok, Arthur Judson, and Ward French were the most powerful musical authorities of the time, deciding what works would be heard and what works would be denied a hearing. On the one hand, their influence was extremely beneficial to our cultural life; on the other hand, they impeded the growth and enrichment of America's own music-making. Also considered is the impact of radio, sound recordings, talking pictures, and critics of the composer and the types of music he wrote. Finally, the essential role played by local, state, and national governments to further the cause of American art music is taken up. Particular attention is given to the Federal Music Project, the brainchild of the first Roosevelt administration, and its encouragement of widespread democratic participation in the musical experience.

An investigation of these years must deliberate on the nature of American audiences. Why did Americans listen to art music? In what ways did they perceive sound as beautiful, or merely pleasing, or puzzling, or even loathsome? How does one explain the astonishing growth of serious-music devotees, from a few thousand in 1925, to several million by 1940? Did the huge increase in listeners vulgarize the excellence of our cultural life? Digging up answers to these questions was the most difficult task facing the author. The fictional audience in composers' and performers' minds had few correspondences with actual people. The real audience was discovered mostly in letters sent to newspapers and periodicals, in mass protest actions against overbearing conductors and overly outrageous compositions, and in person-to-person interviews between the author and individuals who reached adulthood in the years under consideration.

A side consequence of this investigation was a new respect for American audiences. Though their views may not always have coincided with those of composers or conductors, they were equally sincere, equally valid, and equally worthy of attention. To ignore their views, to put them aside as of no consequence, has usually presaged the demise of a healthy music culture; to heed them, to try to reconcile the prerogatives of the artist with the needs of the people, has usually strengthened cultural life. When we examine the musical compositions written between the wars, we clearly see what music remained unloved and why, what music managed to communicate with its audience, and what music achieved the status of the concert-going public's classics. An important conclusion reached is that the integrity of the artistic experience can remain incorrupt, even in those compositions that achieve greatest acceptance. This is the lesson the thirties, in particular, should teach us.

The book concludes with suggestions for strengthening the role of art music in present-day American society. The recommendations are derived from the activities that proved successful in the thirties—with, of course, the expectation that they will be modified to fit current conditions.

Then, Franklin Delano Roosevelt moved quickly and boldly to give musicians employment, composers an ideological framework for their efforts, and citizens musical instruction and performances that increased their faith in democracy and themselves. Today, we dare do no less. Civilization in its present state forms too thin a veneer over the animalism threatening to destroy Western society. Music of excellence ought to be made an indispensable part of our civilization. For our own sake, we must foster it.

1

The Composer Speaks

World War I had ended. The decade of the twenties had arrived. The citizens of the United States were discovering their own authentic voice in jazz, the Broadway musical, and the song and dance pouring from Tin Pan Alley. At the same time, professional performing groups and audiences committed to art music were beginning to reside in the important urban centers. Well-trained and talented art composers increased to more than a handful. (The term "art music," as used in this book, refers to the music of trained musicians that is intended for performance, primarily in a concert or recital hall, or in an opera house. Folk and popular music are not considered "art music" in this context.)

Nevertheless, many of the younger and more forward-looking of the creative artists remained unhappy. Why? Because to be serious musicians and Americans, too, seemed to them an anomaly. They learned that when it came to art music, American ensembles usually performed, and American audiences willingly listened to, European compositions from the past. Contemporary American works, especially the more dissonant ones, remained alien to the general music public. The advanced composers in particular were

1

tempted to see themselves as coming into their own amongst an incurious, even philistine, society that repudiated their efforts.

Several foreign and native critics of American culture were loud on the subject. Quite a few cultured Europeans tended to view the United States as a simpleminded, immature, and inelegant nation. To them, it was peopled by uncivilized buffoons having neither an awareness of the past nor a sense of artistic beauty. This attitude accompanied educated visitors to our shores and grew among many of our own cultivated musicians: instrumentalists, singers, conductors, and composers alike. If our composers failed to hear stories about America's cultural sterility during their years of childhood and adolescence, they certainly were greeted with these tales when they removed themselves to Europe, and Paris, especially, in order to continue their musical studies. They learned from French intellectuals and artists that Paris was the cultural center of the universe, New York City a provincial outpost, and the rest of America a barbaric wasteland.

Regrettably, the indictment of the United States had run on for years. In 1862, Louis Moreau Gottschalk, New Orleans pianist and composer, had written of the French:

> There certainly is an intelligent class who read and who know the truth; but it is not the most numerous, nor the most interested in doing us justice. . . . From Talleyrand, who says that "*l'Amérique est un pays du sales cochons et de cochons sales*" [America is a country of dirty and filthy swine], to Zimmerman, director of the piano classes at the Paris Conservatoire, who without hearing me refused to receive me because "*l'Amérique n'était gu'un pays de machines à vapeur*" [America was only a country of steam engines] there is not an eminent man who has not spat his petty spite upon the Americans.[1]

In 1947, the composer Walter Piston, responding to the author's persistent questioning about his Paris years, said: "I guess there were plenty of arched eyebrows about us young Americans and the sort of country we came from. But in the Twenties, maybe they had reason to be skeptical." He then shrugged his shoulders, made an expansive motion with his arms, and refused to continue.

Fortunately, Paul Bowles has written of his life in Paris during the early thirties and provides information about his own thinking during that period. He states, in *Without Stopping* (1972), that he led "the most pleasant of all possible lives" and wished it to go on forever, since "each day lived through . . . was one more day spent outside [the American] prison." On the other hand, he admits: "I was aware of the paranoia in my attitude and that with each succeeding month of absence from the United States I was augmenting it."

He loved Paris because it provided friends sympathetic to his art and boasted composers in the forefront of innovation. He would have seconded Aaron Copland's assertion that in the twenties and thirties the young American composer "had to be 'finished' in Europe. You couldn't be 'finished' in America." Why go to Paris? To this question Copland answered that after World War I, Germany was no longer the "in" country for musicians. Moreover, Paris contained Claude Debussy and Maurice Ravel: "All the new things seemed to be coming from Paris—even before I knew the name of Stravinsky."[2]

In Paris lived a fabulous teacher of musical theory and composition, Nadia Boulanger. American composers flocked to her classroom: Aaron Copland, Virgil Thomson, Walter Piston, Roy Harris, Elie Siegmeister, David Diamond, and Elliot Carter, to name seven of her American students who later became prominent composers. Only a few, and usually older, musicians failed to take up Paris residence during their formative years: Carl Ruggles, Wallingford Riegger, and Roger Sessions, to name three. Ruggles's early musical influences remain unclear. Riegger studied at the Berlin Hochschule für Musik and learned the current musical styles of Central Europe. Sessions studied with Ernst Bloch, then lived in Italy and Germany for several years; Bloch and Germanic composers would blot out any Italian influences. All three composers would write some of the most dissonant, chromatic avant-garde music of the first half of the twentieth century.

Paris was a dizzying experience to the Americans who sojourned there. They had exchanged the provincial world of their adolescence for the stimulating world of André Breton and Paul Valéry in literature, George Braque and Pablo Picasso in art, Le Corbusier in architecture, and Sergei Diaghilev in ballet. Fauvism, dadaism, surrealism, futurism, cubism, and neo-classicism were the slogans of the European avant-gardists living in France. The advanced thinkers these Americans admired shunned established artistic ways

of doing things and insisted on every individual creator's right
to establish his own first traditions.

Consensus existed that music should reflect the spirit of the
modern age, though nobody clearly defined that spirit or agreed
how it was to be realized. Indeed, it seemed that European
composers were promoting a variety of innovative systems, thus
giving modernity a pluralistic face. Arguments were advanced
against tonality, the octave, triadic harmony, and consonance. One
favored the exploration of the artist's inner consciousness; another
insisted music expressed nothing but itself; still another said
music's appropriate contemporary sound was the clang and clash
of machines. Some composers inveighed against the indifference
of the mass of concertgoers, saying that the honest artist could
please only an elect minority.[3] These were a few of the lessons
absorbed by many of the American neophytes. They discovered
that Arnold Schoenberg, in Berlin, and Igor Stravinsky, in Paris,
were the musical yeast around which most of the cultural ferment
seethed. Therefore it was from these two men, and particularly
from Stravinsky, that most of the newcomers got their bearings.
To compose a work comparable to that of one or the other of
the giants became a part of their aim.

It is no wonder the young Marc Blitzstein began writing
assertive pieces which shocked American audiences. The young
George Antheil grew excited when intellectuals like Jean Cocteau
and Ezra Pound approved his advanced musical compositions and
"adopted him as their favorite son." Antheil felt he had arrived.[4]

Even when, in the twenties, composers like Aaron Copland
tried to write music "that Americans . . . could recognize as their
own" and turned to jazz, much of the inspiration came from
Europe. Copland once explained: "Don't forget that it was the
Hungarianness of Bartok that seemed so fascinating; not only was
he writing good modern music, but it was Hungarian in quality.
Stravinsky was very Russian—a Russian composer, not just a
modern composer."[5] That the jazz in Copland's *"Music for the
Theater* (1925), for example, sounded French and, at the same
time, Stravinsky-like did not take away from Copland as an artist.
Surely this sound established his credentials as an American
composer contemporaneous in outlook and style with the European moderns he hungered to emulate. Moreover, it brought
America up to date in its high culture.

The Artistic Stance

When the American composer thought about himself as an artist, he sometimes became anxious about his prerogatives and about the corrupting effect of the masses on great art, and desirous of an understanding from musically erudite and sensitive listeners, however few they might be.

In the following pages, we will examine the concept of the artist as creator, separate and different from the public, and of his works as significant, light-giving expressions uncorrupted by any intent merely to entertain. This picture of the art composer had commenced in nineteenth-century Europe, especially in Germany, where philosophers and men of letters envisioned works of art, and musical compositions in particular, as vehicles for the profoundest human expression, and composers as ultimate spokesmen for humanity.

The huge migration of educated Germans to the United States, beginning around 1848, and the increasing American admiration of Germanic ideas during the same period acclimatized native intellectuals to this concept. One of these intellectuals, John Sullivan Dwight, was an influential writer on music. Dwight also was an adherent of New England transcendentalism, believing in God's immanence in nature and man's spirit, in intuitive reason as the most authentic source of knowledge, and in music as the truest way to apprehend God and inner knowledge. To a great extent, art music was able to live in this rarefied atmosphere owing to its relative isolation from the main currents of American culture, for almost all of its literature, most of its performers, and considerable numbers of its audience were European and especially German.

This artistic viewpoint carried over into the twentieth century and was accepted by many native composers in the twenties, the early thirties, and the decades following World War II. Some, like Roger Sessions and Carl Ruggles, subscribed to it all their lives; others, like Marc Blitzstein, subscribed to it during the years preceding the Great Depression; still others, like Aaron Copland, vacillated between a desire to win over an American audience through music containing recognizable Americanisms and a conflicting desire to speak individually and authentically in a

ROGER SESSIONS. Drawing by Olga Koussevitzky. Courtesy of Countess Anna de Leucthenberg.

strikingly new manner. And, of course, there was George Gershwin, who did not subscribe to it at all.

During the twenties, the need to sweep away the cobwebs of the past seemed urgent, if only to reflect the spirit of the different world that was emerging after World War I. Their studies completed, the young American composers returned to a United States in the midst of tremendous industrial expansion. Whether they liked it or not, their careers were affected by the economic and social changes this expansion necessitated. They, like other Americans, found their economic and social well-being dependent upon the flighty desires of the marketplace. At the same time, whatever their misgivings, they, like other Americans, were expected to take their chances boldly, since nothing attempted was nothing gained.

Certainly, several of the returnees were bold enough, their creative direction chancy enough. The disruptive musical ideas they returned with from Europe had few ties with the tidy, traditional practices of the older generation of musicians. To the general music public, their compositions contained unpleasant music scrubbed clean of mellifluous consonances and gentle lyricism. These composers rejected the vivid colors, rich resonances, and dramatic rhetoric in favor during the previous century. Soon, conservative critics would hurl the accusation of "ultra-modernism" at them and, in reaction, "ultra-modern" would become the watchword of the accused.

These entrepreneurs in novel music declared that their assertive compositions comprehended not an aberration, a here-today-and-gone-tomorrow style, but a revolutionary way of capturing sound, which eventually would come to dominate all twentieth-century art music in the United States. Taking advantage of the spirit of exuberant individualism that prevailed, they demanded liberty to experiment and to travel creatively in whatever direction they wished, untrammeled by conformity to any one principle.

The consequence of this demand was not entirely fortunate for the composer. The citizenry of the United States left him to travel alone along an unmarked track. Few wealthy patrons came forward to aid him financially, supply him with performers, or find subscribers to attend concerts of his music. For the most part, the composer somehow had to support himself in whatever fashion possible. Most of his compositions took on the appearance of speculative ventures involving high risk and small profit. He had to scramble after scarce grants, prizes, and commissions. He also had to court performers; allay the suspicions of boards of trustees; attract and retain an audience; and convince publishers that his works had some value, if not monetary, at least in the realm of prestige.

The American economy was becoming complex and uncontrollable. It seemed robust enough, and yet the threat of its coming apart was ever present. Population growth was unrestrained owing to native fertility and immigration. As a consequence, anyone with a product to sell had to win the approval of larger and larger numbers of customers in order to remain on top of things. The evolving profit–cost system was such that it had to bypass smaller markets in favor of a mass market unbounded by locality or special preferences. The composer, too, experienced the pressure to cater to and satisfy a huge and indiscriminate public. He could either succumb, or rebel and risk neglect. At first, he rebelled. He saw no virtue in compromise. To him, compromise meant pandering to the lowest denominator in musical taste.

As if this were not enough, the music industry swiftly took on giant dimensions and became interlaced with complications that reflected the new capitalism of the twentieth century. Thus, the composer was confronted with art as big business and with artistic success as the bottom line of financial statements. A musical enterprise, whether symphony orchestra or opera company, consisted of a supervising management responsible for hundreds of musicians, dancers, singers, conductors, assistants, stage workers, and employees involved with publicity, hospitality, program notes, the business office, and the box office. Furthermore, there were the complications of big unions and guilds trying to impose their own rules on the musical world.

The danger was great that the younger art composers might disappear in the shuffle. In the middle twenties, few of them had any reputation. Their music was seldom performed or published. Some tried to band together in New York City and establish colonies, however narrow their membership, of advanced composers, enlightened performers, willing patrons, and attentive audiences. These coteries denounced the conservative tastes of the majority of Americans. *Au courant* music lovers talked up the innovations in free tonality, dissonance, and rhythm, and pushed the avant-garde compositions embodying these innovations. Two musicians, Edgard Varèse and Carlos Salzedo, put together the militant International Composers' Guild in 1921. Six years later, Varèse formed the Pan-American Association of Composers. Affiliated with these two organizations were the ultra-modern composers Henry Cowell, Carl Ruggles, and Wallingford Riegger. Guild and Association struggled to mount concerts despite limited finances and tepid support from the musical kingmakers.

In 1923, Claire Reis and composers dissatisfied with the Guild's direction founded the rival League of Composers. It had more solid backing from patrons and performers and, in 1924, had an admirable vehicle for propagating its views, the periodical *Modern*

Music. Aaron Copland, a director of the League, joined with Roger Sessions in 1928, to commence the Copland–Sessions Concerts (1928–31). In 1932, Copland began the Yaddo Festivals.

Though concerts of contemporary music grew in frequency, the public they attracted remained small and confined mostly to an intellectual group living in and around New York City. No sense of connection with the nationwide mass of concertgoers came about. Nor did such a connection seem possible, owing to the persistent divergence in attitudes about what constituted musical excellence and beauty, what culture was all about, and what valuation to give to the past. The ultra-modern composer's unilateral standards, exclusive behavior, and summary rejection of musical roots destroyed communality and ensured aloneness. Because he identified radical change with progress and uncompromising harshness of sound with honesty, he forfeited the hope of a larger audience, which continued to prefer the hundreds of already sanctified compositions from the eighteenth and nineteenth centuries and took pleasure in their smoother harmony, more comprehensible melody, and warmer emotional ambience.

When it was suggested that a viable American art music required some connection with the American land and its mythology, and some reflection of the American people's demotic song and dance, several of the composers demurred. From the beginning of his career, Ruggles insisted he had no American cultural ancestry at all. For years, the composer Walter Piston termed the pursuit of musical Americanism "a wild-goose chase" and advocated, instead, the achievement of a telling yet individual style. Marc Blitzstein, before his proletarianization, termed folk song a "literary music" and the cry for national compositions an appeal, not for a music, but for a program for music. Throughout his life, Roger Sessions thought any national style to be, at best, "a picturesque mannerism. . . . devoid of significant human content" and "outmoded the moment its novelty has gone." To Sessions, nationalism was a prison shutting the creator off from every "genuine and mature impulse." With the rise of Nazism, Sessions equated national feeling with fascism.[6]

By 1931, Copland had turned away from his aggressive jazz-based manner and was writing in a serious, dissonant, abstract style. The authentic American voice he had sought to cultivate for himself and had advised others to seek was a concept shunted to one side, at least temporarily. After hearing the austere Sessions Piano Sonata, he described it as "music of character," universal in style and devoid "of obvious nationalism." Uncompromising music such as this, Copland declared, was the "cornerstone upon which to base an American music."[7] Unfortunately, beautiful as it was to the sophisticated ear, the sonata was not a foundation upon which to base a widely accepted American music.

At times, the anti-nationalistic stance of composers like Ruggles and Sessions, while ostensibly referring to the lack of cultural precedents or to the enforced local idioms of the Nazis, seemed an unconscious rejection of the ideas that composer and public shared cultural responsibility, and that the composer owed something, anything, to his society, other than the vague imperative to tell it the "truth."

What did "truth" imply in musical terms? Composers like Ruggles, Sessions, and the Copland of the early thirties were seen to be creating a private symbolization in sound unshared by most American audiences. The drive for the significant expression of a private experience, however insightful and universal it was declared to be, frequently resulted in no communication at all with the general public. The musical signposts familiar to the usual concertgoer were absent. Complexity replaced directness; innovation, conventionality.

Writing about the absence of sympathy between composer and audience, Arthur Berger states, in his biography of Aaron Copland:

> It is not always easy to distinguish between those difficulties created by the subtlety and intricacy of the intrinsic relations [in a composition] and those created by elements of novelty, such as dissonance and unusual rhythm. Both types of difficulty are often present in great works of art, and it is obvious that any organized group dedicated to their defense, against a general public that is unwilling to take the necessary pains they impose, will end up by encouraging precisely those aspects of creative endeavor. It was to this tendency that Copland responded around 1930. . . . Demotic elements of jazz are relinquished, or at least not overtly expressed, and the feeling content becomes more rarified.[8]

What is interesting about this statement by Berger, an American composer twelve years younger than Copland, who studied with both Piston and Boulanger, is the linking of off-putting music with great works of art and the assumption that a public should be willing to make a toilsome but requisite effort to understand it. Here is exposed the composer's inclination to attribute to an artistic work what he ardently wishes to believe about it—that its virtues are inherent and have nothing to do with an audience's reactions; that when a work's excellence is confirmed by connoisseurs sympathetic to a composer's cause, then the public is duty-bound to empathize with the artistic statement.[9]

Enthusiasm for novelty excluded any responsiveness to the distress of sincere music lovers, many of them newly won over to symphony and opera. Only recently appreciative of Beethoven, Tchaikovsky, and Verdi, they listened in dismay to works like Copland's Symphony for Organ and Orchestra, Antheil's *Ballet Méchanique,* and Sessions's First Symphony, first performed in America in 1925, 1927, and 1927, respectively.

Commenting on the defense of modernity by the League of Composers and the hostile reactions of listeners to the League's concerts, Claire Reis writes: "Because our 'inner group' was somewhat inclined to be fanatic in the cause of modern music, we did not always sympathize quickly with those who did seem actually to suffer."[10] She included Aaron Copland in the "we."

Indeed, in the early 1930s, Copland sometimes showed little pity for sufferers. In 1931, he wrote of his disappointment in a concert he attended. Save for a Sessions work, "it contained no music that was problematical. One felt, sitting there, that music should be either too hard to write about, or else not worth writing about at all, and unfortunately the larger part of this music fell into the latter category." Surprisingly, even after Copland had lived through several years of his second Americanist period, he was still able to say (in 1952): "I should like to call attention to a curious bit of artist psychology: the thought that my music might, or might not, give pleasure to a considerable number of music-lovers has never particularly stirred me. At times I have been vigorously hissed, at other times as vigorously applauded; in both circumstances I remain comparatively unmoved."[11]

Throughout his life, Roger Sessions has been an articulate critic of American audiences and a defender of the rights of the artist. He has never tried to please the public in any way. Instead, he "demands" the listener's "willing ear," "undivided attention," and submission to repeated hearings of a composition. He insists: "The artist's values . . . cannot be those of the market." The artist must make the public "come to his music," for the composer worth his salt "should always retain the courage of" his "own artistic vision" and insist on "the supremacy of real musical imagination." In short, "contemporary music, and in fact any music whatever, is to be judged in terms of music itself, not of circumstances with which no clear connection can be convincingly demonstrated."[12]

In a letter published in the *New York Times,* 11 March 1934, he insists the composer "belongs in a different sphere [from the public] and demands a different set of standards." He must remain "fundamentally indifferent to criticism for the good of his art," since "the destiny of a work of art is inherent in itself and not in individual opinions regarding it. Its momentary success or failure means precisely nothing."

The depreciation of the listener's independent assessment of an artistic work is further expressed in a lecture Sessions delivered at Juilliard in 1949. He rhetorically asked what the listener demands of the composer. Instead of the expected acknowledgment of the listener's rights, Sessions remained obdurate in claiming the artist's sovereignty:

> The listener wants vital experience, whether of a deeply stirring, brilliantly stimulating, or simply entertaining type. If we understand this we should understand, too, that the composer can effectively furnish it only on his own terms. He can persuade others to love only what he loves himself, and can convince only by means of what fully convinces him. It is for this reason that the artist must be completely free, that such a question as I have stated here can ultimately have no importance to him. His obligation is to give the best he can give, wherever it may lead, and to do so without compromise and with complete conviction.[13]

What Session enunciates is the artistic composer's perceived mandate to discover and describe universals by means of unhampered creative activity. The danger is that here the artist may turn into an infallible high priest beholden only to God, while his music is a kind of religious preachment, understood by an elect who are pure in spirit and believed in by the remainder of the public through an act of faith. One result, according to Ned Rorem, is the exclusion of enjoyable, witty, and accessible music. Instead, Rorem sarcastically observes: "There is room for only masterpieces, for only masterpieces have the right to require the intellectual (as opposed to the sensual) concentration and investigation needed for today's 'in' music. Masterpieces are made by the few geniuses born each century. Yet hundreds now compose *in the genius style.*"[14]

The artist's taste becomes so refined it impedes sympathetic interaction with humbler humans. If the composer is always right, arrogance may infiltrate his thinking. As a case in point, Charles Seeger praises the composer Carl Ruggles and highly approves his music, but notes that Ruggles (like Sessions) insisted that "musical value and the expression and communication of it is primarily the function of the composer." Seeger continues, not only does Ruggles know best, he "knows he knows best." He cares nothing about "the social usefulness of his aims or deeds." What he has is the "conviction—sheer arrogant assertion—of value" in his music. During the twenties and early thirties it was possibly a "Jehovah-complex" that drove Ruggles to seek out what "he preferred to call the 'Sublime'." At any rate, his was "a narrow taste, very particular, and quite of the absolutist type, with no gradations."[15]

Any composer who like Ruggles adheres to a specific set of beliefs in his own creativity, attitude, or taste, is one not free to comment on beliefs held by others, and one disposed to evaluate positively only that creation, attitude, and taste corresponding with his own. Thus, Ruggles demoted the highly popular romantic composer Tchaikovsky to the rank of thirteenth- or fourteenth-rate musician, and cruelly denigrated the more conservative, and recently dead, American composer Henry Hadley at a public lecture attended by Hadley's widow, saying: "I thought that music had reached the lowest possible point when I heard the works of John Alden Carpenter. Now, however, I have been examining the scores of Mr. Henry Hadley!"[16]

Paul Bowles writes that in the summer of 1930, Copland insisted Bowles should come with him to visit Sessions, in part to show him a couple of Bowles's compositions. Bowles found Sessions "formidable." After playing the compositions over, "Sessions confessed that he did not find they had any particular merit. 'Not even freshness?' asked Aaron. Sessions shrugged."[17]

In the early 1930s, Marc Blitzstein, still in his dissonant period, found the tuneful Second Symphony of Randall Thompson to be "banal, poor music," full of "canned yearnings," and lacking "taste, fervor, thought, or original touch." Theodore Chanler pronounced the romantic opera *Merry Mount*, by Howard Hanson, to be decadent and soft in fiber, and the non-dissonant opera *Four Saints*, by Virgil Thomson, to be awkward, without creative volition, and completely inert.[18] All these compositions apparently were insufficiently modern in sound.

Olin Downes, *New York Times* music critic, writes that in the early 1930s he recommended a score for performance by the International Society for Contemporary Music, American branch. He identifies neither the score or its composer. Although he and several musicians that he respected found the work beautiful and well constructed, the music was not in the contemporary dissonant style. To Downes's annoyance, the local American composers' committee unanimously turned it down because it was not "modern" enough. Yet, soon thereafter, one conductor after another performed the composition, and it met with widespread favor. Rejection, Downes claims, was owing to an avant-garde clique "of mutual admirationists" biased against music unlike their own.[19]

Intolerance occasionally prevailed among composers of different modernistic persuasions. John Briggs writes that the International Composers' Guild of the twenties was dominated by musicians like Varèse and Ruggles, who were incapable of making concessions. "Once when there were complaints that Composers' Guild programs were 'too advanced,' Messrs. Varèse and Ruggles telephoned each member of the board of directors and told him he was fired. That was how the League of Composers came to be formed by the ex-directors."[20]

Artistic composers of ultra-modern inclination preferred esteem, not criticism. Because their music lacked wide appeal, their stance was one of righteous militancy. In their scale of aesthetic values, whatever was popular was vulgar and somehow tainted, and only what was tainted could become music of the people. Entertaining and pleasing music required nothing of listeners and therefore was necessarily a compromised art unworthy of serious consideration. For this reason, the *Rhapsody in Blue* and *An American in Paris* were shoddy compositions and George Gershwin an inconsequential cobbler of notes. As Paul Rosenfeld, writer on music and champion of the moderns, said of Gershwin: "We remain unconvinced that he has sufficient of the feeling of the artist." Gershwin lacked "the artist's remoteness from material objects," a "selfless aesthetic touch," and the "impulse to organize his material in conformity" with his own individual artistic experience. Possibly he equated Gershwin's music with jazz, which, Rosenfeld claimed, removed the listener from contact with reality, put him into a drug-like state, and became "just another means of escape." To Rosenfeld, the important American composers were Sessions, Ruggles, Harris, Copland, Chavez, Rudhyar, Varèse, and Ornstein. Gershwin was of a "lower unpretentious order," not worthy of "association with artists." Did not Gershwin's *Rhapsody in Blue* sound like "circus-music," and the Piano Concerto, like "Balaam's ass"?[21]

Vernon Duke, who was composing music both of a popular and a serious nature in the 1920s, says his "versatility, far from being a boon," was in reality "infuriating to most musical people." Artistic critics found "something monstrous and unnatural about a composer writing two different kinds of music." He did not wish to be classified "as an ambitious peasant." Therefore:

> Out of an odd sort of self-defense, I began to torture and complicate the musical dialect in my "serious" output; thus, the simpler and more down-to-earth my tunes, the more cerebral and *voulu* my "good" music became, until it was practically indistinguishable from that of the twelve-tone boys. I sounded off with ten songs on *avant garde* Russian poems. . . . They were exhibited to Nina Koshetz, who attempted to decipher them, couldn't, and worked herself into a violent diatribe against young men who are red-handed with a melody. She was right. . . . The songs, disdained by Nina, were then taken to Eva Gautier, that remarkable and cruelly unrewarded exponent of new music. Madame Gautier . . . liked two of the songs and proposed to perform them at an International Composers' Guild concert.[22]

If well-liked music is debased and its composers suspect, then it is a natural corollary that the mass audience enjoying such music is also debased. Rejected therein is an essential component of the American democratic doctrine that proclaims all Americans to have the capacity to appreciate fine music if only they are instructed in its niceties. Nevertheless, some artists claim that "intelligence and specialized sensibility are not distributed with the voting privilege," and that writing for a mass audience means the lowering

NADIA BOULANGER. Drawing by Olga
Koussevitzky. Courtesy of Countess
Anna de Leucthenberg.

of individual standards and the forgoing of honesty for the sake
of quick popular appeal.[23]

This was the judgment first learned abroad, possibly from the
admired teacher Nadia Boulanger. In a 1939 interview, she states:

> The number of those with some passing acquaintance with the
> masterpieces . . . undoubtedly has grown. . . . But the number who
> really understand them remains static. It is this small minority
> who are indispensable to the creative musician. Amateurs belonging
> to this minority should receive every cultural advantage. Every one
> should have education, but culture should be granted only to those
> ready to receive it. It is useless to attempt to give culture to the
> majority—to those born not to receive it.

Most people, she asserts, "are fooled by their feelings"; only
the emotional aspects of music interest them. Thinking and
understanding are absent. But "art is not emotion," and the

greatness of a work of art always stems from "the judicious process employed in its creation. What is important is how it is made."[24]

Once the composer decides the masses are excluded from the true appreciation of musical artistry, it follows that he may perceive himself as living in a hostile world, surrounded by the benighted and ignoble. This sort of perception comes through again and again in the writings of musicians active in the twenties and thirties. Sessions, to name one, was unhappy he was not accepted as "a cultural citizen, one of the cultural assets of the community, with purely cultural responsibilities." Instead, American society wanted him to be "a cog in the economic machine" and "to justify his existence as a plausible economic risk" and "a possible source of economic profit." To remain loyal to one's artistic vision, he said, meant a life without economic rewards.[25]

Otto Luening testifies to the artist's poverty and unfriendedness in the early 1930s. He says that in 1932 life in New York City had become

> unbearable, and we were on our way to financial disaster. I tried borrowing money from George Houston, but he wrote that he was stranded in St. Louis and couldn't pay his hotel bill. He then asked *me* for a loan, for he could not afford regular meals. Eugene Goossens was guest-conducting the NBC Orchestra and I approached him at a rehearsal. After a handshake he explained how busy he was and moved at a fast pace toward the exit. I trotted after him but he disappeared.

Luening adds that American composers were professionally weak and under attack, citing as evidence an interview with Arthur Judson, manager of the New York Philharmonic and of the Columbia Artists' Bureau, published in the *Musical Courier* under the headline: "Half-Baked United States Composers Menace Music."[26]

Vernon Duke confirms the absence of economic rewards. He states that in the twenties and thirties the bitterness of composers over their neglect by society and over their genuine economic suffering was widespread. It led to estrangement, not only from the American public, but even from each other, owing to the sharp competition for jobs and performances. "Every composer" he met mentioned "a long record of inhuman trials and tribulations, of sums spent and none earned, of eternal promises by publishers,

performers and conductors never fulfilled." One of these composers, who wrote music of "extraordinary merit" (but is otherwise
unidentified), begged Duke for a copying job, he was so destitute.[27]

The disaffected composers charged that, as far as music was
concerned, the United States was a "half-civilized nation" and
its citizenry "semi-somnolent cabbages"-incapable of appreciating
and rewarding excellence. Note the remarks of Edward Robinson,
in the *American Mercury* (1933), on the extreme want and utter
neglect of fine composers like Charles Tomlinson Griffes. Griffes's
plight, Robinson claims, was

> . . . proof that the American spirit, whatever else it may contain,
> certainly does not include the capacity for musical expression.
> Nothing has occurred since his [Griffes's] death to contradict this
> conclusion. More and more it appears inescapable that music, in
> any decent sense, does not run in our blood, that we have no inherent
> psychic necessity for the translation of our cultural aspirations into
> terms of musical thought. All of our instinctive tendencies, in fact,
> point to other directions. Throughout our musical history we have
> always and automatically chosen the wrong elements, and invariably
> supported the worst institutions. A course so consistently erroneous
> would never be pursued by a truly musical people, and no logical
> inference remains but that fundamentally we are totally indifferent
> to the art.[28]

Robinson, of course, mirrored the views of debunking writers
like Henry Mencken, George Nathan, and Sinclair Lewis, who
insisted the United States was mostly inhabited by *Boobus
americanus*—complacent, confident, and utterly stupid. Any
musical composition disliked by *Boobus americanus* had to be
good; any musical composition favored by *Boobus americanus*
had to be bad.[29]

The artistically minded minority looked back with nostalgia
to the era of Haydn and Mozart, forgetting that composers then
were lackeys of the mighty, and erected the fiction that serious
musicians and the powerful who sponsored them had shared a
highly developed taste for fine music: "Princes played with it and
with musicians," writes Alexander Fried. What if "they paid the
expenses of their pleasures from the pockets of their subjects?"
Aristocrats were cultivated persons whose "standard of music was
high." For this reason, the rich and mighty were exonerated from
the charge of exploiting the commonality. With something like

approval, Fried says: "So far as their humbler contemporaries heard music it was either imposed upon them in church service, or they reverently followed the taste of their betters. Then good music did not have to explain itself; it was in power."[30]

What is conspicuously evident in statements like the above is the approval of elitist–autocratic attitudes, with more than a hint that social rank matches distinctions in human sensitivity, and that persons incapable of appreciating contemporary music of a demanding nature are of no cultural consequence.

A supreme virtue of rational men is the ability to compromise. Unfortunately this virtue was miniscule in composers like Ruggles and Sessions, and writers on music like Fried and Robinson. They preferred to argue to no purpose. Confrontation, not compromise, was their chosen way to conduct relations with the American society. The polarization could only harm artists. They were engaging in a contest which they could not possibly win.

The Conservational Position

Despite the fact that books and articles on twentieth-century American music give over a preponderance of their pages to the advanced composers, assuredly the larger number of composers active in the twenties and thirties had little inclination toward the ultra-modern styles. Determinedly they held on to time-honored musical procedures and regarded their own creations as more vital to their era than those by the modernists. They considered themselves evolutionists, not revolutionists. They held that anything of value had to grow out of the best thought of the past; music that spurned its historical roots could never survive.

In contrast to the avant-gardists, musical conservationists affirmed a definite sense of connection with earlier musical practices. Whatever changes took place in music, they believed, had to be gradual, else composers and their compositions would be divorced from the cultural mainstream. A life of artistic isolation was abhorrent to them.

Among the conservationists were older composers, born in the 1870s and 1880s, who were still composing in the era following World War I—Henry Hadley, Arthur Farwell, Daniel Gregory Mason, John Alden Carpenter, Charles Wakefield Cadman, John

Powell, and Deems Taylor, to name seven. More in the public eye in the middle decades of the twentieth century were composers born between 1893 and 1911, who continued composing in the decades following World War II—Douglas Moore, Howard Hanson, Randall Thompson, Paul Creston, and Samuel Barber. George Gershwin, born in 1898 and dying in 1937, belongs in this second group.

These were composers under constant attack from ultramodernists. Wherever the latter had control over performances, they excluded works that followed traditional practices. Charles Wakefield Cadman and other conservationists complained about the gradual disappearance of their music from concerts. Adherents of "the extreme modern movement," writes Cadman, were completely intolerant, unable to compromise, and hostile to every composer not revolutionary.[31] (The modernists, on the other hand, would have voiced the same complaint—that *they* were discriminated against when it came to performances.)

The typical avant-garde criticism of the conservationists was that they are artificers of music and remained aloof from contemporary problems. Their compositions provided escape into an unreal world characterized by sentimentality, genteelness, and sterility. They purported to offer idealized and profoundly felt statements on human experience; but they were actually rhetoricians, adept at passing off empty eloquence as poetic insight.

It was an accusation whose surface of truth concealed unfairness. The conservationist felt that to be more traditional and in favor of tonal organization, judicious dissonance, and mellifluous melody did not necessarily compromise one's integrity. A refusal to deal in uncongenial idioms simply for the sake of a current fashion could have its own kind of honesty. A great deal might be said for music with direct emotional appeal. Randall Thompson insisted "a composer's first responsibility [is] to write music that will reach and move the hearts of its listeners in its own day." George Gershwin confessed: "To me feeling counts more than anything else. In my belief it eventually determines the greatness of any artistic effort. It means more than technique or knowledge, for either of these without feeling is of no account."[32]

Howard Hanson, conductor, teacher, director of festivals of contemporary music, and an out-and-out romantic composer, once said: "Though I have a profound interest in theoretical problems, my own music comes from the heart and is a direct expression of my own emotional reactions." Composers, he insisted, should write "music for everyone, music for every mood, music for laughter and tears, music frivolous and music serious, music for joy and music for hope and faith. . . . We need it all." Of his Second Symphony ("Romantic"), he said in 1933 that unlike the predominantly "bitter type of modern musical realism which occupies so large a place in contemporary thought," his music is anti-cerebral, "a manifestation of the emotions," and "simple and direct in expression." It was a position he had held ten years earlier when he completed his First Symphony ("Nordic"), and continued to hold in 1937, at the completion of his Third Symphony: "Like my second or 'Romantic' symphony, so the third one, too, stands as an avowal against a certain coldly abstract, would-be-nonsentimental music professed by certain composers of high gifts."[33]

Samuel Barber, fourteen years younger than Hanson, had no crisis of creative identity when he first set up as a composer. He accepted without hint of revolt the romantic style from the late nineteenth century, possibly aware that his genius was centered on lyrical writing based on tertian harmonic procedures and a definite tonality. Additionally, he was sensitive to vocal and instrumental colors (though of a traditional nature), wrote idiomatically for singers and instrumental players, and created sounds that appealed to great numbers of concertgoers.

In 1971, Barber explained the attitudes that had guided him over the years: "[When] I'm writing music for words, then I immerse myself in those words, and I let the music flow out of them. When I write an abstract piano sonata or a concerto, I write what I feel. I'm not a self-conscious composer. . . . It is said that I have no style at all but that doesn't matter. I just go on doing, as they say, my own thing. I believe this takes a certain courage."[34]

The "courage" Barber mentions was frequently accompanied by anger and even depression over the relentless attacks against his music and person that commenced in the early thirties and would not cease until his death in 1981.

Describing his beliefs concerning the writing of music, Paul Creston goes beyond the composers mentioned above and says music is not merely an exploration of feeling but, more importantly, "a spiritual practice" that gives "justification of my pursuit of art." Asked if he regarded himself as an innovator, Creston replied that no such person existed, since "the things that we create today are built upon the beginnings of many yesterdays. The works of Bach himself evolved from patterns that men before him had set down. In short, I believe in evolution—not revolution." He himself has striven "to incorporate all that is good from the earliest times to the present." While his music is inspired by song and dance, he attempts an integration "of melodic design, harmonic coloring, rhythmic pulse, and formal progression." Finally, and in contrast to the already quoted statement on musical culture voiced by Nadia Boulanger, Creston believes that all people should try their hand at musical composition and should have a chance at receiving solid musical instruction.[35]

The Great Depression and the Changing Viewpoint

The Great Depression began with the stock-market debacle of 1929 and intensified with the painful economic dislocations of the early thirties. Its persistence and its imposition of extensive privation and suffering on the American people were without precedent. As a result, society ceased regarding itself complacently. The balance of ideas that gave the United States stability had vanished with Black Tuesday. A new balance had to be discovered. The aggressive individuality of the twenties was now a luxury. Aloofness and indifference to the well-being of others had proved America's undoing. Compassion and the concomitant need to unite in a time of crisis became imperatives to be ignored at one's peril.

Artists could not help feeling the icy winds blowing over America. How could modern composers proclaim themselves superior sorts of humans worthy of serious attention in the face of starvation, homelessness, and incipient revolution? To remain isolated, not to change, grew impossible for many. Out of necessity, composers reexamined the basis of their art in order to discover how they might serve the times. Some were convinced that the public could no longer stand the menckenian attacks on their beliefs and customs. To satirize the insufficiencies of ordinary humans during their struggle for survival seemed senseless, undiscerning, and irresponsible. A preponderance of intellectuals and modern artists reviewed their assumptions of the twenties, questioned their role in society, and wondered about the real value of what they were saying, writing, and creating. There arrived for many of them a chilling awareness of the futility of their labors.

On the other hand, a conservationist like Gershwin, however far-out his private tastes, continued to write music of wide popularity and saw no need to reexamine his creative premises. Still others, like Howard Hanson and Henry Hadley, however personally they might feel averse to overly dissonant music, continued to champion contemporary music by Americans of diverse persuasions, while at the same time remaining, as composers, true to the conservative style, which they loved, and which they prayed the public might find easy to accept.

Unchanged, too, were one or two of the truly advanced composers. Ruggles, for example, continued to go his own crusty way, refusing to accept the idea that the times and his music impinged on each other. And Sessions was convinced that especially in time of chaotic and conflicting beliefs, a composer should remain honest with himself and avert his eyes from the main chance.

In contrast, other modern composers like Blitzstein and Antheil felt they should either cease writing altogether or strive to arrive at a different purpose for creative activity. Hectic meetings, several of them arranged by Aaron Copland, took place, where musicians gathered to discuss their attitudes and compositions. Often the exchanges between composers were neither calm nor rational, as Paul Bowles testifies. Some composers remained defensive; others savaged the works of associates.[36] Gadflies like Virgil Thomson, uneasy about the music-making around them, now made others so. Thomson assaulted artistic assumptions concerning dissonance, chromaticism, texture, and, above all, originality, to the discomfit of his colleagues. He could not be dismissed as an old fogy, or an incompetent musician, or an inconsequential composer. Several composers heeded his strictures. One or two modernists realized that they had become superfluous anomalies, and that taking in one another's washing had earned them a most precarious position in society.

The depression drowned out the voices advocating rugged individualism. Indeed, to insist on the artist's right of absolutely free expression was a throwback to affectations (as they were now viewed) practiced in the twenties. Art could no longer survive if it were merely ornamental, exclusive, and self-condoning. Rights were secondary to the alleviation of human distress. Joshua Taylor, Director of the National Collection of Fine Arts of the Smithsonian Institution, writes that the depression shocked the artistic community and wiped out "what patronage the American artist enjoyed," while "talk of 'pure' art and of conflicting isms had begun to wear thin." The concept "of an art community with its special values and private heroes," and of the creative person "as a professional living apart" faded. "More and more the artist wished to identify himself with society as a whole, to find his place in a broadly based culture."[37]

Changes were imminent, if not already taking place. Emotion, for one, was "in" again. Roger Sessions wrote, in 1933, that American music was in crisis and there was growing talk of a return to expression in music. In the same year, Marion Bauer, an influential member of the League of Composers, wrote that the American composer had had too great a "fear of being sentimental" and had "sacrificed sentiment." She acknowledged that the composer had revolted "against the nineteenth century, the epoch of romantic thinking and belief in a soul"; he had tried to establish "an affinity with the eighteenth century, when art and thought were intellectual, classic, and 'pure.'" However, the composer had built on "a false foundation for his declaration of faith," if he thought "that Bach, Mozart, or Haydn were coldly classical and chastely intellectual. They were expressing their emotions in the means at their command." Finally, Virgil Thomson, writing at a later date about the results of the self-examination in the early thirties, stated: "We had long since lost taste for its [the twenties'] bar-stool discussions of courage, its pride in banal misbehaviors, and had moved into a range of sentiment that seemed to us fresher. Our new romanticism was no nostalgia for the warmth of World War I or for the gone-forever prewar youth of Stravinsky and Picasso, but an immersion complete in what any day might bring. *Mystère* was our word, tenderness our way, unreasoning compassion our aim."[38]

Life overseas, cultural and otherwise, diminished in attractiveness. In part, the lessening drawing power of things European was owing to the rise of fascism, first in Italy, and next, after the Reichstag fire of 1933, in Germany. Another world war menaced Western civilization. Europe appeared devoid of strength politically and economically; also culturally and spiritually. Emboldened conservatives like Arthur Farwell attacked American modernists whose music "European-born and European-matured thrusts itself into every ramification of American musical life." He warned that "many young and gifted Americans, lacking the safeguard of a sufficient art-historical background, follow these shallow vagaries and are brought to confusion and failure." A second conservative, Randall Thompson, demanded a music based on American colloquialisms and denounced those avant-garde "musical Solons" who wondered if Europeans would accept their works. Why seek European approval? Europeans had never waited for our endorsement of their artistic output. "The European yardstick," Thompson said, 'is no measure for the things we do." Nor does it help us "achieve artistic autonomy." It represented "a tyranny of opinion under which we struggle to please Europe but only succeed in displeasing and aping it. The value that a given work has for us," he insisted, "is the important thing, and that value is only to be estimated by its relation to other works of our own."[39]

Olin Downes, writing in the *New York Times,* said that "European musical fashions of the hour" and "sophistications borrowed from overseas" had to be replaced by an American pioneering spirit. Through "trial and error" and "rigid self-criticism," the American composer would eventually "reveal what we are and shape beauty as we see it. . . . In our so-called 'art' music," we seem in past years to have turned "away from frontiers" in order "to seek the shelter and the rather pretty prizes of the sophisticated schools of composition overseas." Like Downes, Henry Hadley saw the nervous jazz-oriented music that some modernists found indigenous in expression to be merely a faddish sound with a pronounced European accept and dependent on European approval for its continuation. At best, it could represent only a small portion of America. Note also Charles Seeger's assertion, in 1932, that though he was "one who *does* appreciate good jazz . . . there has not come to my notice one single treatment of jazz in so-called 'art-music' that did not lower the value of the work of art and fail utterly to be one-tenth as good music, arty or otherwise, as the half-asleep improvisation of any good Negro dance-hall band."[40]

Americans living distant from the Atlantic Ocean added to the criticism of the avant-gardists. They urged artists to pay less attention to Europe, and more to the vast America west of the

eastern seaboard. Artistic people tended to cluster in New York
City, said the midwestern painter Thomas Hart Benton. They were
forever forgetting that this city is an appendage to the "much
greater U.S.A." and mistaking their New York "interests, wishes,
and hopes for those of the whole country." New York City was
not America; it harbored both a "great parvenu class" who "look
to Europe for the paraphernalia of their pretensions," and "a large
group of young intellectuals who are not happy unless they are
expressing ideas consecrated by a birth overseas."[41]

Nelson Price of Salem, Ohio, was one of several writers to
the *Times* who advised composers to resist foreign influences:

> In this respect the East has been more at fault than the Middle
> West and the West, largely because of susceptibility and proximity
> to European ideas. . . . While it may be doubted whether the Middle
> West is the real United States, yet ample proof can be cited that
> composers of our nation had better turn their eyes westward rather
> than eastward in order to write indigenous works. The depression
> has already done much to nationalize United States composers.
> . . . [who are] fast becoming United States-conscious.[42]

A sinking economy, both in America and Europe, forced
American expatriates to return home, where they found nothing
to resemble the 1920s and saw "themselves not a little like Rip
Van Winkle." They heard creative people who had stayed in
America, like Stieglitz and Georgia O'Keeffe, state that they had
no use for expatriates, and that a truly American artist could
function only in the United States; otherwise he could not be taken
seriously. When George Antheil returned from a long residence
in Paris, he lamented: "I am an American composer. I did not
grow up here, but I was born here. Everybody in Europe always
said I was very American. Now everybody in America . . . said
I was very European."[43]

The possibility existed that modern composers might grow
indignant in their resistance to a belief contrary to their own,
especially if they were in an unsettled state of mind and saw some
truth in the criticisms levelled against them. One belief of this
kind, waxing strong after 1930, was that in the existence of a
legitimate democratic audience for art music, whose needs had
to be met. While in percentage of the total American population
it might never amount to more than the single digits, in actual

count it could reach some twelve to fifteen millions, certainly not an inconsiderable number. Only a few obstinate composers (Ruggles and Sessions have already been mentioned) resisted the idea.

Resistance was likely to have been greater if composers of ultra-modern bent had received support from a prestigious minority. In the early thirties, however, such support dwindled. Writing in 1939, Copland, perhaps the most influential leader of the younger composers, explains his own *crise de foi* as follows:

> During the mid-'30s I began to feel an increasing dissatisfaction with the relations of the music-loving public and the living composer. The old 'special' public of the modern-music concerts had fallen away, and the conventional concert public continued apathetic or indifferent to anything but the established classics. It seemed to me that we composers were in danger of working in a vacuum. Moreover, an entirely new public for music had grown up around the radio and phonograph. It made no sense to ignore them and to continue writing as if they did not exist. I felt that it was worth the effort to see if I couldn't say what I had to say in the simplest possible terms.[44]

Enthusiasm for avant-garde experiment ran low; the continual onslaught of economic disasters decimated the array of devotees. One after the other, modernists abandoned the notions of the twenties. Their move was toward a rediscovery of America and a partnership with the popular-front coalition. Optimism and patriotic sentiment grew "chic" in the ranks of the avant-gardists.[45]

The disconsolate George Antheil, once the infamous "bad boy of music," returned home to Trenton, New Jersey, where he tried to reacquaint himself with his roots: "Daily. excursions over the native fields and beloved haunts of my childhood . . . produced a strong feeling: one of hearth and home, of 'belonging' here on this native soil, my America. One evening, feeling quite 'mystical' and in touch with the immediate universe about me, I began some sketches, hardly knowing what they were. The next morning I discovered . . . that they were the opening bars of my Third Symphony."[46]

Once adamantly in favor of the avant-gardists, the distinguished ethnomusicologist and teacher Charles Seeger told Sidney Cowell that he first realized that American folk songs actually existed and could be beautiful when at one of Thomas Hart Benton's weekly get-togethers, in the winter of 1929–30, he heard the Kansas City painter Bernard Steffen play "Pretty Girl Milking Her Cow" on the harmonica. . . . Almost singlehanded the two Seegers, Charles as trail breaker and his son Peter as musical activist, laid the foundations for today's free interplay among our many worlds of music.

After his indoctrination at the Bentons' entertainments, Seeger increasingly insisted that composers listen to and utilize their own country's traditional music.[47] Later, in the late thirties, when he was appointed assistant director of the Federal Music Project, he was in a strong position to advance his views.

The Last Best Hope

Franklin Delano Roosevelt, with his fervent advocacy of a New Deal for all Americans and his election to the presidency, spurred the imaginations of the despondent. He put novel and radical stress on the needs of ordinary people, on concentrating all resources toward the aid of the jobless and moneyless rather than toward the bolstering of business establishments.

By 1933, the year Roosevelt assumed the presidency, intellectuals and artists had already moved a considerable distance to the political left. They had heard about or witnessed the first Communist protests in New York City, against hunger and indifference to the worker. They contributed to the mounting agitation against the capitalistic system. Proletarianism was the dominant watchword. Communist-inspired groups like the John Reed Clubs, the League of American Writers, and the American Student Union achieved notoriety. The term "popular front" came to describe a combination of leftist associations whose ideology, directly or indirectly, originated in the Communist Party. Yet, as Charles Hearn explains, though

the faith of the thirties was to an extent, of course, a Marxian faith . . . except for the orthodox and now mostly forgotten party-line proletarian novelists, our writers did not merely substitute the

Communist dream for the American dream. Their idealism was largely an indigenous American idealism and their real hope was to define a new American dream out of a synthesis of the sense of communalism and the traditional American belief in personal freedom, equality, and the dignity of the individual.[48]

The philosopher John Dewey, in *Art as Experience* (1934), was one of several writers who took his cue from the spirit of the times and criticized the belief in art for art's sake. A vital art, he wrote, drew its inspiration from the social events taking place around the artist. It had to make palpable the aggregate sentiment of the American people. If exclusive, overly somber, and self-oriented, art was no longer vital but offensive.

Caught up in the excitement, composers joined the nation's move to the left. Virgil Thomson, Roy Harris, and Aaron Copland, among others, absorbed the atmosphere of the popular front and heard over and over again that they must bring forth "a specifically American music," qualitatively excellent yet having wide appeal. The pressure to rethink their art continued unabated. A large number of these composers' acquaintances leaned far to the left or were Marxists. The concerts of contemporary music of the thirties, including the several Yaddo Festivals, found a major part of their audiences made up of listeners of radical persuasion. Some composers, like Paul Bowles, even joined the Communist Party. Others, like Marc Blitzstein, went through a creative crisis, then opted for the proletarian side. Marriage, in 1933, to Eva Goldbeck, a confirmed leftist, caused Blitzstein to reject his earlier problematical works.[49]

Everywhere composers heard Roosevelt's New Deal slogan for the N.R.A., "We do our part." Were they doing theirs? Burgeoning guilt was a secret affliction of socially aware artists during 1932 and 1933. They perhaps recalled Roosevelt's campaign warnings not to stand still: "It is common sense to take a method and try it. If it fails, admit it frankly and try another. But above all try something." Were composers too timid to try anything different?

Elie Siegmeister was one composer who took these admonishments to heart. He wanted to come out of isolation and create a "powerful art that reached out to a wide spectrum of humanity. Was there a kind of modern music that might" achieve this result?[50] How was he to make contact with the mass of Americans? "Art with a capital A is a menace," he decided. It was "alien and meaningless to the people" he knew and liked. He explains:

> In the early 1930s I found myself quite dissatisfied with performing for the narrow and oversophisticated audiences of the 'élite' organizations, and turned to making music for the wider audience of people who never came to modern music concerts—never even heard of them, in fact. I organized a chorus of shipping clerks, house painters, stenographers, and college students (their enthusiasm was greater than their note-reading ability) and, together with another group of young composers, gave concerts of newly written American music in empty lofts and abandoned stores in Brooklyn, the Bronx—wherever we could get people to listen. Although the admission (usually 25 cents) was just about enough to pay the performers' carfares, contact with the fresh audience of common people was stimulating. They only paid a quarter to hear us, but always insisted on getting their money's worth. After the official program was over, the fireworks usually began. The members of the audience would rise and fire questions at the composers: "Where is the melody in your work?"—"Why did you write that composition?"—"What has your music to do with us?" Those questions sometimes made us pretty mad, but after it was all over, we realized that we had gotten the most honest and direct music criticism of all.[51]

The newly installed Roosevelt Democrats made patriotic appeals to the poor, middle-class, and rich alike to come to the aid of the country, bury their differences, and pull together for a swifter recovery from the depression. In similar fashion, socially conscious musicians like Charles Seeger appealed to the composers. Help the recovery, he begged; make contact with the laboring classes. To Seeger, the proletariat included workers, intellectuals, and musicians. Music worth anything, he said, "is a social force. It is propaganda" to assist the proletariat achieve a better life. By recognizing the proletariat, composers would find their talent strengthened, technic purified, and music given content. Do this, he urged, and composers will "have a wider hearing—not of sophisticated individualists who half disdainfully tolerate them, but of the great masses who [will] welcome them with hungry ears—not an audience of hundreds, but of millions."[52]

The reborn Marc Blitzstein agreed with Seeger. In 1931, he had completed his forbidding Piano Concerto. Then, in 1932, forsaking his harshly dissonant style intended for a select audience, he presented *The Condemned,* whose theme was the Sacco-Vanzetti trial. He continued to try to shape a recognizably indigenous work that would combine effective propaganda for the worker's plight with power-packed drama and contagious music. Finally, in 1936, he would achieve his purpose with *The Cradle Will Rock.*

Not just Siegmeister, Seeger, and Blitzstein recognized the need to cultivate a broader public. In the fall of 1933, composers at the Yaddo Festival buzzed with the idea. They were concerned that scarcely anyone wanted to play or hear their music. In their discussions they emphasized the necessity for ending their separatism and their catering to only a handful of people. What is also significant is the way various writers thought the Yaddo discussions so important that they reported on them fully in the large metropolitan newspapers and in the music periodicals.[53]

No transformation can effectively take place until one or two influential leaders confirm what the advocates for change are urging and convince the majority of people who hold them in high regard that reformation is urgent. One such leader was Aaron Copland. The organizer of the Yaddo Festival agreed with the conclusions reached in 1933. Possibly Oscar Levant had quipped at him during the festival what he later wrote in his *Memoirs.* Describing that year at Yaddo, Levant writes: "I had an amiable relationship with Aaron Copland. I found refuge in being a serious composer. It is similar to being an architect—nobody asks an architect what he's built lately—the same thing goes for a serious composer." At any rate, Copland recognized that music was in a "hybrid and unhealthy condition" and needed to shake off its foreign trappings in order to "speak directly to the American public in a musical language which expresses fully the deepest reactions of the American consciousness to the American scene." The lesson was painfully brought home to him when his difficult-to-perform and dissonant *Short Symphony,* completed in 1933, failed utterly to interest any audience and was put aside.[54]

The example of Roosevelt's "fireside chats" before him, Copland turned to lecturing, writing articles, and organizing colloquies among composers in order to resolve the creative dilemmas of the thirties. Like the president, Copland realized he had to explain the issues to the people. He asked musicians "for action, and action now," and impressed upon his colleagues his own sense of emergency.

In 1933–34, the question remained in the minds of most musicians: what kind of music was appropriate to the decade? Composers had agreed to give up excessive intricacy and dissonance in order to cultivate a wider audience. Yet a great many of the compositions they were writing, despite the will to change, remained unattractive to music lovers in general. How could their newfound empathy with America's masses be translated into a viable music?

It is necessary to keep in mind that the problem American artists faced and the question they asked were common also to several European composers. In 1930, the Russian composer Serge Prokofiev, while visiting the United States, was quoted in the *New York Times* (2 February 1930) as saying he was abandoning his dissonant style in favor of a simpler, more melodic style. Counterpoint, he admitted, had no effect if too complicated, since only when the lines are clearly differentiated can the ear follow more than three melodies at a time. During the same year, Igor Stravinsky completed his *Symphony of Psalms*, commissioned for the Boston Symphony Orchestra. The work projected a depth of feeling within a powerful yet simple context. A year later, Béla Bartók, resorting to a plainer, more available musical language, completed his Second Piano Concerto and, three years later, his Fifth String Quartet. Arnold Schoenberg's essay, *Style and Idea* (1933), confessed the composer's yearning to employ a simpler style, which was realized in the *Suite in G* for string orchestra, completed the next year. At the same time, Paul Hindemith's advocacy of *Gebrauchsmusik*, rather than music for its own sake, was winning over more and more Americans.

If American composers had cast about for compatriots who might guide them toward their goal, acquaintanceship with six composers in particular would have proved useful. The George Gershwin of the *Rhapsody in Blue* (1924) and the Piano Concerto (1925) had been looked down on by the intolerant aesthetes of the twenties. Then, in 1931, he mixed political satire with infectious melody and unmistakably American rhythms and came out with the very popular Broadway musical *Of Thee I Sing*. It and *Porgy and Bess*, which he would complete in 1935, were not intended for "the usual sponsors of operas in America" or "the cultured few." Rather, Gershwin "hoped to have developed something in American music that would appeal to the many." This was the very thing the musical converts also desired to accomplish.[55]

In addition, William Grant Still and his music would have been valuable to study. He was a black American composer resolved on integrating the music of his race with that of the Western art world. White composers of the twenties had often sounded inexpert in their use of Afro-American materials. Still, in contrast, had attempted to saturate himself with the spirit and musical sounds of his heritage and translate them into characteristic compositions: *From the Black Belt* (1926) and *Darker America* (1927) for orchestra, the ballet *Sahdji* (1930), and the *Afro-American Symphony* (1931).

Then there was the admirable craftsmanship and native-inspired tunefulness of Douglas Moore: *The Pageant of P.T. Barnum* (1926), *Symphony of Autumn* (1930), and *Overture on an American Tune* (1932). Requested in 1931 to comment on the *Symphony of Autumn*, Moore said his contemporaries worried too much about idioms and aesthetics and were fearful they were not modern enough or too modern, or they were not American enough or too American. Why so self-conscious? Try to reflect American naturally, he advised. Cease imitating Stravinsky, Ravel, and other Europeans. American audiences would go more for music filled with sentiment and a sort of romantic realism, less for pure cerebration. "The best of what we accomplish is usually achieved by dint of high spirits, soft-heartedness, and a great deal of superfluous energy." These are not the qualities of the Europe-derived modern school. Yes, learn from Europeans, condense, simplify, objectify, but never "avoid a good tune" or neglect the "creating of atmosphere."[56]

Next there were the compositions of the musical iconoclast Virgil Thomson. His *Sonata da Chiesa* (1926), *Symphony on a Hymn Tune* (1928), Violin Sonata and First and Second Quartets (1932), though Parisian in several aspects, manage to display the high spirits and superfluous energy Moore recommends. Thomson's ability to mix outrageous statement with sincere melody and still make a work sound integrated was unparalleled. American hymn and folksong, hints of jazz and blues, solemn proclamation and pun rubbed against each other, as they did in Thomson's home town, Kansas City. Finally, in 1934, he produced *Four Saints in Three Acts,* which thumbed its nose at the avant-gardists, the musical mystics and philosophers, and the somber asses of music. Cliché, absolute consonance, incongruousness, sounds from the dance hall and meeting house and street corner thrust sharp pins into the afflatus of the modern-minded artists.

When Copland decided to write simple works for general audiences, lengthy talks with Thomson may have helped him find his new direction. As Thomson tells it:

> Themes appropriate to a time of protest and of trade-union triumphs seemed just then far more urgent, especially to Copland, surrounded as he was by left-wing enthusiasts. He wanted populist themes and populist materials and a music style capable of stating these vividly. My music offered one approach to simplification; and my employ-ment of folk-style tunes was, as Copland was to write me later about *The River,* "a lesson in how to treat Americana".[57]

Not to be overlooked were the First and Second Symphonies of Randall Thompson, performed in 1930 and 1932 respectively. They sounded genuinely American with their jaunty sound patterns, relaxed impromptu-like (sometimes barbershop) harmo-nies, and melody rooted in some kind of American soil, popular and traditional. Reject "literal and empty imitation of European models," Thompson advised composers, in favor of inspiration from "our own genuine musical heritage in its every manifestation, very inflexion, every living example."[58]

Last to be mentioned is Roy Harris. In the early thirties, he was important for his potential rather than for his accomplish-ments. In 1932, several spokesmen for American music expected him to become the most genuinely American composer of the decade. Arthur Farwell, in the *Musical Quarterly* of January 1932 announced: "Gentlemen, a genius—but keep your hats on!" Harris had around this time written his Concerto for Clarinet, Piano, and String Quartet (1927), a piano sonata (1929), a string sextet (1932), two string quartets (1930, 1933), and a symphony (1933). These works had their rough, amateurish, boring, and incongruous moments. Yet here and there were flashes of originality and passages of beauty which recalled for some listeners the lands that stretched from the Mississippi to the Pacific. The mantle of the West Harris wore as if it were all his own. He wholeheartedly believed that he was capturing the West in his compositions and that he could convince more than a minority of listeners of his authenticity.

He wrote articles, gave talks, and provided explanatory prefaces to his compositions. Not only did he speak about himself, but also about his compositions, describing his aims and what meanings his music contained. Arthur Mendel, writing in *The Nation* (6 January 1932), says that he knew the composer still had to arrive at "a clear and powerful medium of expression" in a period when all former guidelines had proved moribund. Nevertheless, he thinks Harris is to be praised for "trying to work out an idiom in which the structure shall be based on the self-determined growth of the melodic material, not on any super-imposed form." If only Harris could accomplish his task, Mendel says, he would arrive at a method for evolving logical structures suited to American-inspired materials.

All things considered, composers chose among three alternatives. First of all, they could take a sympathetic interest in the lowly city dweller—the disesteem rendered him by the snob, the exploitation of his labor by the industrialist, and the subservient conformity forced upon him by the powerful. The composer, in song and stage work, would become a proponent for democratic justice and social reform. Torch song, blues, popular ballad, American ballroom dances, jazz improvisation, and the pulsing drive of the big swing band would help flesh out the creations of the art composer. Gershwin's, Duke Ellington's, and other popular composers' compositions that mediated between plebian and artistic music might serve as models. What was out was the splintery, dissonant, glass-like compositions of the twenties, which now seemed dated as well as overly beholden to Europe and only superficially American. These compositions, it was thought a decade later, specialized in a dehumanized and crabbed sound which excluded warmth, and failed to attempt a rapprochement between the composer's need for artistic expression and the audience's need for a singing music that could draw forth its deepest feelings.

Second, composers commenced an exploration of the strengths inherent in uncomplicated country life, despite the fact that many of them were city-born and -bred. With the blindness of urbanites fed up with the indignity and corruption of urban existence, they failed to see the pecksniffian morality and narrow-mindedness that hid behind picket fences and lace curtains. They wanted to gather regional myths and customs uncontaminated by the cities. They asked who were the celebrated figures immortalized in rural song and story. They studied the melody and rhythm of folk ballads, sacred songs, and dance tunes that had lived on, year after year, in isolated communities. The unique harmonies, crude but indigenous, originated by the eighteenth-century Yankee tune-smiths and nineteenth-century shape-noters came under scrutiny. Soon ballet, opera, concert overture, and poetic symphony would embody this research. Assuredly, the exploratory endeavors of composers like Moore and Thomson provided precepts by which the compositions of the thirties might be guided.

Third, a few composers could opt to mirror a special culture, not necessarily American, for which they had an affinity, whether owing to ancestry or preference. True, they might not include the American people as the dramatis personae of their compositions. On the other hand, a traditional music with connection to some specific society would help give life and purpose to works that otherwise might turn out sounding private and artifical. Thus, in subsequent years Henry Cowell would try sounding Celtic; Colin McPhee, Balinese; and Alan Hovhaness, Armenian.

At any event, whether the composer favored music and myth reflecting the American countryside, the American city, or a special people, he hoped he was leaving behind him the hothouse isolation of the twenties, with its embarrassing incarnation of the artist as the navel of civilization.

The Democratic Composer

Twenty-five years after the end of World War II, Virgil Thomson reminisced about the old days and concluded:

> Succeeding developments will need all they can muster of energy and fresh ways to match those of the 1930s. For that was surely in American music the definitive decade. After 1910, everything led up to it, and after 1940 everything was different. The survival today of Copland's commando and their continued creation of viable

works each in his own style is evidence both of their individual strength and of that of the time in which they ripened. For their music—along with that of Ives, Ruggles, and Varèse—is what anybody anywhere means by American music.[59]

The comment is a little self-serving, since Thomson regarded himself as one of the most vital contributors to the music of the thirties. In addition, critics might demur about the inclusion of Edgard Varèse, who, despite his participation in American musical life, was after all French born and educated, thirty-two years of age when he arrived in the United States, and a composer of French-titled works whose ambiance is Paris.

Nevertheless other writers confirm Thomson's general conclusions. For example, Paul Broder, in *One Hundred Years of Music in America*, writes of "an explosion of creative energy in the 1930s. Several forces joined to sustain a great upsurge of musical creativity and experimentation. . . . American music had finally come of age."[60]

Certain conditions had to be met, according to Aaron Copland, to make possible a native music of great human consequence. The composer had to have a sense of belonging to and acceptance by a country recognizably different from other countries. Furthermore, he had to have experienced and understod all types of music in depth, advisedly including those in the folk and popular idioms. These requirements satisfied, he would be encouraged to work unstintingly only if groups ready to perform his music were available.[61] It was especially during the Roosevelt years that these necessary circumstances for musical creativity truly coalesced.

Performers in the thirties could choose between a rich assortment of American works, all of them skillfully put together and engrossing. Performing groups organized under the aegis of the Federal Music Project willingly scheduled this music. American audiences crowded the concert halls, theaters, and outdoor stadiums where these groups played, lured by curiosity, love of music, and nominal admission fees. On occasion, an established orchestra premiered a work or two.

Fortunate were those composers who had worked their way into the graces of a world-famous conductor. To cite a significant instance, the conductor Serge Koussevitzky became a champion of several American composers. In the month of November 1939, for example, he appeared in Carnegie Hall with the Boston Symphony Orchestra and gave concerts that featured American works: Arthur Foote's Suite in E, Roy Harris's Third Symphony, Randall Thompson's Second Symphony, William Schuman's *American Festival Overture*, Edward Burlingame Hill's Violin Concerto, and Howard Hanson's Third Symphony. Knowledge-able attendees at these concerts came away impressed. Olin Downes reported in the *New York Times* that the music was interesting, full of variety, and well written. Some of it was "put down with sheer virtuosity." The craftsmanship had an impeccability rarely evidenced in works written twenty-five years before. "Technique, style, approach and development of subject matter" differing from work to work demonstrated the versatility of the composers. "The day is past," concluded Downes, "when any American composer need be told that he doesn't know his business."[62]

The day was past, too, for composers to favor art for art's sake. In the atmosphere of feverish optimism encouraged by the Roosevelt presidency, their watchwords took on populist char-acteristics. Now it was "art for humanity's sake." The vast citizenry, composers believed, required access to art works in order to restore their spiritual well-being. Reveal the world of good music to Americans and they would actively embrace it as an antidote to the grimness of everyday existence.

Composers generally agreed not just any music would do. People wanted compositions to articulate what they yearned to express but could not. At the same time, they desired recreation, a cheering of their minds through attractive melody, rhythm, harmony, and poetic subject matter. To be avoided, however, was mere popularization, the condescending write-down to an audience for the sake of comprehensibility and acceptance. This approach would result in cheap shoddy, supposedly derived from high culture but debased and mangled. The object instead was to render music into another style of expression while maintaining qual-itative excellence. Achievement of this goal would mean not only a pleasuring of humans eager for civilized enjoyment, but also an increased demand for new compositions and encouragement for composers to work to their utmost.

Undoubtedly, the avant-garde experimentation of the twenties had helped unfetter imaginations. At that time it had been more valuable than not to have a small supportive group applauding every effort to eradicate the tired language of the nineteenth century in order to introduce fresher ways of capturing sound. Now that supportive group had shrunk to nothing. Moreover, despite its salutary effects, the music itself was out of touch with circumstances. Only a few diehards still openly favored it. Most composers had turned themselves into populists anxious to make contact with the rank and file.

One of the first to abandon the modernism of the twenties, doing so before the social upheavels brought on by the Great Depression, was William Grant Still. Around 1925, he began to identify strongly with black Americans and to feel that his and their lots were one. He has commented on his changeover from avant-gardist to populist as follows:

> I learned a great deal from the avant-garde idiom and from Mr. Varèse but, just as with jazz, I did not bow to its complete domination. I had chosen a definite goal, namely, to elevate Negro musical idioms to a position of dignity and effectiveness in the field of symphonic and operatic music. This would have been extremely difficult, or even impossible, had I chosen the avant-garde idiom. Through experimentation, I discovered that Negro music tends to lose its identity when subjected to the avant-garde style of treatment. I made this decision of my own free will, knowing very well that pressures would be brought to bear to make me follow the leader, and compose as others do.[63]

Elie Siegmeister also admits to the usefulness of the education he got, not from Varèse but Nadia Boulanger. That education, taking place from 1927 to 1932, ended after the depression's onset and (perhaps owing to the situation in the United States) with a rejection of the Boulanger circle's values: "The early years of study in Paris were valuable for training received in some areas, but not the total blessing one might imagine. I never quite felt at home in Europe, did not care for the precious and somewhat effete atmosphere of 'society' musicians clustered around the Boulanger studio."[64]

In 1926, Marc Blitzstein had left America to study with Nadia Boulanger in Paris and Arnold Schoenberg in Berlin. He had started his career as an avant-gardist scornful of easy, unchallenging music. In part, it was Kurt Weill's graphic use of popular-music idioms in order to bring dramatic scenes to life that gripped Blitzstein and caused him to repent what he considered to be his obtuseness. After attending a performance of Weill's *Johnny Johnson*, he confessed: "I have written some harsh things in the past about Kurt Weill and his music. I wish now to write a few good things. He hasn't changed, I have. The touchoff is the production the Group Theatre have given of his and Paul Green's *Johnny Johnson*. Whatever its fate at the hands of New York audiences (I have seen a preview of the work) I wish to go on record as being grateful to it for having shown me values I didn't know about before."[65]

The year 1936, when Blitzstein attended the performance of *Johnny Johnson*, Copland completed his first composition in his altered style, the *El Salón México*. Arthur Berger claims that this coincidence of late depression year and Copland's turn toward simplification and a broader audience was hardly accidental. It was about this time, Berger says, that discussion among artists and intellectuals peaked in America and that the liberal viewpoint gained complete ascendency. It was then that the influence of the Group Theater and the Federal Music Project was strongly felt for the first time. It was then that ordinary people constituted a primary source for the subject matter of all sorts of artistic works simple and direct enough in appeal for the common man to recognize himself, whether in paintings, novels, dramas, or concert works.[66]

If the composer failed to make contact with his audience, the federal government provided mechanisms for him to learn why he had failed. Give-and-take between composer and listener was encouraged. The principal vehicle for achieving this contact was the federally funded Composer's Forum-Laboratories, where, after a new work was presented, the composer had to respond to questions from the floor. Ashley Pettis, director of the Laboratory in New York City, observes that composers reacted variously to the grilling to which they were subjected:

> Some, usually the weakest, are on the defensive, frequently defiant towards what Mr. [Elliott] Carter calls [in *Modern Music*, November–December 1938] the "pitiless questioning of the audience." As it should be, many of the composers have "first and last" performances at one and the same time, in the Composer's

Forum-Laboratory. But your real composer is made of sterner stuff. He weighs the criticism, determines what is applicable to and for him, develops his power of self-criticism, and—his inner conviction undimmed—goes ahead.[67]

It was generally agreed that music was in a healthier state when composer and audience had an equal freedom, a mutual trust, and a common bond of responsibility. Ideally that was what the Composer's Forum-Laboratories fostered. Musician and listener learned what was on each other's mind. They communicated. Together they could penetrate the veneer of politeness and get at the basics of art, and the way art touched people.

Although in the quotation that follows the speaker is Thomas Hart Benton, it might well have been any one of the populist composers instead:

We symbolized aesthetically what the majority of Americans had in mind—America itself. Our success was a popular success. Even where some American citizens did not agree with the nature of our images . . . they understood them. . . . The fact that our art was arguable in the language of the street, whether or not it was liked, the proof to us that we had succeeded in separating it from the hothouse atmospheres of an imported and, for our country, functionless aesthetic. . . . In the heyday of our success we really believed we had at last succeeded in making a dent in American aesthetic colonialism.[68]

Elliott Carter may have wondered whether the success claimed by Benton was more than skin-deep, and whether the composer's attempt to communicate widely was worth the effort. But Carter would belong to the post-World-War-II generation of composers who rejected all that the populists, from around 1935 to 1945, stood for. In the second half of the thirties, most composers were heady with the thought of oneness with the populace. They believed that the bridges they were building to America's own present and past—in works given titles like *The Plough that Broke the Plains* (Thomson, 1936), *Billy the Kid* (Copland, 1938), *When Johnny Comes Marching Home* (Harris, 1935), *Song of Democracy* (Siegmeister, 1938), *American Festival Overture* (Schuman, 1939), *The Peaceable Kingdom* (Thompson, 1936), and *The Devil and Daniel Webster* (Moore, 1939)—were not necessarily idle fancies.

For composers, the populist approach meant the discovery of musical traditions that would stimulate new and vital compositions. Comprehensible melody, functional harmony, clear structures—all inspired by America's own characteristic traditional and popular musics, yet different—imbued their pieces. As George Antheil explains, when he was completing his Second Symphony in 1936, his music was "American" and he was living in a new creative era with new values for himself: "I began to realize that no young artist starts the world all over again for himself, but merely continues . . . the heritage of the past, pushing it if possible on a little further." Later, he would say to the program annotator of the Philadelphia Orchestra: "The objective . . . of my creative work has been to disassociate myself from the passé modern school of the last half century and create a music for myself and those around me which has no fear of developed melody, real development itself, tonality, or understandable forms."[69]

The passé modernism he disassociated himself from included his own *Ballet Mécanique,* performed in Carnegie Hall, in 1927, which unleashed cacophonous airplane propellers, thunderous percussion instruments, and clanging pianos at a startled audience. In 1927 his rallying cry, aping that of his French mentors, had been *épater les bourgeois.* In 1937 it was music for the people. He had learned the lesson that antagonizing the public paid no dividends, for the composer was in no way its master. Roy Harris, for one, knew this and would have advised Antheil that the audience "of every young, growing culture has always been increased with righteous indignation whenever 'upstarts' from their midst challenged the canons which they have so conspicuously sponsored and cherished."[70]

In the thirties, if a composer felt his creative work had to challenge his audience, he could expect to do battle with them. In 1927, Antheil had invited them to battle and lost. (Who can say whether the content of the *Ballet Méchanique* had more than shock value?) But even if the composer thought he had written something excellent and sincerely meant to engage a large audience's attention, he sometimes had the problem of convincing the public to meet him halfway. To solve this problem some composers turned to teaching the public what this music was about and how to listen to it. So long as the instruction was democratically

AARON COPLAND. Drawing by
Olga Koussevitzky. Courtesy
of Countess Anna de Leuc-
thenberg.

inspired, unpatronizing, and genuinely informative, it was welcomed. For example, Aaron Copland believed that if his art
compositions, however carefully fashioned to reach a wide public,
proved difficult to comprehend, it was up to him to explain himself
and his music to the bewildered auditors. "Do not denounce the
inexperienced listener; educate him" became a Copland motto.
His books, *What to Listen for in Music* (1939) and *Our New Music*
(1941) were intended to enlighten the inexpert and win a following
for his and his associates' music. Educating the layman was also
on Elie Siegmeister's mind when he published *A Treasury of
American Song* (1940) and *The Music Lover's Handbook* (1943).
And educating both layman and musician was Virgil Thomson's

intent in *The State of Music* (1939), *The Musical Scene* (1945), and *The Art of Judging Music* (1948).

What kind of new music did the composer hope he was writing and elucidating to the public? Roy Harris makes clear his own position in a letter to the *New York Times,* 31 December 1939. He says that the music has to grow "in the midst of . . . people, succinctly expressing a time and place." It should exhibit "new qualities" that mark "its authenticity," since "no skillful pastiche has ever reconstituted an art or added a new room to the archives of tradition."[71]

Composers said they were no longer ashamed to use their own native folk and popular music as a basis and stimulus for their own compositions. They had a conviction that when the unique American idiom becomes, in the words of William Grant Still, "an integral part of the composer," he will develop an individual art style "influenced by" the "people's idiom." The quality of America's vernacular music was no less excellent than that of art music, it was now maintained. Blitzstein, for one, saw no qualitative difference between a popular song heard on the Broadway stage and an art song heard in the recital hall: "I have heard the former, being 'plugged,' need only be 'pluggable,' while the latter can take its time, make its points more musically; in other words, don't be too good a composer, and you may write a successful theatre song." Such a claim does not make sense, Blitzstein said. Good theater songs of the past have lasted; poor concert songs have died, which proves that "time and tarnish go their own sweet way, plucking off the cheaper products without regard to category."[72]

Simple music based on the vernacular is no better or worse than complex art music, Copland writes, and it has the added virtue of "making a connection between" the composer "and the life about" him. A great deal of modern music is "too involved and pretentious." It is fascinating, therefore, to see Virgil Thomson go "to the opposite extreme and deliberately" write "music as ordinary as possible," in order not to "overwhelm the listener but to entertain and charm him . . . [through] absolute simplicity and directness."[73]

The desire to entertain through art music was by no means limited to Thomson. He had colleagues who felt similarly and acted accordingly. They cited as precedent the music of the thousands of composers who had lived before Beethoven. In the centuries before the romantic era, composers had always written to please—so claims Olin Downes. He had come away from hearing Bernard Wagenaar's Triple Concerto for flute, cello, and harp, performed by the New York Philharmonic in 1938 to a delighted audience. "Wagenaar," Downes writes, "was no longer an ego in a tower of ivory. He was writing for the public" and aiming to please "in a modern and artistic way." He demonstrated a mastery of compositional techniques, skillfully exploited the capacities of the instruments, and showed "taste and ingenuity in orchestration." Whatever Wagenaar might compose in the future, Downes says, this was "one occasion" when "he wrote to entertain and . . . produced an art-work of value. He did not sacrifice his standards in so doing. He composed with skill and enthusiasm, with a concrete purpose that reached his audience."[74]

Because listeners valued sound that stimulated their feelings, the music that addressed this very human requirement was again in favor. The new music, Copland said, in a statement published in the *New York Times* (1955), shares with the music of older times "the expression of basic human emotions, even though at times it may seem more painful, more nostalgic, more obscure, more hectic, more sarcastic. Whatever else it may be, it is the voice of our own age and in that sense it needs no apology."

The new sound, in significant ways, modified the neoclassicism (à *la* Stravinsky) of the twenties, which purposely curbed emotionalism. Note Louis Gruenberg's artistic creed, which he enunciated around 1940. By this year his rejection of emotionally reticent neoclassicism is complete. Melody is the "blood of a composition," he says, and emotion is essential to it. He tries to compose easily recognizable melodies. Even if trivial, they are "better than none at all." He concludes: "I reject as emphatically as I am able, ALL systems that tend to cramp the emotional sweep of one's impression. This includes fugues, third-tone, fourth-tone or twelve-tone systems, trick orchestrations, and other easily acquired technical matter."[75]

Melody and emotion were wedded to exalted themes in many compositions of the late thirties and early forties. Thomson notes the abrupt restoration of "noble subjects" that had been "taboo in the twenties." Especially during the years of World War II did composers take up "noble subjects" to express their feelings for country and suffering humanity: Harris's *American Creed* (1940), Copland's *Lincoln Portrait* (1942), Thompson's *The Testament of Freedom* (1943), and Moore's *In Memoriam* (1944). Composer and public possessed in common during these years a group of musical ideas and a set of symbols that aroused strong feelings, expressed a common conviction, and embraced a shared aesthetic. Nothing like this unanimity had ever been experienced before in the world of American art music. Nor would it continue to be experienced in the post-war years.

Throughout the Roosevelt years, composers also wanted to write functional works, music for use wherever and however needed. At the same time, several essayists in *Modern Music* advised formats that made new music more comprehensible to the public— ballet, which united eye and ear; play-operas, where sound, sight, and words explained each other; motion pictures, where appealing drama and background music fused in viewers' minds. Isadore Freed, in the October–November 1939 issue, urged the writing of teaching pieces. He warned that music teachers had to turn mostly to older European materials, thus training up their students to have a taste only for foreign music from the past. He also urged the creation of easy works for amateurs, maintaining that "turning out simple pieces is [not] an inferior practice"; nor does it involve any "degree of 'writing down.'"

Copland once was asked whether he liked writing music for use, and movie music, in particular—the questioner hinting Copland had demeaned himself and his artistic principles by writing for profit. Copland replied that he loved doing so: "Film music constitutes a new musical medium that exerts a fascination of its own. Actually, it is a new form of dramatic music—related to opera, ballet, incidental theatre music—in contradistinction to concert music of the symphonic or chamber music kind." He said he reveled in the thought that people were actually asking to hear his music. To feel "needed as never before," Copland said, was "heady wine." Why? "Previously, our works had been largely self-engendered; no one asked for them." But all at once functional music was in demand—music for movies, dance companies, radio, schools, and the theater. For film, Copland wrote the music to

Our Town (1940); for high-school singers, the play-opera *The Second Hurricane* (1937); for radio, *Music for Radio* (1937); for high-school band, *An Outdoor Overture* (1938); for ballet, *Billy the Kid* (1938).[76]

Elie Siegmeister points out how psychologically important and creatively energizing it was to write for someone who wanted his music. He writes: "I eagerly sought the opportunity to write for the dance, teacher, and radio, for schools, amateur performers, and children." The experience was fructifying: "At the same time, contact with these various agencies stimulated me to think along new lines, musically speaking. What might be called the 'American' flavor in some of my scores: *American Holiday, Abraham Lincoln Walks at Midnight* (a cantata to words of Vachel Lindsay), and *Created Equal* (music for one of the Federal Theater's Living Newspapers), was probably a result."[77]

Some compositions united professional and amateur performers. Harris's *Folksong Symphony* (1940) is one instance. Its author says: "I am trying to write a music which expresses our time and period in America and which is serviceable to our musical life. By serviceable I mean music which effectively uses the instrumental and choral and other resources available at present." The *Folksong Symphony* is purposely designed "so that the adults and young people of our cities could sing and play the folk songs of our nation for pleasure. I wrote the choral parts for the range of good high school choruses, with the thought in mind that such choruses might have a work to prepare with the symphony orchestras of their cities."[78]

Curtainfall

The decade 1935–45 was without doubt an intoxicating period for most creative people. However, like any cultural movement, music populism contained its own seeds of destruction. For one thing, its very leaders had carried on with no absolute conviction of the rightness of their actions, with no carefully thought out and unifying program which related all concerned parties to each other, and with no anticipation of the necessity to explore ever-new and fresh forms of expression even while maintaining their Americanism. Composers remained restive above the unadventur-ous taste of the public. Harris, for example, complained that concertgoers countenanced only symmetrical melody in the major-minor keys and the simplest folk materials (preferably European, not American). Harmony, he claimed, had to be triadic and never intrude upon the melody; while orchestration had to be "very colorful or heavy and lush." Opera lovers and concertgoers alike lived in the previous century and idolized not music, but singers' voices and virtuousos' skills.[79]

On the other hand, Harris himself came in for criticism, as did other composers, for using Americanism to propagandize himself and his music. In the background of such criticism always lurked the suspicion that their love of country was lip-deep and self-serving. In 1940, Thomson wrote: "Roy Harris's *American Creed* invites kidding, as all of his programistically prefaced works do. . . . No composer in the world . . . makes such shameless use of patriotic feelings to advertise his product. One would think, to read his preface, that he had been awarded by God, or at least by popular vote, a monopolistic privilege of expressing our nation's deepest ideals and highest aspirations."[80]

Now and again, a composer grew fearful of becoming "overly commercial." Arthur Berger gives this as the reason why Copland wrote his abstract Piano Sonata (1941) and Violin Sonata (1943). Furthermore, Berger implies that Copland's most serious and intense interest centered in abstract compositions like these, rather than in works meant for popular consumption: "He [Copland] took advantage of the fact that they [the two sonatas] would not be at the mercy of commercial forces of orchestras, radios, etc., and put some of his most earnest effort into them."[81]

Copland had his own full share of contradictions. He wanted to feel needed, yet feared commercialization. He liked popularity, but preferred to be completely understood by the musically erudite. Gratifying the general public was all right, he once said, but he still favored the "gifted listener" who divined "whatever it was the composer tried to communicate." He admitted to not being particularly stirred by the pleasure of his music might or might not give the listener, since once a work was completed, he felt detached from it.[82]

Regarding these contradictions Thomson remarks that in the thirties, while Copland hungered for a large public, subscribed to "social-service ideals," and decried the "over-intellectualized and constricting modernism of his Paris training," he also did not want to lose his "intellectual status." That, Thomson says, was Copland's problem.[83]

The bugaboo of originality, the perceived necessity for each composer to have his own distinctive music, also bothered Copland. He was afraid that the premium set on creative togetherness might compromise artistic vigor and independent expression. It was an anxiety that hung over him from the previous decade, and was in evidence during a conversation he had with Antheil in 1939. Copland told Antheil that he liked Harris's music because it was "always written in his own style, nobody else's."

Antheil asked, "Is individual style as important as all that?"

"Yes," replied Copland, "you must always know whether or not this page of music belongs to this or that composer; that comes before everything—except, of course, sincerity."

After mulling over the conversation, Antheil dismissed "sincerity," because in his experience all composers were convinced they were sincere. As for originality, a caustic Antheil concludes that too many American composers "believe they must, from bar to bar, 'trade-mark' their music. They all seem to believe they must initial each bar with their own musical idiosyncracies (or 'idiom,' if you prefer) in order that, before all else, they can establish their 'musical personality'—whatever that is."[84]

In addition to the dilemma of a national style versus originality there was the problem of intolerance toward conservative composers reluctant to subscribe to one or another contemporary style. Simplicity was acceptable to reformed modernists; but nineteenth-century romanticism was decidedly not, for their outlook, however transformed by the impact of the thirties, had taken essential shape in the decade before. The young Samuel Barber, in particular, upset the musicians who approved only current styles that were modifications of those fashionable in the twenties. Barber's *Adagio for Strings* and First Essay for orchestra ignored the innovations of the twenties, featured singing melody of marked emotional appeal, and received the enthusiastic approval of noted conductors and countless listeners. An upset Ashley Pettis, director of the New York Composer's Forum-Laboratory, damned Toscanini's sponsorship of Barber's compositions, in a letter the *New York Times* published on 13 November 1938. For Pettis, it was not sufficient argument to perform Barber's works because audiences demanded them. In the querulous voice of the twenties, he spoke of Barber's music as if a neanderthal had composed it. He asked, where was Barber's originality? Why was he important enough to perform, while Sessions, Copland, Ives, and Harris receive far less attention? "One listens in vain for evidence of youthful vigor, freshness or fire, for use of a contemporary idiom (which was characteristic of every composer whose works have withstood the vicissitudes of time)."

Barber was an anachronism to Pettis, his music replete with clichés, empty of the spirit of adventure—and a philistine to boot.

The next week, Barber's friend Gian-Carlo Menotti sent a rebuttal to the *New York Times* (20 November 1938). He inquired why art had to toe a narrow "modern" line derived from Paris, and why a variety of styles could not coexist. Barber was courageous "to defy the servile imitation of" the Parisian "style (which has been called American music)," and "that has bored concert audiences for twenty years." Presumably Menotti was referring to the modern music composed during the pre-populist era.

A second letter, written by Alexander Kelberine, Russian-born pianist resident in New York City, appeared in the same *Times* issue. According to Kelberine, Pettis was defending, not the cause of all American composers, but "a specific group . . . of his own masterly choice." Kelberine continues:

> Mr. Pettis obviously belongs to that group of thinkers which believes that its particular brand of understanding of what comprises a contemporary idiom is absolute and should prevail. . . . Must a work be cacaphonous in order to be of today? . . . How can one be so all-fired sure that Messrs. Aaron Copland, Roy Harris, Roger Sessions will withstand the "vicissitudes of time"? Must an artist always portray what goes on about him? Or is it possible that an artist be impelled to record the inner turmoil that wells within him as he views reality?

Leave it to time to winnow out the good from the bad, advises Kelberine.

Two weeks after the Pettis statement, a letter appeared, written by Franco Autori, who had been active as a conductor for the

Federal Music Project, and who now headed the Buffalo Philharmonic. Autori counseled common sense in the dispute: "Who is to decide what constitutes the modern idiom and what difference does it make what particular idiom a composer chooses to use? The real issue is whether the composer has a message to deliver, whether he is competent to deliver it, and whether, in delivering it, he is sincere and true to his purpose." He suggested that Pettis's favored music was also full of clichés, though of a contemporary sort.

More ominous that the criticism of Pettis was that voiced by Elliott Carter in 1938 and 1939, since Carter would be a dominant American composer in the post-war years. With words that remind us of Copland's declaration to Antheil, Carter comes down strongly on the side of "personality or individuality" in musical compositions. Without it, he believes, a composition exists in a flawed state. He finds Harl McDonald's Fourth Symphony "derived from Tchaikovsky" and possessing "no personality behind it." Dante Fiorillo's Triple Concerto for piano, oboe, and horn is dissonant yet imperfect; it "seems to have a personality but has not learned to express it convincingly." Henry Hadley's romantic works are deeply felt, but display "lack of strong individuality."

Carter comments on the Barber–Pettis squabble, showing annoyance at the letters refuting Pettis. The letters, he complains, fail to discuss whether Barber's *Adagio* is "good or bad in its reactionary style." Carter measures a work's goodness by the imagination and vitality revealed: "I believe none would be more disappointed than these critics and correspondents who so glibly tell the composers what to do, if musicians followed them and wrote scores in strict accordance with their ideas. Certainly neither Henry James nor Walt Whitman ever fulfilled a previous 'should,' and no important composer, past, present, or future may be expected to do the same." Nowhere does Carter demonstrate a willingness to accommodate different points of view, and his disdainful argument distorts the meanings of the letter writers.

Carter believes that few important contemporary composers are "easy on their audiences" and that "one kind of new music does not always lead to comprehension of another," since "usually each is a new attack on a new problem of expression." To Carter's way of thinking, it follows that audiences understand composers only if they "compose the same piece over and over again under different titles." Being "well-trained in nineteenth century hero-ics," audiences "will stand for a lot of tedium in music." Carter never explains why important works have to be insular, difficult to comprehend, and like scientific propositions requiring argumentation.[85]

It goes almost without saying that if younger composers like Carter, owing to the prevalent populistic attitudes of the time, tried to write for a large public, they would half-heartedly produce pieces that failed in their objective. Carter's ballet *Pocahontas* (1939), First Symphony (1942), and *Holiday Overture* (1944) he says he wrote "in a deliberately restricted idiom," not from conviction. He admits Copland termed the overture, despite its intended effect, "just another one of those 'typical, complicated Carter scores.'"[86]

After Richard Goldman heard the *Holiday Overture,* he wrote: "It is . . . a truism that popular culture and intellectual populism actually never meet; it is perhaps sadder that in practice the 'intelligentsia' seldom knew which is which." The overture was an effort to appeal to a large audience within "the limits of a highly self-conscious and conventionally modern" style. "But the piece needs, for a smashing success in our concert halls, an admixture of witlessness and vulgarity which its composer will never, even with the best intentions, acquire."[87]

Other composers, who would be significant in the post-war movement away from the intent to gratify audiences, condescended to write for the gallery during their early years. In 1941, Milton Babbitt received the Bearns Prize for his *Music for the Masses.* Babbitt says: "This work was a *pièce d'occasion* which embodied deliberately idiomatic conservatism, as a momentary respite from the twelve-tone composition with which I had already become deeply involved."[88]

In the fifties, when composers like Carter and Babbitt would hold sway, a new internationalism replaced the commitment to things American. Many of the musical classics of the Roosevelt years were rejected by influential members of the upcoming generation. A work like Copland's *Appalachian Spring* now had "a homeliness . . . which borders on the cloying," and his *Tender Land* only a "flaccid content." Thomson's *The Plough* and *Louisiana Story* now sounded like tiresome "hymns for irrigation canal and orchestra," which dripped with a distasteful "jus' folks sentimentality."   William Schuman was advised that he could please discerning critics only if he eliminated "the embarrassing Americanism that stands in the way of easy acceptance by those for whom the best ballads of Americans never wave a flag or even name their patriotic purpose."[89]

The new message from Europe was that the styles cultivated by most of the American students of Nadia Boulanger were passé. The mystical eclecticism of Olivier Messiaen and the twelve-tonal writing of Arnold Schoenberg and Anton Webern were the vogue. In 1946, Nadia Boulanger returned to Paris, after a residence of six years in the United States. She "found Pierre Boulez's clique booing Stravinsky; as Stravinsky's staunchest appendage, the outmoded Boulanger also came under fire." To Boulez, "the important figures" were Messiaen and René Leibowitz, a champion of twelve-tone music.[90]

The old American heroes of art music were replaced by new European gods—Anton Webern, Luciano Berio, Karlheinz Stockhausen, and Pierre Boulez. Copland, who had labored unstintingly for American composers, was forgotten.

One year, Karlheinz Stockhausen was in New York for a series of performances featuring his compositions. Local intellectuals and aesthetes lionized him. He was attending a rehearsal with a woman companion when he caught sight of Aaron Copland in the hall. Without hesitation, Stockhausen introduced Copland to his friend with these words: "I'd like you to meet the great American composer Virgil Thomson."[91] *Sic transit gloria mundi.*

2

The Intermediaries Between Composer and Listener

The composer of only art songs and chamber music felt that his reputation would be limited to one or two localities and a special audience. To break away from this confinement, reach a wider public, and gain what he considered meaningful recognition for his creative efforts, he felt he had to write and have performed compositions for symphony orchestra, opera association, or ballet company. Several superb musical organizations existed in the United States. The problem was how to interest their charismatic directors, men like Leopold Stokowski, Arturo Toscanini, and Serge Koussevitzky, in the compositions of an unknown and disparaged American composer. Unless this problem were solved, the public would not even know that a body of native music existed.

What were the ensembles and institutions, and who the musicians, managers, trustees, and critics mediating between composer and listener? The New York Philharmonic was founded in 1842; the Boston Symphony, 1881; the Chicago Symphony, 1891; the Cincinnati Symphony, 1894; and the Philadelphia Orchestra, 1900. In 1940, sixteen major orchestras existed, employing professional musicians on a full-time basis for a stated number of weeks during the year. In addition, there were hundreds of metropolitan, community, and college orchestras giving concerts.[1]

Early in the century, the personnel of most orchestras were German. After World War I other nationalities contributed members. Gradually room was found for American musicians. However, it was not until after World War II that significant Americanization of the symphony orchestra took place. At the beginning of the thirties, the *New York Times* reported on the nationalities represented in New York City's Philharmonic Orchestra, Metropolitan Orchestra, Roxy Symphony, and Manhattan Symphony: of a total of 375 musicians, only 23 percent were American. The greater number were European-born, most of them from Italy (24 percent), Russia (21 percent), and Germany and Austria (10 percent).[2] If we examine the roster of soloists singing in the Metropolitan Opera, the absence of Americans is painfully obvious. As for the touring virtuosic instrumentalists, foreigners usually were treated as celebrities; Americans were slighted.

The conductors who headed orchestras of more than passing importance also were Europeans. Interestingly, several of the most famous of these conductors—Leopold Stokowski, Eugene Ormandy, and Hans Kindler, to name three—had little reputation before Americans engaged their services. Qualified American conductors, in contrast, rarely received a push upwards. Indeed, what few there were might experience a push *out* of a major position in favor of a foreign conductor, as did Henry Hadley in 1926. Hadley, whose wish was the close association of the New York Philharmonic with American music, found himself replaced by luminaries like Arturo Toscanini and Wilhelm Furtwängler, whose interests excluded American music. Nor, for that matter, did these foreign conductors, save for one or two, show any real interest in American life or values. A writer in the *New Britain Herald*, 6 May 1933, noted what was common knowledge about foreign conductors: "These worthies stay in the country only long enough to earn their money. The moment they are free to travel, they depart, always to Europe."[3]

When foreign conductors on occasion unbent to perform an American work, as often as not they misunderstood its idiom or gave a lukewarm rendition. Aware of the shortcomings in interpretation, Serge Koussevitzky in a lucid moment once remarked to Aaron Copland that American audiences "would never understand American orchestral compositions until they heard them conducted by American-born conductors."[4] Regrettably, the nurture of American-born conductors had a low priority in American musical circles.

To illustrate the low valuation of things American: when the New York Philharmonic's centenary celebration came around in 1942, no American-born conductor was honored and no new American composition was commissioned. The insult to American music provoked Virgil Thomson's comment, on 23 March 1941, that the orchestra really was not a part of New York's intellectual life. He suggested a reform of the orchestra's attitudes and an attempt to cultivate an audience for American music. He said further that the repertory played for that audience required interpretation by American-born conductors.[5]

One can understand the complete frustration of so many American composers and their exasperation with the American cultural establishment when one considers that whatever they composed, whether in an up-to-date European style or in a native idiom, and however skillfully they structured their compositions, the most honored conductors, orchestras, and opera companies were arrayed against them. The people in America possessing the authority to pass judgment on their music were, more often than not, European-born or wealthy and unadventurous members of boards of trustees.

Even the foreign conductors most sympathetic to native music had less than a comprehensive awareness of the American scene, however long their residence in the United States. What is more, they had a notion of their own infallibility, which allowed for no correction of this lack of knowledge. Vernon Duke relates a story about Serge Koussevitzky that underlines this point. In 1932, Mrs. Eugene Meyer offered to sponsor an annual composers' festival. A composers' committee discussed a suitable conductor sympathetic to contemporary music. Several of those present judged that one man—Serge Koussevitzky—stood out for his sponsorship of American composers, even though he excluded some important men whose styles he found unappealing. Consequently, the committee (which included Vernon Duke, Aaron Copland, and Nicolai Berezowsky) proposed Koussevitzky's name, despite Nicolas Slominsky's warning that the conductor would displace the committee and assume complete control of the festival.

It happened as Slonimsky predicted. Influenced by his wife Natalya, Koussevitzky insisted on supremacy, feeling he, not the composers, should determine the festival's programming. Moreover, "it appeared that Sergei Alexandrovitch was greatly vexed by 'unknown amateurs' who wrote him offering program suggestions, and—in parenthesis—asking him to listen to their music." Duke continues: "When I asked the identity of so bold an amateur, Mrs. Meyer checked . . . and said it was 'somebody called Wallingford Riegger'. I gasped. Riegger . . . was one of America's outstanding composers."

Yet, when Koussevitzky was apprised of Riegger's stature, he got angry and resigned. Fearful of antagonizing the conductor, Copland and Berzowsky also resigned. Finally, Mrs. Meyer abandoned the idea of a composers' festival.[6]

Conductors and Other Performers

However gifted an American composer might be, he was always scaled at much lesser weight than either the foreign conductor or the virtuosic soloist in the opinions of musicians, managers and trustees of musical institutions, and the preponderance of the concert-going public. One of the sorriest spectacles in the musical life of the thirties was the American composer enduring the injustice of nothing or very little paid him—even as reimbursement for out-of-pocket expenses to music copyists—when an established orchestra condescended to perform a work of his. Depression and budget deficits were the usual excuses given. Nevertheless, to quote Minna Lederman, "the curious thing about those deficits is that while they make it impossible to pay the composer anything, conductors go on receiving a total of hundreds of thousands of dollars and soloists are paid fees commensurate with their place in the concert field."[7]

Conductors and soloists certainly were compensated for their services during the darkest depression years and some were compensated handsomely. Europeans wondered at the fat salaries granted the more glamorous musicians who crossed the Atlantic

LEOPOLD STOKOWSKI. Drawing by Olga
Koussevitzky. Courtesy of Countess
Anna de Leucthenberg.

to sojourn in the United States. One of these was Arturo Toscanini.
Though Toscanini claimed he was disturbed by the New York
Philharmonic's mounting losses, he declared that the federal, New
York State, and New York City governments should not hesitate
to impose special taxes to meet the deficits. At the same time,
he demanded his full pay, which ran around $100,000 for some
ten weeks of work. His advocacy of a special tax demonstrated
an ignorance of American democratic processes, and his appetite
for money showed a lack of concern for the plight of the
Philharmonic players, who agreed to lesser wages in order to permit
the orchestra's survival. During the full season—not the ten weeks
alluded to above—the average player received $2,700.[8]

In the early thirties, Leopold Stokowski, another glorified
conductor, headed a Philadelphia Orchestra whose season sub-

scriptions fell off 15 percent and whose orchestra players experienced a 10 percent cut in salary. Yet Stokowski high-handedly continued to force additional debts on the orchestra through costly performances that required larger-than-normal forces and through idiosyncratic programming which turned off concertgoers. Throughout these years his own earnings were between $200,000 and $250,000 a season. In 1932, a worrisome year for the board of directors, he proved himself incapable of accepting any responsibility for the economic problems faced by the orchestra. On the contrary, he brashly insisted that he was underpaid and that it was up to the board to turn out a mass audience for him.[9]

Their mercenary commercialism notwithstanding, quite a few of the foreign musicians who came to America held that music was not entertainment but an art; performers not entertainers but artists; and audiences not guests awaiting entertainment but students needing education. They behaved as if questioning their fees was an affront to good taste, and questioning their programs and their performances an affront to artistry. That music belonged to people and had a human function, they disputed; that it should endure the democratic give-and-take of popular criticism, they found incredible. Artur Schnabel, noted concert pianist, voiced the shared artistic view of music: "We should not say . . . that music is for the people. The people are for music. Art cannot be brought to them; they have to be brought to art; they must climb." Like other foreign musicians, Serge Koussevitzky railed against criticism of his performances, however censorious he might be of other conductors: "My profession is aristocratic, my art is aristocratic," he said. "Critics, like the artists, must be aristocrats of the spirit." It is the critics' duty to help the public understand clearly the aim of the artist."[10]

Here again we find the image of the artist invoked, but not as previously, to enhance the position of the composer. Now it is invoked to enhance the position of the performer, to the exclusion of the composer.

Without question, conductors like Koussevitzky behaved autocratically. One reason for this behavior was that they constantly lived amidst adulators. Halina Rodzinski wryly writes of the Koussevitzkys and of herself: "Natalie and Olga attended him [Serge Koussevitzky] as if he were the Tsar himself. I thought it all very funny, but only because I recognized myself doubled in them, for I waited on Artur just as obsequiously." Once, an effusive woman said: "Dr. Koussevitzky, I know who you are. You are God!" Koussevitzky sedately considered her assertion, then replied: "I know my responsibilities." Later, when asked if the incident actually happened, he said: "Sounds like me."[11]

Those daring to oppose Koussevitzky's will did so at their own peril. In 1933, he had a falling out with his nephew Fabien Sevitzky. Sevitzky, despite his uncle's order to refuse the offer, had accepted the directorship of the People's Symphony Orchestra of Boston. Moses Smith writes that an American composer (otherwise unidentified), who was starved for performances, incautiously agreed to have Sevitzky conduct one of his scores. Koussevitzky warned the composer that he would boycott the composer's entire orchestral output. The work was not withdrawn. From then on, Koussevitzky and the Boston Symphony Orchestra ostracized the composer. As for Sevitzky, his tenure in Boston (1934–36) was made most uncomfortable by his uncle.[12]

The lesser mortals—composers—befriended by conductors were frequently treated to negligence. Oscar Levant tells of Stokowzki's deciding one year to play one of his compositions. However, Stokowski took his own good time about scheduling it, until at the end a fed-up Levant asked for the return of the score.

Stokowski was a law unto himself. Nobody could tell him what to do—neither composers, nor trustees, nor the public. In 1932, despite the drop in ticket sales and the mounting debts of the Philadelphia Orchestra, he presented Arnold Schoenberg's *Gurrelieder* in Philadelphia and New York City, employing an augmented orchestra of 123 instrumentalists, three male choruses, a mixed chorus, and five soloists—532 participants in all. The next year, he indulged himself again when he decided, at a youth concert, that the children should sing the Communist "Internationale." It provoked anger, controversy, and protest. Most unfortunately of all, it left a lasting residue of bitterness against and suspicion of the arts.[13]

A third example of a conductor ruling as if possessed of unlimited authority is Arturo Toscanini. In 1930, when unemployment proliferated and America teetered at the edge of catastrophe, Toscanini insisted on a European tour with the New

York Philharmonic and forced the orchestra's board to accede. George Marek, a Toscanini biographer, says the trip was meant to negate the "old accusation of American commercialism," to demonstrate pridefully our "musical excellence," and mollify Toscanini, who "wanted it badly." Perhaps so; but no American composition was performed during the trip.[14] Without doubt, upon seeing the conductor and orchestra able to ignore them with impunity, New York composers felt an increase in their feelings of outrage and isolation.

Two years later Toscanini, possibly deciding a sop should be fed to American composers, scheduled two native works for performance, a symphony each by Bernard Wagenaar and Howard Hanson. However, he had no great affection for the works and felt it his right to alter arbitrarily where he saw fit: "The Wagenaar symphony was filled with advanced harmonies and with dissonances that bothered Toscanini because they seemed to him often to have no purpose. In a moment of exasperation he wrote a concluding C major chord on the last page of the score, circled it in red ink, and scribbled under it, 'My chord, Arturo Toscanini.'" The act underlines Paul Lang's conclusion that the modern orchestra leader thinks composers exist for his sake, "and with few exceptions he has little respect for the composer's property."[15]

Though Toscanini hated fascism, he detected no contradiction when he himself acted dictatorially. Friends feared to vex him and constantly acquiesced to his prejudices. Samuel Chotzinoff invited him to dinner, then got into a fluster over who else should be invited: "We made a list of possible guests. Many turned out to be questionable: one was divorced; another was addicted to ultramodern music, which the Maestro heartily detested, and so on, and so on. We finally decided to take no risks. We invited three of the Maestro's closest friends . . . who, as far as we knew, had not at the moment incurred his displeasure."[16]

As for foreign performers, too many of them, given a modicum of reputation, browbeat not only friends but audiences into meekness. Music was art; audiences had to listen in worshipful silence. For this reason, soloists interrupted their performance and sulked off the stage, or conductors silenced their orchestras when the tread of latecomers, the rustle of programs, or the coughs of the foolhardy distracted them. In 1928, Schnabel left in the midst of the performance of a Schubert piano sonata because a radiator hissed and a person coughed. When, at last, he returned to the stage, "people sat breathless and nearly died for want of a breath or a cough. The rest of the evening, which seemed to last forever under these conditions, no one listened at all to the music, for watching his neighbor."[17]

Stokowski exhibited a similar temperament when he and the Philadelphia Orchestra performed the Schoenberg *Variations* for orchestra at Carnegie Hall in the fall of 1929. At the work's conclusion, some listeners applauded; others hissed. An irked Stokowski lectured the audience, saying he would go on giving what he thought was the best music. If any in the audience were reluctant to agree with him, they should leave never to return and thus make room for the more open-minded. When he ceased his harangue there was some applause and also "sullen silence from those who resented his admonitory remarks."[18]

Protocols of proper behavior for audiences increased amongst the more imperious performers. More conductors forbad hissing altogether and discouraged applause between movements of a symphony or a concerto. A few conductors wanted to eliminate all applause, feeling that it destroyed the devotional attitude toward masterpieces, which they wished to foster. As might be expected, none of these masterpieces were of American origin.

In January 1930, Ossip Gabrilowitsch arrived to lead the Philadelphia Orchestra. He revealed a more liberal attitude than that of Stokowski. Gabrilowitsch told his symphony audience: "When you like something, jump in with both feet and show it." He praised "those countries in the south of Europe where they shout when they are pleased and when they are not they hiss and throw potatoes." He carefully added, however, that a broad-minded Stokowski had given him permission to state his opinion.

A woman in the audience arose and asked for "a rising vote" for Gabrilowitsch's viewpoint. A quarter of the audience stood up. The remainder, probably dumbfounded by the suggestion or cowed by Stokowski, remained seated. However, when the concert continued, "spirited applause" broke out at the conclusion of every number."[19]

The editors of the *New York Times* thought the matter important enough to remark upon, under "Topics of the Times," 3 February 1930. Their editorial states that most audiences are

DRAWN BY " MIKE " ANGELO

Someone Drops a Handkerchief During a Performance of the Philadelphia Orchestra

Reprinted from *The Saturday Evening Post*, April 20, 1929. Drawn by "Mike" Angelo. Copyright © 1929 by the Curtis Publishing Company. Reproduced with permission.

good natured and receptive when they enter a concert hall. They like to clap their hands in appreciation of a fine performance. "Now a new factor" has been introduced, in that they "must keep track of tastes of orchestra conductors if they hope to please them." On one hand, Stokowski "had created something of a sensation by demanding silence after a selection had been played. He wanted no applause, no cheers, no huzzas, and no hisses." On the other hand, Gabrilowitsch said that musicians liked applause and that "hisses and other signs of disapprobation are necessarily the right of an audience entitled to applaud." The editors' sympathy was not entirely with Stokowski.

News of Stokowski's demands reached London. Francis Toye, in the *London Post*, wondered at the American musical public, which let tyrants like Stokowski treat it "like dirt" by making it earn "the privilege of listening" through absolute obedience to their whims, however pretentious and absurd.[20]

Deaf to all protests, Stokowski increased his demands. Latecomers to concerts must be punished, he decreed. They were to remain excluded from the auditorium until intermission. In addition, nobody was to be allowed to leave the auditorium, once inside, until intermission or the concert's conclusion. A furious concertgoer, Jerome Alexander, expressed outrage at the treatment accorded some people who arrived late for a Stokowski concert given in New York City. The night, Alexander writes, was one of unusual traffic congestion. Thirty men and twenty women—many of them old and feeble—had been held up through no fault of their own. Yet, instead of the customary permission to find their seats between numbers, they were made to stand in the lobby of Carnegie Hall, "like dumb driven cattle" for three-quarters of an hour, while four separate pieces were performed. Stokowski had proved himself "unwise and inhuman."[21]

Shortly after Alexander's letter appeared in the *Times,* the results of a questionnaire sent to subscribers of the Philadelphia Orchestra were published. Three-quarters of the respondents favored applause. At last, Stokowski relented and allowed some handclapping.

The controversy over applause refused to die. Conductors continued to rule over their public, scolding it and telling it what was permitted. On 24 January 1932, the *Times* published a letter from Frank Norris, who was responding to an article by Olin Downes on applause, which had appeared on 10 January. It seemed to Norris that all people in music considered "the majority of the audience" to be "ruled by habit rather than intelligence." Sarcastically, he suggested: "It would seem fitting" therefore "to print on the programs—underlined in heavy red—which movements should be applauded." From time to time, other letters and other comments on applause appeared. One of Olin Downes's last lengthy articles on the subject was published in the *Times* in 1938. He wrote that Toscanini, Stokowski, Klemperer, Koussevitzky, and "the small fish" were still forbidding audiences to applaud between movements and labeled the ban a "modern form of snobbery." True, it was inappropriate to applaud until the end of such works as Tchaikovsky's Sixth Symphony. However, where once an audience might have released its emotions and expressed enthusiasm between movements, if it felt so moved, it now sits ill at ease, fidgets, whispers, and resorts to a variety of other means to relieve its tension. "How anti-musical it is! Snobbism in excelsis! An unnatural and sterile exhibition in the name of high art!" If an occasional work requires it, Downes advised, request no applause in the program; else permit it. "Music is composed for people. People are not assembled merely to observe a musical ritual," was Downes's conclusion.[22]

If conductors were cavalier in their attitudes towards managers, trustees, and audiences, they behaved with even greater arrogance when dealing with composers. This arrogance was touched on earlier, in describing Toscanini's tampering with a score by Wagenaar. As previously noted, most conductors were European and had scarcely any acquaintance with the American scene, and therefore they tended to spurn American compositions or rely on friends to suggest a work or two. As often as not, the friends had narrow tastes and little insight into, or curiosity about, American music. The occasional native piece a conductor did produce was given a first performance for its "novelty effect," and rarely given a second one. The wise composer took care to keep his music brief, since too much costly rehearsal time might be necessary and because conductors believed that audiences would react hostilely to a lengthy modern work. If fortunate, the composer might receive royalty of seventy-five dollars for the performance.

Composers agonized over their problems with foreign conductors, Roy Harris, for example, writes:

> Conductors do not like the emotional content of our most serious characteristic music; and above all they resent the technical difficulties of its rhythmic patterns and forms. It requires a new receptive approach in which neither the conductor nor his orchestra men can rest on their experience. It requires conscientious work; it must be felt, and European conductors and orchestral men rarely have the time, the patience, or the desire to study our music thoroughly enough to feel it. They can play all the literature of the masters from memory; why should they sweat over a young American upstart? . . . If enough pressure is brought to bear to force their [i.e., American compositions] production they are very often given . . . a scratch performance. . . . When [American audiences] . . . hear an American work poorly performed they conclude that the work was not good.[23]

The unhappy native composer needed sympathetic intermediaries to realize his works. Only by hearing his music could he evaluate what he had done, find stimulation to continue writing, and develop new ideas. In a letter to the *Times*, Edward Potter asks how the "budding American Beethoven" could be discovered and encouraged if conductors decline to play his music? "A real problem," he complains, "is the matter of getting a composition brought to the attention of orchestra conductors. How does one go about it?" Citing his own personal experience: "I take a score to a conductor—or, rather, to the conductor's secretary, for one never contacts His Highness—in the Fall, only to be told that the programs for the entire season have been made up and it will be impossible to consider additional works. I then defer my attack until the following Spring after the season is over, and then I am told that the conductor is on the eve of leaving for Europe and cannot be bothered with the consideration of new works."[24]

When fortune attended a composer's campaign to have a composition accepted for performance, it denoted no achievement of respect for the person of the lucky one. Vladimir Dukelsky (who used the pen name Vernon Duke for his popular music) writes of his elation when Koussevitzky scheduled his Second Symphony for performance. But:

> Rehearsals in Symphony Hall were closely guarded secrets with only special appointees permitted to attend. . . . Composers, troublesome and nosy creatures, were relegated to the first balcony and tolerated on condition that they remained silent and respectful. To correct a glaring mistake in the orchestra parts, or an erroneous tempo by the conductor, meant standing up and shouting—a daring feat attempted by few. I remember leaping to my feet when the coda of the finale was tackled *twice* too fast, and screaming: "No, no! slower, please." Koussevitzky stopped the orchestra, turned to me with a terrifying scowl, screamed back: "If too slow, I play faster!" and did. I screamed louder this time, in genuine anguish. Sergei Alexandrovitch rapped the stand with his baton and hissed: "*Personne* play!" (which was his way of saying: "Nobody plays"), then added in tragic tones, addressing me: "You conduct," and crossed his arms on his chest. "But I cannot conduct, Sergei Alexandrovitch," I wailed. "Then you compose and I conduct and you—SILENCE!" Koussevitzky summed up grandiosely and resumed the offending coda. It was now taken at the correct tempo, but the episode looked like a Koussevitzky victory.[25]

On the whole, performers preferred old to contemporary, conservative to progressive, and European to American works. Why

SERGE KOUSSEVITSKY. Photo: Copyright © 1948 by William Whitaker. Courtesy of the Boston Symphony Orchestra.

the old? Deems Taylor explains that the score and parts of an old piece, say by Mozart, cost only "a fifth of what you'd pay for a modern work." Old music entails no performance fees, necessitates fewer rehearsals, is easier to play, and meets with the approval of leading supporters of the orchestra. Aaron Copland points out that because audiences are kept from experiencing new music, and are fed nonsense about a few masterpieces from the past, which they hear over and over again, they cannot help feeling apprehensive about contemporary sounds. They return to the performer the prejudices he has promoted. Furthermore, as Peter Korn mentions, since the public hears very few American works, usually in the shape of "a curtain raiser, seldom longer than a few minutes," it may conclude that the United States has "few really important symphonic composers, and that these 'specialize' in overtures, essays for orchestra, and similarly brief programme dividends."[26]

A quotation from the conductor Walter Damrosch indicates the kind of antagonism performers accorded contemporary works. In 1932, he wrote: "In regard to modern tendencies in creative music, I am not very optimistic. There have always been periods in the world during which an art has stagnated." Such a period, he said, has been in progress since Wagner. "The ultra-modern composers of today seem to negate the entire past. Many of them seek to eliminate human emotions altogether from their works, and all their efforts seem based on creating a kind of nervous excitement which soon tires and finally bores the listeners." One might assume that Damrosch was referring principally to the grating music of Schoenberg, Stravinsky, and their American followers; but apparently his disapproval was more extensive. A look at Damrosch's concert programs and the music he aired during his "Music Appreciation Hour" on radio reveals compositions almost entirely from the past that, he said, had "proven worthy" and would not "distress . . . his adult audiences."[27]

Contemporary American music competed for program space not only with the thousands of well-understood works from the past, but also with the numerous contemporary works from Europe, toward which the conductors felt a closer affinity. For example, Eugene Ormandy, who replaced Stokowski as conductor of the Philadelphia Orchestra in 1938, said the greatest modern composer he knew of was his fellow-Hungarian Béla Bartók, followed by the Russian Sergei Prokofiev, the German Paul Hindemith, and the Russian Igor Stravinsky (from his early period). Pressed to mention American composers, he named the more immediately understood ones—Paul Creston, Samuel Barber, and the young William Schuman. Not that he championed their music. As did most other conductors, he avoided doing so. Why? Because the "staid audiences" of Philadelphia countenanced only pleasing music. He would not alienate them with overdoses of modern works.[28] Ormandy's stand was certainly a contrast to Stokowski's, but no improvement as far as native composers were concerned.

Toscanini was notorious for ignoring American compositions. Between 1926 and 1936, the years he directed the New York Philharmonic, he performed only five works by Americans. Native composers, he said, possibly had technical ability but lacked heart. "There will be composers [in America] in time," he added. Yet he did manage to perform the works of several twentieth-century Italian composers—Ottorino Respighi, Victor de Sabata, Vincenzo Tommasini, and Ildebrando Pizzetti, among others. He refused in 1931 to put on Gershwin's popular *Rhapsody in Blue,* despite the urging of William Paley, head of CBS. When Toscanini finally did do it eleven years later, he made a miserable botch of the music.[29]

Sir John Barbirolli arrived from England to replace Toscanini as conductor of the Philharmonic. On his arrival in New York, a writer in *Musical America* said that he hoped Barbirolli would differ from other conductors who scheduled more than Americans wanted to hear of their countrymen's compositions. The writer could not know that later the same year Barbirolli would boast in a letter to Charles Parker, in England, that he had begun to propagandize the cause of English music. Michael Kennedy, Barbirolli's biographer, would admit that the few American works Barbirolli used were lesser compositions pressed on him by others and that he included altogether "too many English works" on the Philharmonic's programs.[30]

In 1931, Olin Downes was praying for "the brilliant and authoritative American conductor" to appear, who would be "sympathetic as a European conductor hardly can be to characteristic phrases of American creative talent." Proving Downes's point about European musicians lacking sympathy for American music, Arthur Fiedler speaks of having "a devil of a time" when he started to conduct American music. "The musicians who were mostly foreigners looked down their noses; they wouldn't get into the right spirit. 'Now look here!' I told them, 'You're in America, you're making American money, you're playing to American audiences, and you're going to play American music.'"[31] Fiedler, fortunately for native music, had been born in Boston.

John Mueller, in his study of the American symphony orchestra, found that the programs of foreign conductors normally contained 6 percent or fewer American works. To illustrate this he writes that American composers "by and large, did not profit from [Stokowski's] explorations." How could they, while Stokowski stated that "American music will take several centuries to reach its first great flowering period"? He held that it needed to mature gradually and fuse "all the cultural elements" before it could sound like a truly "American idiom," one "with American feeling about life."[32]

Note the patronizing attitude of Halina Rodzinski when she claims that her conductor–husband, the Polish-born Artur Rodjinski, found that "quality . . . was not often or easily come by" in contemporary American compositions. She says that he performed works by Barber, Schuman, Harris, Herrmann, Bernard Rogers, Still, Creston, and Dukelsky. Heard once, they "never had another Philharmonic hearing as far as I can discover," for they "promptly fell into a desuetude which they probably merited." She concludes: "The best to be said of all these pieces is that they were well made."[33]

American composers and some critics never ceased their complaint that foreign musicians were biased and thought European trivialities of greater consequence than serious American works. As a result, the fate of the native piece occasionally heard in concert was "a first performance and then complete oblivion . . . even though critics praise [it highly]." The more truly American a composition sounded, the more apt was it to be misunderstood; the more European, the more apt was it to be performed. Moreover, they claimed, extraordinary and highly successful American works did exist; to name three of one composer, Aaron Copland, there were *El Salon Mexico, Billy the Kid,* and *Rodeo.*[34] Yet these works did not quickly reach concert audiences. "They were not sought after by symphony orchestras as the latest Shostakovich or Prokofieff symphonies at the time—although they are more original and imaginative as music. Americans, even Copland, never receive the kind of cultural acclaim reserved for foreigners in our country."[35]

As for the canard about audiences remaining adamantly opposed to contemporary American works, composers could cite several instances in which, given the chance to familiarize themselves with the music, Americans reacted positively. That kind of chance was given by the dance companies who commissioned contemporary ballet music and performed it repeatedly in New York City and while on tour. Lincoln Kirstein and the Ballet Caravan had thus popularized *Billy the Kid;* Agnes de Mille and the Ballet Russe de Monte Carlo, *Rodeo;* Martha Graham and her Ballet Company, *Appalachian Spring.* In all three instances, Copland was asked or voluntarily decided to utilize traditional American music and modify his own style in order to give verisimilitude to authentically American scenes.[36]

In all fairness, it should be mentioned that a handful of European conductors did play more than a token amount of American music, while they were active in the United States. Immediately coming to mind are Eugene Goossens, Fabien Sevitzky, and Serge Koussevitzky. Koussevitzky alone, in the years 1924 to 1944, gave a first hearing to sixty-six American works and brought to the fore composers like Copland, Piston, Harris, Hanson, Barber, and Schuman. True, he favored works that showed a French or Russian influence, not a German one. But he boldly went ahead and performed what he considered meritorious new music, even though audiences might dislike it. Unfortunately, he did have the weakness of liking novelty for its own sake; save for some favorite works, after a second or third presentation his interest would cease.[37]

To his credit, he actively sought out American unknowns. When he heard that the young Walter Piston lived nearby and composed music, Koussevitzky asked Piston to see him and learned he wrote only chamber music. "Why not for orchestra?" Koussevitzky asked. Piston replied, "Because nobody would play it." Said the conductor, "I will play it." And he did Piston, composition after composition, beginning with the *Symphonic Piece* of 1928.[38]

A few years later, Koussevitzky met Roy Harris. "You must write something for me," Koussevitzky said. "What?" asked Harris. "Something big," came the reply, "from the West." Harris compiled with his First Symphony (1933).[39] Harris, along with Piston and Copland, became one of Koussevitzky's most favored *protégés*—a composer whose talent the conductor admired and whose music he responded to emotionally.[39]

As for American performers of American music, three names stand out: John Kirkpatrick, Henry Hadley, and Howard Hanson. Kirkpatrick from 1931 on became a vigorous publicist for the piano compositions of native composers, especially those of the neglected Charles Ives. In the thirties and forties, contemporary American composers could depend on him to include at least one or two of their works in each of his piano recitals. It must be kept in mind that these were years when most soloists assiduously avoided any contact with American music. Reviewing a concert given in November 1943, Virgil Thomson succinctly states the argument for American performers. (Kirkpatrick had played pieces by Ives, Harris, and Theodore Chanler, among others). He writes: "John Kirkpatrick, who gave a piano recital last night in Times Hall, has a way of making one feel happy about American music. He does this by loving it, understanding it, and playing it very beautifully."[40]

Henry Hadley was associate conductor of the New York Philharmonic from 1920 to 1927. When he was crowded out of his position by foreign musicians, he took over the Manhattan Symphony Orchestra, where he remained until 1932, conducting a goodly number of native compositions. In order to win the public over to art music, he insisted on low ticket prices for concerts (fifty cents to two dollars, students twenty-five cents), occasionally gave free concerts, and allowed the music to be broadcast over radio station WOR. From 1933 to 1935, he conducted the orchestra of the Berkshire Music Festival, where he again scheduled American works. He and his Festival orchestra would be superseded by Koussevitzky and the Boston Symphony Orchestra in 1936.[41]

Enough cannot be said in praise of Howard Hanson's efforts to familiarize Americans with their own music. Appointed director of the Eastman School of Music in Rochester, New York, in 1924, he commenced a series of concerts that placed emphasis on American works. For some forty years, he himself would direct the performance of countless American orchestral compositions both during the annual American Music Festival at Rochester, when a guest conductor of other orchestras in the United States, and while on tour with the Eastman Orchestra in Europe and the Middle East. The many recordings he has made of twentieth-century American compositions remain benchmarks for younger conductors who wish to interpret the American repertoire. Virgil Thomson accurately puts his finger on what constituted Hanson's excellence as a conductor, in a commentary about "Americanisms," written in 1946. His subject was both Howard Hanson and the young, up-and-coming Leonard Bernstein. The two men, Thomson writes, conduct American works pleasurably. In contrast, foreign conductors who perform this music usually build a resistance to it because of "a complete lack of adaptation . . . to American speech. They understand its international grammar, but they have not acquired its idiom and accent." They think "idiom and accent" are "localisms of some kind. They are nothing of the sort; they are a contribution to the world's musical language."[42]

Who were the American composers most often performed? Fortunately, John Mueller has taken the trouble to summarize the incidence of native works in the repertoire of the ten oldest major symphony orchestras in the United States. He found that the most popular native composers, as seen in the performance of their compositions in the years 1925 to 1950 were first Aaron Copland, second Samuel Barber, third George Gershwin—followed, respectively, by William Schuman, Morton Gould, Walter Piston, Virgil Thomson, David Diamond, George Antheil, Randall Thompson, Paul Creston, Howard Hanson, John Alden Carpenter, Norman Dello Joio, Roger Sessions, and Roy Harris. All ten orchestras have performed Barber, Carpenter, Copland, Diamond, Gershwin, Hanson, Harris, and Piston. Nine have done Gould and Schuman; eight, Creston and Thomson; seven, Thompson. Of the 280 American composers who have appeared on the programs of these orchestras, 50 percent of them were represented in performance by only one orchestra each. Owing to the usual one or two performances of any given work and the regional concentration in each orchestra's native repertoire, few composers managed to achieve any national representation or recognition.[43] When we consider the endless scheduling of European works, including twentieth-century ones, the record for performances of American music is dismal indeed.

We might hope that community and other orchestras less exalted than these ten would represent native culture more fully. These orchestras were multiplying in number, despite the depression, or possibly because people were seeking release from their everyday anxieties, and local orchestral concepts served as palliatives. These ensembles had no costly star system of prominent conductors and soloists. Wages for professional orchestra players were modest, and often competent amateurs contributed their services. Nor were concerts expensive to produce, since some community or school auditorium or gymnasium was normally available for use. Artistic aloofness and pretension formed no part of the makeup of these groups, which drew freely from, and existed only for the sake of, their communities.

A typical instance of how one of these orchestras came into being is furnished by the Pioneer Valley Orchestra of northwestern Massachusetts, conducted by Harold Leslie. In 1939, a few dedicated people tentatively organized a Young People's Symphony. Interest was so keen that an adult orchestra started up the next year. The Kiwanis Club of Greenfield offered to manage the budget—which was $2,500 for the year, all of it, save for five hundred dollars met through ticket sales. The orchestra numbered about seventy-five to eighty musicians from every walk of life. The first season, five public concerts were given in the towns of Greenfield, Northfield, and Brattleboro (Vermont). Virgil Thomson, who heard the orchestra in April 1941, reports that the playing was musical and glowing. The program consisted of Mendelssohn's *Hebrides Overture,* Haydn's *London Symphony,* and Dvorak's Ninth Symphony, "From the New World." The Pioneer Valley Orchestra, Thomson says, is an amazing example of the some thirty thousand symphony orchestras founded since the beginning of the depression.[44]

Experimental ensembles were also formed from time to time. One was the eighty-member Woman's Symphony, conducted by Antonia Brico, which made its debut on 18 February 1935, performing a Handel Concerto Grosso, Schumann's First Symphony, and Tchaikovsky's *Romeo and Juliet Overture.*[45]

Unfortunately, the proliferation of American orchestras did not mean the proliferation of performances of native works. Whether community or experimental, these orchestras aped their prestigious counterparts and confined themselves to playing European compositions from the eighteenth and nineteenth centuries. When a book like Herbert Roussel's *The Houston Symphony Orchestra* (1972) is read from beginning to end, one realizes how insignificantly American music figured in the history of the regional orchestra.

As for their operas, American composers had even fewer expectations than they did for their symphonic works. The Metropolitan Opera of New York was a desert of futility. Deems Taylor's *The King's Henchman* (1927) and *Peter Ibbetson* (1931);

Louis Gruenberg's *Emperor Jones* (1933); Howard Hanson's *Merry Mount* (1934)—these works were about the extent of its commitment to Americana. The minor opera companies, like those of Alfredo Salmaggi, Fortuno Gallo, and Charles Wagner, did nothing at all. And the various civic opera associations, like those of Flint (Michigan), St. Paul (Minnesota), Omaha (Nebraska), and Milwaukee (Wisconsin), which were formed in the late twenties and the thirties, did very little. The mounting of Charles Wakefield Cadman's opera *Shanewis* in 1932 by the Flint Community Music Association is an exception to this rule, as also is this association's performance of Randall Thompson's *Solomon and Balkis*.[46]

When the evidence from the thirties is sifted through, one is left with the conclusion that, on the whole, American composers had applied themselves with a will to create well-crafted and attractive works that would appeal to a widespread public. Cultural prejudice, ignorance, and incuriosity combined to keep these compositions off the concert and opera stage. Until performer and public willingly fostered the composers about them, who in good faith tried to accommodate their interests and desires, a viable art-music culture could never come into being in the United States.

The Financing of Music Organizations

Commencing with the twenties, music organizations in America, however artistically oriented, were capitalistic business enterprises. They were privately controlled by a board of trustees, which set policy and made decisions, usually after consultation with the orchestra's or opera company's manager and director. From this standpoint, members of the public were considered customers. Therefore, music lovers had to be enticed into purchasing tickets by means of attractive programs and, to the extent they were affordable, noted conductors and soloists. Since it was thought that a considerable number of people attended concerts and operatic performances mostly for the sake of the personalities on view, the presence on stage of one or more widely celebrated performers might secure higher profits. Unfortunately, art music was not a necessity, like bread and milk, nor a product with mass appeal, like the movies. For many of the men and women who made

Edward Hopper, *Two on the Aisle*. The Toledo Museum of Art, Toledo, Ohio. Gift of Edward Drummond Libbey. Reproduced with permission.

up the art-music audience, attendance at performances was a luxury indulged in good times, but postponed in reduced circumstances. Moreover, competition had to be countered. Music was available free over the radio, at minimal cost at the movies, or as a permanent possession on disc recordings.

Admission prices to concerts and operatic performances remained lower than the amount required to meet expenses. Traditionally, music organizations had depended on the bounty of a limited number of wealthy patrons to cover their deficits. But as the Great Depression wore on, fewer people purchased tickets, deficits grew, and depleted private fortunes deterred patrons from exercising their customary largess. For organization after organization, survival meant broadening the base for its support. Thus, in 1936 the Metropolitan Opera Association set up the

Metropolitan Opera Guild in order "to develop and cultivate a wider public interest in opera, to further musical education and appreciation, and to promote the activities of the Metropolitan Opera Association." The first year, the Guild's membership numbered 11,000 people from all walks of life. (In 1949, membership would stand at 40,000.) Members subscribed to *Opera News,* received a variety of inducements to attend operatic presentations, and were asked to contribute whatever money they could to help defray the opera company's expenses. The Guild itself worked to interest public-school officials in the educational values of opera, underwrote matinee performances, and sold low-priced tickets to students so that they would attend these performances.[47]

When Arthur Fiedler attempted to launch his Esplanade Concerts in Boston, he originally had expected about sixteen well-to-do contributors to assume responsibility for expenses. The depression intervened; Fiedler had to fund the series with money from several hundred contributors, in addition to what he could raise through appeals to the general public.[48]

In 1934, the New York Philharmonic also went public, in a drive to raise $500,000 for support of the orchestra over the next three years. Harry Harkness Flagler, president of the board, reported that former patrons "could no longer be expected to bear the burden of increasing losses . . . and that part of the responsibility of continuing the work of the orchestra must be shifted to the public." He claimed that all possible economies had already been made in orchestral salaries, administrative expenses, and hall rentals. At the same time, receipts had fallen off by $60,000; the deficit stood at $150,000.[49]

Not everyone accepted Flagler's explanation. A writer in *Musical America* suggested that the big-name conductors used by the Philharmonic were receiving exorbitant salaries, which required cutting. Bruno Walter, the writer said, was drawing only small audiences, and Toscanini was failing to pack the hall. If the board dismissed the "stars," hired capable conductors at reasonable salaries, and reduced ticket prices, it would develop an audience of genuine music lovers interested in the compositions played and not in the glamorous conductors.[50]

A more radical suggestion came from the composer Douglas Moore. He said that if the board wanted money from the public it should be willing to share its control over the Philharmonic. The orchestra ought to play contemporary music and cease being only "a symbol of the past." Both "the Philharmonic and the Metropolitan [opera] stand unalterably opposed to any progress in the new principles of music." Since Moore represented an opposition with little power, he went unheeded. In fact, about the time he made his suggestions, a firm of financial experts was recommending that the Metropolitan Opera select the "best-selling operas" of the past ten years and make them the basis for future performances. And Edward Johnson, the new director of the Metropolitan, was announcing that the company could no longer afford the risk of performing any new works.[51] It was an announcement that was being made by one director after another in these years.

In 1934–35, the San Francisco Symphony seemed about to die. All of its funds were spent, and it had ceased giving concerts. Then, in May 1935, voters amended the city's charter so that a one-half-cent tax could be levied for the orchestra's benefit. An art commission set up by the city purchased concert performances and sold tickets at low prices to the public.[52] However, nobody came forward to suggest public control over the orchestra. It would seem that for the most part what the San Francisco Symphony and other orchestras were performing on a regular basis, mainly romantic and classical works, met with general approval; or so the conductors and boards of directors claimed.

The trustees, on the other hand, could not always be relied on to know what the general music public approved. Furthermore, some of them did not care to know. Customarily, they held themselves aloof from the community, associating with people of power and wealth like themselves. The board of the Philadelphia Orchestra, for example, was an unliberal cliquish group drawn from old local families who shared similar values, lived in close proximity, and maintained personal relationships exclusively with each other. Among them were financiers, industrialists, and corporate lawyers. Absent were musicians, educators, and representatives of the larger concert audience. Edward Arian writes that most trustees of the Philadelphia Orchestra were certain that comparatively few people had the capacity to understand fine music and appreciate the high excellence of their orchestra. When the question arose of trying to enlarge the audience reached by the orchestra, one board member said: "This talk of playing for more people in the community is nonsense. Let's face it, most of the people in this town aren't interested in hearing your kind of music, let alone being able to appreciate how well you fellows play it."

The trustees then voted against expanding the orchestra's communal activities, fearing the action would, first, meet with a loss, and, second, vulgarize what the orchestra stood for. One trustee commented: "We'd have to be pretty desperate before we'd stoop to making a circus of this institution."[53]

Attitudes nowise different were held by the board of the Metropolitan Opera Association, though in this case the members were not all from old New York families. This board, too, was inclined to turn a deaf ear to people's desires. Just before the arrival of the depression, excited discussion was going on in New York over the value of operas sung in English. The proponents said it would win larger audiences for the Metropolitan by increasing comprehension of the drama. Otto Kahn, chairman of the board and wealthy financier, spoke against catering to popular needs. Opera in English, he said, would distort the sound and rhythm of a music conceived for a different language. Librettos were sometimes inane and absurd; operas were better enjoyed if not literally understood. In addition, by keeping operas in a foreign language, the Metropolitan could bring in the best singers in the world and use them to finest advantage. Kahn cited a final and most extraordinary reason against presenting opera in English: Yes, he agreed, the French, Germans, and Italians did hear all opera in their native language. However, the explanation for this was that they could not afford the expense, as could the Metropolitan, of presenting operas in their original language.[54]

If a foreign conductor arrived in the United States with insufficient sense of his own worth, trustees communicated their patrician point of view to him. John Barbirolli, for instance, though he avoided meeting with the "pompous music patrons" of the New York Philharmonic, "and kowtowing to them," did have to listen to Ruth Pratt, one of the friendlier trustees, advise him not to socialize with members of the orchestra but to live and behave "much more grandly." The reporter of Pratt's conversation with Barbirolli, Michael Kennedy, adds that most of the Philharmonic's directors and patrons "were Republicans with a deeply grained isolationism which upset" Barbirolli. (World War II had started and, of course, Barbirolli was worried about England, his native land.)[55]

As has been pointed out, the Philharmonic's board at this time was notorious for employing no native conductors, commissioning no native music, and making no sincere attempt to schedule American works for the celebration of the orchestra's centennial. Although criticized, "the Philharmonic board did not so much as sniff its disapproval of this radical vision. It just went right ahead with its stodgy plans for the Centennial."[56]

Schickel, Arian, Mueller, Graf, and other writers on the American symphony orchestra and opera association are in agreement on how the conservative, backward-looking programs of the orchestras and opera companies mirrored the tastes and met the needs of upper-class patrons. Board members protected their class's cultural concerns and expected, by so doing, to add to their own reputation and position of rank among their fellows. As for contemporary music, they disliked it. Exploring unmarked musical territory required a curiosity they lacked.[57] Theirs was an illusory, copycat, provincial acquaintanceship with music acquired through imported compositions from the past and interpreted by imported musicians. They and the directors they hired were becoming caretakers of musical necropoles.

Every now and again the rare exception to the narrow-minded patron is discovered. Elizabeth Sprague Coolidge (1864–1953) deserves praise for her commissioning of chamber works by native composers and her sponsorship of chamber concerts that included native music. Another of this scarce breed was George Eastman (1854–1932), who put his fortune at the service of American music. He funded the Eastman School of Music, in Rochester, New York, and brought in Howard Hanson in 1925 to be its director. Eastman's money made possible the many years of annual American Music Festivals organized by Hanson; he gave it despite his friends' warning that it was money wasted. Composers, they said, would benefit creatively if made to confront the real world on their own. Howard Hanson states: "One ultraconservative critic remarked to Mr. Eastman that the concerts had been going on for five years and he had not yet observed that we had discovered any Beethoven."

George Eastman replied: "If we discover one Beethoven in fifty years I shall consider the venture an enormous success."[58]

Like the patron and trustee, the professional manager of musical activities was not a public musical performer. His job came into being because his services were useful to the thousands of American communities that wished for art music but needed some outside agency, knowledgeable about cultural matters, to bring performances to them. The manager's functions were to determine where these communities were, organize and oversee concerts for them, furnish the musicians, and offer carefully chosen programs designed to have a high rate of acceptance. As an entrepreneur, he had to plan with care and exhibit a shrewd business sense. Altruism could have little place in his calculations; a manager's motivations had to center on financial gain.

Roger Sessions observes that after World War I, when a mass audience came into existence for art music, a hugely increased number of musical performances came into demand as well. Entrepreneurs became necessary to count costs, consider profits, and predict the tastes of millions of individuals: "Those who furnish the products [concerts] are obliged to produce as efficiently and as cheaply as possible the goods which they can sell to the most people; they are obliged, furthermore, to try to persuade the people to whom they sell that it is preferable to buy the goods that are the most cheaply produced; it is furthermore necessary to do everything possible to enhance the value of the goods sold."[59]

The first significant entrepreneurs of this sort were Harry Harrison and Dema Harshburger. In the first third of the century they began to offer programs entitled the "All-Star Series" to smaller cities and towns. By 1930, they had organized 182 Civic Music Committees in thirty-two states, and each committee purchased an annual series of concerts from Harrison and Harshburger. The strategy of the two managers was to discover the most prominent members of a community, convince them of the benefits their town would derive from active participation in musical culture, and request their assistance in rounding up subscribers for a concert series, although no townspeople would know beforehand what programs they would actually hear. Once sufficient subscribers had pledged their support and sufficient profit was assured the managers, then the town was provided with performers, known and unknown, playing tested and familiar compositions similar to those current in the metropolises. Fortunately for the managers, at the other end were musicians anxious to sign up with agents able to line up concerts and make travel arrangements for them.[60]

The success of Harrison and Harshburger encouraged others to enter the field. Into existence came the Community Concerts Corporation, the National Broadcasting and Concert Bureau, and the Columbia Concerts Corporation, to name three of the most important. Scores of salespeople were sent out to locate new towns desiring music and to package concerts for them.[61]

The early years of the depression slowed the recruitment of communities. However, by 1934 and coincident with Roosevelt's assumption of the presidency, more and more towns fell into line. Ward French, in January 1935, reported that the circuit he managed for Arthur Judson, Community Concerts, had experienced a 20 percent increase in membership, and as far as his "campaign directors" were concerned, there was "no more talk of depression." The fear that radio would take away customers evaporated; people wanted to get out of their houses. Indeed, concerts over the radio had created many additional music lovers who were anxious to see live artists like those heard on the air. Five years later, Ward French's organization had experienced tremendous growth and was servicing 365 communities and "upwards of several hundred thousand persons."[62]

By the end of the forties, ten influential men controlled almost all the musicians of any ability and reputation who were concertizing in America. Seven men in Columbia Artists Management commanded 150 soloists and thirty-five ensembles. Two men in the National Concert and Artists corporation and Sol Hurok commanded 118 soloists and twenty-one groups.[63]

Since musical taste in the communities served by these managements appeared to be unformed or unconfidently voiced, the concert managers themselves began to surmise the preferences of their audiences and to prepackage performers and programs for them. The attitude of these impresarios was set forth by K. Howlett of Radio Air Service Corporation when speaking before a gathering of school-music supervisors. Howlett asserted that 75 percent of the public was familiar only with dance music and could not be blamed for a lack of taste, since it "did not know any better." In New York, Sol Hurok concurred in opinions like Howlett's. Moreover Hurok constantly took the public's pulse and if it seemed to express a strong preference for a limited number of art compositions, he acted in compliance with its wishes. His musicians, however angered they might become, were made to eliminate unloved works from their repertoires and play mostly the dependable winners.[64]

The works of contemporary composers were unknown and not dependable winners. Managers normally excluded them from the repertoires of the artists on their roster. Vernon Duke (Vladimir Dukelsky) tells the story of Arthur Rubinstein, around the middle twenties, asking him for a piano concerto. The young composer enthusiastically wrote the composition and hastened to Rubinstein with the manuscript:

> He grabbed the manuscript and began looking it over page by page, his large bulging eyes shining. "It's amazingly good, far, far better than I expected. Forgive me, but I expect very little from new composers," he said. "They all have two faults which make their works hopeless for a pianist who must earn his bread; firstly, they have no melodic gift or are ashamed to display it, and secondly, they don't know how to write for the instrument. They think the piano is a kettledrum. Thank God, you don't. Also, the concerto is full of tunes." He sat down at the piano and essayed the first solo, then added: "Yes, I'll play this music—only not here; the managers won't let me play what I like—they're always complaining about poor Karol's [Szymanovski's] things, which I love. As for concerti . . . it's always Tchaikowsky, Beethoven, or Liszt. No, the place for you and your concerto is Europe. Go to Paris, where I'll be this summer'."[65]

The search for winners restricted the repertoire to just a few pieces played over and over again. An annoyed Virgil Thomson, in the *Herald Tribune* of 21 January 1951, writes a protest against the lack of imagination displayed by concert managers: "With concert business bigger than ever (by volume) the concert repertory gets smaller year by year. There are only five sonatas by Beethoven that the central offices will accept without a row. . . . A little modern music, if short and not too 'advanced' in style, will sometimes be passed." If Thomson had hoped to stir up some public disapproval of this practice, he failed. Instead, at least one letter appeared in the newspaper in opposition to Thomson's stand. The letter, from Scranton, Pennsylvania, reads, in part: "The musical tastes of inland audiences vary unbelievably and they are rarely sophisticated. It is certainly the wish of the management group to provide what the public wants badly enough to pay for, and this is obviously what they do."[66]

Clearly, contemporary composers got short shrift under this system of managed concerts. The commercial imperative that compelled an expansion of every management's market for music, if only to lessen risk and cushion expenses, likewise forced the businessmen involved to avoid innovation and to promote works of proven popularity. Regrettably, by taking no chances and endlessly presenting the same surefire works, they denied the public those exercises in listening to the new that could improve its powers for understanding contemporary works. The result was management's ministering to the wants of audiences conditioned by the marketing conservatism of management itself.

One manager, Arthur Judson, became a powerful figure in American music. From 1915 to 1935, he managed the Philadelphia Orchestra; from 1922 to 1956, the New York Philharmonic. In 1928, he assumed charge of the Wolfsohn Musical Bureau, a firm that he consolidated with Columbia Concerts Corporation in 1930. Later, the corporation was reorganized as Columbia Artists Management and Community Concerts Service. As manager-advisor to Stokowski, Toscanini, Barbirolli, and a number of the greatest instrumental and vocal soloists, he had a great deal to do with what music was performed and who performed it throughout the United States. He did feel it was only sensible to repeat popular classical works several times a season and not to perform often those compositions the public had not enthusiastically accepted. As for the complaints about lack of variety and repudiation of new native compositions, he said it was his experience that a loudly vocal minority grumbled endlessly, no matter what was programmed.[67]

The managerial viewpoint here expressed also guaranteed a complete lack of sympathy for new composers. A budding American Beethoven, if he appeared, stood no chance of sponsorship by the Judsons of this world, unless money could be made from his genius. Men like Judson would respect only money and power, and these composers had neither the one nor the other.

Facing Reality

What was the actual state of things confronting the unperformed serious composers? Most of them endured existences both financially shaky and psychologically disheartening. Unlike painters and sculptors, they could not sell their works to collectors. Unlike painters and sculptors, their art evanesced after being exhibited in performance, leaving behind nothing more concrete than the critical reviews—scant incentive for a would-be patron. Moreover, a musical composition could not be exclusively owned; it had to be shared with performers and audiences. Only rarely did a piece become so popular that conductors clamored to perform it, phonograph companies to record it, and publishers to print it.

In a free-enterprise economy and democracy, patrons such as Prince Esterházy who shared a composer's aesthetic views and purchased his services were an extinct species. Religious or secular oligarchies in control of affluent parishes or towns and seeking music to reflect their power and glory had sundered with the revolutions that convulsed the Western world, beginning in the late eighteenth century. The United States was neither fascist Italy and Germany, nor communist Russia, to find value in works apotheosizing a "folk" or a "proletariat." As Harrison Kerr stated in 1934, the American art composer, after a long, arduous, and costly training of some ten to fifteen years, ended up with an "unsalable knowledge," since "no one will pay . . . a red cent for his work." He remained an outsider to American society and a person of insignificance to the unsympathetic performer, conservative trustee, and profit-conscious manager.[68] Sessions's comments, quoted in the previous chapter, on the arts as subject to the laws of commerce, and the composer existing as a mere cog in the industrial scheme, are borne out here.

When money was needed for food and shelter, and none was to be had, composers could no longer pretend that they were somehow entitled to special consideration. To make a living, they often had to turn their faces away from creating new musical compositions. They taught, played instruments, conducted orchestras, arranged or edited or copied other people's music, or wrote about musical matters for newspapers and periodicals. They became door-to-door salesmen, house painters, or restaurant waiters. Wealthy women or women willing to work and support an artist, they wooed. Sponging from parents and friends grew into a highly developed skill. Failing all this, they went on public relief.

We can understand Paul Bowles's utter astonishment when once he was actually paid to play some passages from his own music. He writes: "The Friends and Enemies of Modern Music gave another bash during the summer of 1935, this one taking place in the Hartford house of Chick Austin. Virgil [Thomson] had long been stressing the importance of music as a commodity which must be paid for; a composer who gave away his music was simply a scab, he maintained. This applied even to being cajoled after dinner by one's host or hostess into playing a few excerpts from one's work in progress. Austin agreed with Virgil's point of view; accordingly he hired Aaron [Copland], Virgil, George Antheil and me to perform in Hartford."[69]

The stand urged by Thomson was bold enough. Regrettably, hardly anyone would pay, and even giving the music away found few takers. Paul Bowles ended up on relief.

An advertisement in *Musical America*, 10 January 1938, is instructive regarding the composer's plight: "Prominent Composer desires to become associated with an outstanding music school or institution as teacher of theory, counterpoint, and composition." A Juilliard graduate, he has "won many of the major awards in international competitions." His works have received the "unanimous acclaim of press and public in Europe and America, and are being constantly programmed by the leading musical organizations everywhere." Moreover, his music has been "published by foremost American music publishers and is enjoying great sales the world over." Yet, all this said, the composer was not making it financially and needed a job! Regrettably, the advertisement fails to name him.

For some time now, various state and federal laws had existed that protected the worker against the exploitive industrialist. Nobody thought, however, to protect the composer against gouging by the directors and managers of concerts and operatic presentations. Note Charles Repper's assertion in *Musical America*, 10 February 1936: "At present we have the ridiculous state of affairs in which composers, on whose existence depend the occupations of conductors, singers, instrumentalists, music teachers, critics, and publishers, are the only ones who cannot, except in rare instances, make a living at their jobs. And to cap the climax, even their fellow-workers in the musical vineyard expect them to accept this absurd situation as inevitable."

The average royalty paid by the New York Philharmonic to a composer, who had to supply the score and a set of parts, was $29. Other major orchestras might pay from $20 to $50. The remainder paid nothing. And to have a set of parts copied might cost the composer $250. The composer could substantially lower his cost of living by not seeking any performances!

Not much better was the Metropolitan Opera Association. Despite the fact that its production of Louis Gruenberg's *The Emperor Jones* was a hit, in 1933 the composer received an average of $91 a performance, and the Metropolitan presented the opera only eleven times.[70]

A work had to bridge the gap between art and popular music to make a great deal of money. The *Rhapsody in Blue* of George Gershwin was one such work. Gershwin could be indifferent to critics who denounced it as an example of serious music when at the same time it earned over $250,000 from record and sheet-music sales, parts rentals, and subsidiary rights. For allowing its use in the 1930 movie *The King of Jazz*, Gershwin received $50,000; for soloing in it for two weeks at the Roxy Theater in New York City, he received $10,000.[71]

Occasionally an established publisher asked native composers for music, as did the H. W. Gray Company in 1940. Requesting short pieces for organ, Gray published the contributions of Copland, Jacobi, Moore, Piston, Sessions, Sowerby, and Wagenaar. G. Schirmer experimented with issuing a new series of study scores of recent music, including Carpenter's *Sea Drift*, Harris's *When Johnny Comes Marching Home*, and Barber's *Dover Beach* and *Music for a Scene from Shelley*. The composers, to be sure, were most grateful.[72]

The Gray and Schirmer actions were exceptional. Other publishers felt hostility to new music; publishing it, they said, guaranteed them financial loss, and no firm could survive on losses.

Composers had to push hard for the publication of their music. They courted the affluent for the necessary money, or they contributed their own earnings. One of the first enterprises devoted to issuing new native music was Arthur Farwell's Wa-Wan Press, which the composer operated on a shoestring, in Newton, Massachusetts, from 1901 to 1911. After its demise, a handful of organizations, most of them directed by composers, specialized in issuing the new music spurned by regular publishers: the Eastman School of Music, the Juilliard Foundation, Cowell's *New Music*, Alma Werthein's Cos Cob Press, and the Arrow Music Press. None expected to reap a profit; deficits were annual occurrences. But at least they did print and offer the public contemporary-music scores. Lehman Engel writes that he, Copland, Thomson, and Blitzstein started the Arrow Music Press in order to offer "composers an opportunity to print and distribute their music inexpensively, and with virtually no bank account we published in the first five years, through composers themselves and friends, fifty-four works, most of them of major proportions and importance."[73]

In addition, composers and their friends (fortunately, some of them monied) pooled their efforts to put on the concerts of contemporary music that established ensembles avoided performing. Marion Bauer states:

> In 1921, a small group of young American composers founded the American Music Guild. Our object was to learn each other's music and to present worthy works by other American composers to the New York public. This organization was short-lived because of lack of funds, but it existed long enough to accomplish its purpose and to open the way for other societies with similar aims, such as the International Music Guild [1922] and the League of Composers [1923].[74]

The League of Composers, oriented toward American composers with Parisian training, presented its first program on 11 November 1923 in New York City. One year later it gave two concerts of "the younger generation in music," including Antheil, Rogers, and Copland. Eventually, more young composers were given hearings, and a continuing interchange of music and ideas was established with composers of Latin America.[75]

Aaron Copland, who had helped found the league, in 1928 commenced with Roger Sessions the Copland–Sessions Concerts (1928–31); and, in 1932, he brought about the Yaddo Festivals held at Saratoga Springs. Indefatigable in the cause of new music,

Copland and other leaders in the league evolved a plan to promote American composers by commissioning works targeted for specific ensembles. Money from wealthy backers underwrote the plan. In 1934, Gruenberg, Harris, Piston, Sessions, [Randall] Thompson, [Virgil] Thomson, Berezowsky, and Citkowitz were the composers designated to write the works. Stokowski and the Philadelphia Orchestra, Walter and the New York Philharmonic, Stock and the Chicago Symphony, Rodzinski and the Cleveland Orchestra, Davison and the Harvard Glee Club, Dessoff and the Adesdi Chorus, the Pro Arte Quartet, and the Stradivarius Quartet were the performers agreeing to premiere them.[76]

A year later, Copland had gotten the New School for Social Research in New York City to agree to give five one-composer concerts: Copland, Harris, Piston, Sessions, and Thomson. This was the first time a series of concerts, each devoted to one American composer, had been attempted in the United States.[77]

Later, on 17 December 1937, Copland, Thomson, Harris, Sessions, Moore, and forty-three other composers met in New York City to form the American Composers' Alliance, whose objectives were to protect composers' economic rights, to stimulate interest in the performance of American music, and to regulate and gather all performance fees. Though the alliance was not totally effective, it did bring about some improvement in composers' dealings with performers.[78]

While Copland was active in New York City, Howard Hanson was active in Rochester. Through the Eastman School of Music and the munificence of George Eastman, he not only published new American works but also performed and recorded them. His annual American Composers' Concerts, begun in 1925, allowed composers to meet, discuss music, and hear one another's latest creations. In his four decades of concert-giving, he performed more new native compositions than did all other conductors combined. Seven years after Hanson's initial concert, Emanuel Balaban noticed the audiences had grown considerably. Baliban observes: "If there is to be a future for American music . . . Dr. Hanson's fruitful work in Rochester will have a great share in making it possible."[79]

A limited amount of recognition and money came to composers through commissions, prizes, and outright stipends meant to encourage creativity. At no time, however, were such rewards as widespread and munificent as those granted authors, painters, and sculptors. For example, by the mid-thirties, several foundations, like the Oberlaender Trust, Pulitzer Foundation, American Academy in Rome, and Guggenheim Foundation, were coming to the aid of creative people, among them composers. Yet a study of where the monetary awards went demonstrates that American composers received only a small amount of the total. The Guggenheim Foundation, to name one, had by 1934 given out 222 fellowships, of which only 10 had gone to composers.[80]

Another problem for composers, particularly the unknown ones, was the subjective if not arbitrary nature of the decisions made by awards committees responsible for winnowing through submissions in order to discover the potential American masterpieces. In 1934 Samuel Barber, still without wide reputation, was refused the Prix de Rome. Amazingly, the next year the American Academy in Rome urged him to apply again for the prize. Barber submitted the same works that had been rejected the previous year, namely his Cello Sonata (1932) and *Music for a Scene from Shelley* (1933). But this time around he won the prize and heard extravagant praise for his music from the committee. Asked to explain the judges' about-face, Barber pointed to the performance by the Philharmonic of the *Shelley* music, and its favorable reception.[81]

If committee members had conservative tastes, or the fashion of the time was to reject ultra-modern sounds, then neo-romantic or only mildly dissonant works would find favor. Stung by criticism that the New York Philharmonic never played or encouraged American music, the orchestra's cautious board tried from 1936 to 1938 to give awards for orchestral works by native composers. Singled out for recognition were Gardner Read, Quincy Porter, Philip James, David Van Vactor, Charles Haubiel, and Robert Sanders—all of them either romanticists or moderates.[82]

On balance, the inclination of performers, managers, and trustees was to ignore American music and to make no financial overtures to American composers. This neglect persisted during the 1939 New York World's Fair, in which the United States concentrated on proving beyond doubt the preeminence of democratic culture in every sphere of human activity. In the sphere of music, an international music festival was to feature fine American performing groups whose playing finesse would dazzle transatlantic visitors. Concerts were to be devoted to the art music of individual foreign countries; the Metropolitan Opera Association would contribute nine performances of Wagnerian opera. But American art music would not be honored. By March some Americans had become so offended at the slight given native music that they took action. Sigmund Spaeth headed a coalition to protest the absence of American works. Belatedly, the New York Philharmonic played Griffes's *The Pleasure Dome of Kubla-Khan* (on the 30 April), Barber's Overture to *The School for Scandal* (on the 7 May), and Walter Damrosch's *An Abraham Lincoln Song* (on the 7th May). No other American works were to be performed, however, in the ten scheduled Philharmonic concerts, despite the inclusion of many contemporary European compositions. The furore over the debarment of native art music grew. Finally, on 24 May the World's Fair management cancelled the international festival altogether.[83] It had no interest in providing any sort of showcase for America's own musical culture.

Fresh Possibilities for Music

Three new mediums for bringing composer and public together became significant in the thirties: phonograph recordings, motion pictures, and radio. The first machine to record sound was demonstrated by Thomas Edison in 1877. Nineteen years later, Emile Berliner patented the first disc record. Then, in 1924, the electrical process for recording sound was discovered. The annual purchase of discs grew to over 100 million by 1927. However, with the Great Depression, sales dropped; in 1932 only 6 million discs were purchased. At first, the record companies issued mostly music that was tried and true. Then, around the mid-thirties, the companies charily began to market American art music. By 1941, a small but significant amount of American music was available on disc, including portions of Blitzstein's *The Cradle Will Rock* and *No for an Answer*, Copland's *Piano Variations*, *El Salón México*, and *Music for the Theatre*, Harris's Third Symphony and *When Johnny Comes Marching Home*, Piston's *The Incredible*

Flutist, and Schuman's *American Festival Overture*. Unfortunately, just when the possibilities for recording American works seemed most promising, the United States entered World War II and concentrated its resources on the war effort. In addition, owing to disagreement with the recording companies, James Petrillo, president of the American Federation of Musicians, barred members from making any recordings at all. Disc recording ceased to seem promising.[84]

Meanwhile, movie technology was growing apace. Projection machines designed to show motion pictures were used in New York City in 1896, and six years later America's first movie house opened in Los Angeles; when, in 1927–28, the sound track was added to film, the first great decade of the talking picture began. In the mid-thirties, at the time that American music was finding its way onto disc recordings, writing musical scores for sound films took on importance—the more ambitious the film, the more essential a striking score for the soundtrack.[85] But regrettably, knowledgeableness and taste in music met with disesteem in Hollywood. Throughout the thirties and forties, producers like Darryl Zanuck valued only musical commonplaces and popular tunes that encouraged foot-tapping and might prove to be hits. The movie audience, they were convinced, lacked sophistication, would tolerate no novel sounds, and approved completely sentimental music. Irwin Bazelon, a film composer, once told Leonard Rosenman that if an art composer, even a winner of the Pulitzer Prize, competed with a successful popular-song writer to do a motion picture, the latter would invariably win out. Rosenman replied: "The chances are that they [the producers] never will have heard of the concert composer, even if he had won the Pulitzer Prize—or, for that matter, of the Pulitzer Prize."[86]

The Hollywood situation was not one to attract many serious composers unless they were anxious about money to pay bills. The temptations of Hollywood for the impoverished composer are vividly described by Otto Luening. In his autobiography, *The Odyssey of an American Composer* (pp. 344–46), he writes that in May 1941 he went to visit Bernard Kaun in Hollywood, and found him and three other "wild-eyed men surrounded by ashtrays filled with cigarette butts," the four of them busily writing the musical score for the picture *Of Human Bondage*. He was invited to help, at a wage of $1 per measure of orchestration, and $30 per measure of composed music. Within seven hours Luening had made $240 ("every time I passed a bar line I could hear the cash register ring"), which was the fastest money he had made since he was born. Kaun asked him to come to work in Hollywood, guaranteeing him $1000 a month, and the possibility of a wage of $50,000 a year. But, Luening realized, he would involve himself in "a pressure job," with no time "to write serious music." He declined.

Luening and other serious composers, had they worked exten-sively in Hollywood, would have felt apprehensive about producers' attitudes and their own isolation, physical and spiritual, from the artistic mainstream. The typical composer who did go to Hol-lywood and remained there was considered tainted with the producers' philistinism. He received the sobriquet of movie composer and, as often as not, was no longer considered a true art composer. Denigration of this sort accompanied George Antheil's move to the West Coast. Earlier, in 1926, his outrageous *Ballet Mécanique* had earned him the epithet of charlatan from American concertgoers with no pretentions to avant-gardism. Later, his musical style modified, growing more warmly melodic and less dissonant. He claimed that the change was owing to his inner need to communicate with the larger American audience; detracters in the artistic world claimed it was owing to a flaw in his character. In the mid-thirties, after he took up his Hollywood career, musicians on the Atlantic coast denominated him a compromised composer lacking in intellectual depth. In 1935, Antheil wrote music for his first two films, *Once in a Blue Moon* and *The Scoundrel.* Next came music for *The Plainsman* (1936), *Spectre of the Rose* (1936), *Make Way for Tomorrow* (1937), and *Angels Over Broadway* (1940).

George Gershwin, highly successful as a popular composer, was of course courted by producers and paid well for his music to the pictures *Shall We Dance* and *Damsel in Distress* and for individual songs interpolated into other films. But in most artistic circles, Gershwin had always been regarded more as a song writer, less as a serious composer.

One of the more important film composers was Alfred Newman, who started off as a vaudeville pianist before going to Hollywood in 1930. When the principal tune in his music for *Street Scene* (1931) achieved great popularity, Newman became the darling of the producers. As composer, conductor, and, eventually, director of all musical activities at Twentieth-Century Fox, he would be responsible for about three hundred film scores and gain fame for his music in *All Above Eve, The Egyptian,* and *Love is a Many-Splendored Thing.*[87] Yet his rating as an artist remained low. Witness his exclusion from both the fifth edition of *Grove Dictionary* (1954) and the supplement to the fifth edition which came out in 1961.

The serious composer of greatest stature who wrote for films was Aaron Copland. After he achieved a large measure of popular success with *El Salón México* (1936), *Music for Radio* (1937), *Billy the Kid* (1938), and *An Outdoor Overture* (1938), he was asked to write the musical scores for several commercial pictures and documentaries, including *The City* (1939), *Of Mice and Men* (1939), *Our Town* (1940), *North Star* (1943), *The Cummington Story* (1945), *The Red Pony* (1948), and *The Heiress* (1949). Three suites drawn from films, *Music for Movies, Our Town,* and *The Red Pony,* have been successes with concert audiences; his music to *The Heiress* received an Academy Award. Though the motion pictures containing his music have turned into "textbook studies" and become profound influences for the majority of film-score composers, Copland himself was later "given something of a cold shoulder by Hollywood." His aesthetic attitudes were too earnest to please producers.[88]

Another highly regarded composer, Virgil Thomson, became noted for his music to three documentaries and for the orchestral suites drawn from them: *The Plough that Broke the Plains* (1936), *The River* (1937), and *The Louisiana Story* (1948). He also wrote the scores for *Tuesday in November* (1945), *The Goddess* (1957), *Power Among Men* (1958), and *Journey to America* (1964). Thomson, however, did not strive to attract the attention of the Hollywood producers. Nor did these makers of commercial films devote any effort to enlisting his services.

We must conclude that, with few exceptions, the more serious the composer was about his art, the less he wanted to go to Hollywood, and the less the producers wanted to fetch him there. With these attitudes prevalent, motion pictures could scarcely loom large as a viable medium for artistic music during the thirties and forties.

Commercial radio began life in 1920 with the establishment of the first commercial broadcasting station, KDKA of Pittsburgh. In 1924 came the first coast-to-coast hookup, and five years later Americans were listening in on ten million sets. When the thirties began, broadcasting stations blanketed the country and were rapidly coming under the control of giant networks—RCA, CBS, and Westinghouse. Between them, NBC and CBS had signed up 108 stations in seventy cities, and were reaching an audience of millions. In the same way that cultural control of the movies was centered in Hollywood, cultural control of radio was centered in New York City.[89] This location was a potentially valuable one for American music, since many major composers and a number of America's finest instrumental and vocal groups resided in, or within a 250-mile radius of, New York.

As profits from broadcasting increased, more and more voices were raised against radio's excessive emphasis on making money by pandering to the crassest tastes. The demand grew that the federal government force radio to greater cultural responsibility and awareness of its public service functions. The directors of the networks could no longer afford to ignore their critics after the election of Roosevelt, who believed in an active government role on the part of American citizenry. To appease their critics, radio's directors programmed concerts by symphony orchestras and other instrumental ensembles, and operatic performances as well. Wryly, Louis Reid commented on this phenomenon in 1938: "The listings of the symphony orchestras permit the radiomen to solace their artistic consciences, harried from prolonged occupation at the sales counters. Invariably entered in the red side of the ledgers, they give the broadcasters' bow to artistic idealism and potent support of the principle of public service under which they are allowed by a benevolently censorious government to operate."[90]

Reid went on to say that the Sunday broadcast of the New York Philharmonic was the outstanding musical program on radio, whose "heavy cost to the Columbia Broadcasting System has been balanced by the enormous prestige it has brought its radio backers." He said further that radio had rescued the Metropolitan Opera Association when it was on the point of bankruptcy. How was it done? "The radio panjandrums dipped again into their heaping treasuries, thumped their publicity drums, and, abandoning their custom of condensing everything to fit a time clock, brought grand opera in its full length to the firesides of the nation."[91]

Contemporary commentators frequently stated that the credit for the remarkable growth of an audience for fine music in the thirties belonged, along with the Federal Music Project of the WPA, to radio, which demonstrated "the ancient truth that if you throw at people enough of the products of any art, good, bad, and indifferent, some of these people will in time learn to prefer the good." When in 1938, after four years, the General Motors Sunday evening radio concerts ended, the editors of *Musical America* wrote: "Radio represents one of the most important fields of activity for the musical profession and is today the most powerful single factor in shaping public taste. Consequently, whether America is to have good music or bad, whether the radio is to present serious musical artists or merely entertainers, whether, in a word, music on the air is to go forward or backward depends primarily on the establishment and maintenance of "programs like the one discontinued."[92]

What did radio's reluctant interest in programming art music mean to contemporary American composers? Unfortunately, very little. First, composers heard the same traditional works performed on the air that were featured in regular concerts; second, the occasional playing of contemporary compositions won negligible support from the radio audience. For example, around the beginning of 1937 CBS introduced a weekly program on Saturday night from 8:00 to 8:30 called Modern Masters, and gave first radio hearings to works by composers like Harris, Hanson, Thomson, and Sowerby. Whenever possible, the composers were on hand to explain their compositions. Regrettably, after three months, CBS cancelled the program, explaining that not enough interest was created to justify its continuance.[93]

Third, the commissioning of new compositions designed for broadcast over the air was, at best, a sporadic occurrence, and never involved more than a tiny number of composers. Late in 1936, CBS commissioned Copland, Gruenberg, Hanson, Harris, and Still to write "works especially for the microphone," and this move was the "first substantial gesture for utilization of radio as a specific medium" for music. During 1937, CBS had the six works performed over the air. In addition, its Columbia Workshop did a radio music-drama by Blitzstein, *I've Got the Tune*. Listeners wrote to discuss the meaning of the compositions. One Ohio writer, for instance, said Copland's work meant: "First part fast . . . work; second part quiet . . . lunch; third part fast, work." The letter came from a "source seldom considered music-conscious." An enthusiastic Baltimore listener wrote: "Vigorous and prolonged applause for the two-hour broadcast this afternoon. Add stomping of feet and even standing on the chair." A writer from Chattanooga, Tennessee, said: "It was a rare treat. The music was full of variety, interest, and color, and gave the vast audience a splendid idea of what our American composers are able to do."

This support was not enough. Profits had to be engendered. Since CBS lost money on the project, its interest in new American compositions quickly subsided.[94] Because all of the above quotations are taken from *Modern Music*, a journal dominated by contemporary American composers, and because CBS and other networks did not afterwards hasten to commission many other new works, we must conclude that the majority of letters sent to CBS were not laudatory. Like disc recordings and motion pictures, radio proved to be an unpromising outlet for native art music.

Music Critics

From the 1790s on, American music lovers relied on the music reviewers of periodicals and newspapers to attend concerts and evaluate the quality both of the performances and of the works heard. If the music was new, they wanted a description and characterization of its general sound. They also welcomed an explanation of passages that the public might find inexplicit on first hearing. Finally, they appreciated a judgment of the music's worth, since they might mistrust or be uncertain of their own appraisal.

Ideally, the reviewer should have had musical training and familiarity with diverse literatures, old and new, and should have been aware of the guidelines widely accepted by past composers as well as the major innovative trends pursued by contemporary composers. Such awareness, nevertheless, ought not to have become a straitjacket on critical thinking, but rather a broad experimental background for calm, deliberative contemplation of any work. One could also expect the sensitive reviewer to be aware that he wrote not truths but subjective conclusions about the music he heard, colored by the limitations of his background, personal tastes, and biases for or against a particular style, composer, genre, performer, or audience.

Is it true then that American music reviewers of the past were, as a whole, far less than ideal critics where new native works are concerned? Certainly most American composers have thought so. Typical was Roy Harris's complaint in 1933 that conductors like Toscanini could safely exclude American compositions from concerts both in the United States and during foreign tours with American orchestras, because neither American critics or music lovers noticed the absence of native works. Five years later, Elliott Carter was claiming that newspaper critics invariably dismissed contemporary American works as inept. The reason for this, Carter felt, was in large part economic. Critics were offered no money and experienced no compulsion from superiors to spur them into showing interest. And their superiors sat on their hands because neither advertisers nor public cared—the former having nothing to gain, and the latter having "succumbed" to the critics. The result was that critics needed to "make no effort to understand, or even to be literate" in their condemnation.[95]

On occasion, the economic factor was admitted to by the critics themselves. In 1939, Olin Downes of the *New York Times* responded to Paul Henry Lang's censure of critics for rarely attending concerts of contemporary American music, saying: "It is . . . true that critics 'cover' too many performances of the same works by the same artists. Here news enters in. A concert of standard works which attracted three thousand people is more important to the city editor than one which assembled five hundred connoisseurs." But Downes makes no admission of bias on the part of reviewers.[96]

Conductors, virtuosic instrumentalists, opera stars, and the like were eminently newsworthy. Their doings, opinions, and music-making received careful and continuous attention from reporters. In contrast, little attempt was made to describe the type of audience in attendance at concerts, or the character of its reaction to a new work, beyond a curt reference to applause or the lack of it. Nor was care taken to study the musical score beforehand, if an unfamiliar work were scheduled for performance. In fact, critics' lives were burdened with too many concerts to attend, too little time to prepare for listening to a new composition, and too pressing a deadline for filing in order to make the next morning's edition. They had no leeway to think over what they had heard, so that they could write carefully matured opinions.[97]

Unfortunately music critics, as often as not, lacked musical training, had a cursory acquaintance with American musical works, and regarded as worthless what they could not understand. To give an instance, the writer on music Olga Samaroff, addressing a conference of music teachers, "told of her experiences as music critic of the *New York Post,* when a plethora of concerts necessitated sending out uninformed assistants, who put debutantes at their mercy with their flippant reviews, and stated that such reviewers were known in New York as 'the polytonal chain gang.'" Keeping her comment in mind, we can sympathize with Copland's lament over the superficial reviews by critics, while American composers were "in dire need of criticism, real criticism," which would "point out their shortcomings and weaknesses as well as their qualities." We can also understand Harris's assertion that composers, if their music was reviewed at all, were likely to be the recipients not of valid criticism but of snap judgments by incompetents.[98]

The most highly regarded critics, however knowledgeable they were, would attend the same performance and yet write oppositely about a contemporary composition. A case in point was critical reaction to the premiere performance of Louis Gruenberg's opera *The Emperor Jones,* presented at the Metropolitan Opera House on 7 January 1933. Lawrence Gilman of the *Herald Tribune* reported that while "the orchestral commentary" was "skillful, discreet, and ingenuously adapted to the action and discourse," the music itself did not "truly contribute" to the drama, but was "superfluous and intrusive." Olin Downes of the *Times* found the music to be dramatically conceived, masterly, "prodigiously sure, headlong, fantastical, brutal in its approach." William James

Henderson of the *Sun* hated the opera's score because it contained "no melody." He heard "crass dissonance, raucous shouts," but "no beautiful music." And Oscar Thompson of the *Evening Post* said what he saw acted was impressive; what he heard played and sung was unimpressive. The opera, Thompson added, owed little of its success to the music, which he found trifling.[99]

As can be gathered from the above, scarcely a critic cared for music that abrogated the practices common in the previous century. To hear one modern piece on a program took all his patience. To hear two or three hours of modern music was a punishment avoided if possible, a justification for negative writing if attendance was necessary. One critic "mildly sympathetic with the 'modern' idiom in music" had to sit through a concert in 1933 at New York's School for Social Research. He found nothing interesting in the program, through which, he writes, "the orchestra waded manfully, though not uncomplainingly." To him, the music sounded overly beholden to Stravinsky and Schoenberg. Lastly, the reviewer reports that he was "informed on reliable authority that during the concluding four minutes of . . . Elie Siegmeister's *May Day* . . . the instrumentalists played *ad libitum*, having lost their places irretrievably." His ears found "the result "not appreciably different from what had gone before."[100]

Censure of this sort echoed what some of the ultrafashionable intellectuals had been saying about American music, especially in the decade and a half before 1935. Had not George Jean Nathan, a founder of the *American Mercury* with Mencken, pronounced all American art composers to be "trivial men" and "psychically, mentally, and . . . emotionally commonplace"? They had no heart, no intelligence, and no depth of feeling.[101]

Though reviewers as a whole were not as irretrievably sharp-tongued as Nathan, they showed their disesteem of American composers in other ways: first, by attending a concert of native works and reporting in detail everything save for the nature of the music itself, which, if mentioned, appeared as a brief afterthought—as in the report of a *Times* journalist on a concert given 10 November 1933 at the American Academy of Arts and Letters; second, by sending lower-echelon reporters who might or might not listen to the entire concert. Elliott Carter, after saying that critics were ill informed about native music and failed to cover concerts devoted to it (like those of the Composers' Forum Laboratory), states that as far as he could see only the *Times* and *Tribune* "bothered to send even their second-string reviewers, who were perfunctory enough to come late or leave early. Other papers made the kind of passing mention accorded to third-rate artists." The comment appeared in the January 1939 issue of *Modern Music*.[102]

Another way critics did disservice to native music was to write about it in meaningless generalities while avoiding any detailed consideration of the composition at close hand. This charge came from Aaron Copland, in 1940, after reading reviews of compositions by Roy Harris. Copland had hoped to see a discussion of the music's "merits and shortcomings," of Harris's significance in American musical culture. He writes: "I have never seen a single newspaper column that sums up and critically estimates the work of a man who, at the moment at least, is more frequently played, more praised, and more condemned than any other living American composer."[103]

Indicative of the problem composers faced, even with the more sympathetic of the prominent musical journalists, was the perplexing position of Sigmund Spaeth. In 1939, he had led the coalition that protested the exclusion of American music from the plans of the New York World's Fair. The ensuant publicity forced the director of the musical activities at the fair, Olin Downes of the *New York Times*, to resign. Five years later, Spaeth published his book *At Home with Music*, which gave the American public advice on what to listen for and whom to listen to in art music. Claiming to write on contemporary American music, Spaeth granted a paragraph each to the Swiss-born Ernest Bloch and Alsatian-born Charles Loeffler, and similar space to a handful of native-born composers, among them Charles Griffes and Charles Ives. He allowed Carl Ruggles one sentence. Then, most astonishingly, he required only one paragraph to deal with Copland, Sessions, Schuman, Creston, Harris, Saminsky, Diamond, Varèse, and Dello Joio, allotting each a couple of words of general description. Immediately after, he added insult to injury by listing the names of [Randall] Thompson, [Virgil] Thomson, Herrmann, Moore, Piston, and Hanson, with no attempt, even the feeblest, to characterize their music. In the sections of the book entitled

"What Every Music-Lover Should Know" and "Music to Enjoy," he recommended Ponchielli's *Dance of the Hours* under both headings. Furthermore, Spaeth felt Americans "should know" Gounod's *Faust* waltzes, Prokofiev's *Peter and the Wolf*, Ravel's *Bolero*, Saint-Saens's *Danse Macabre*, and Weber's *Invitation to the Dance*; and that Americans would "enjoy" Rubinstein's *Melody in F*, one of Elgar's marches, Beethoven's *Country Dances*, and Ippolitov-Ivanov's "March." Most of these approved pieces are of the lightest weight. Beside them, and often qualitatively superior to several of them, might have been placed the well-received Barber's *Adagio for Strings*, Piston's *The Incredible Flutist*, Gould's *Latin-American Symphonette*, Copland's *El Salón México*, *Billy the Kid*, and *Rodeo*, and Gershwin's *Rhapsody in Blue*, *American in Paris*, and Piano Concerto. Surely, American composers deserved better in a book written in 1945 and aimed at informing the general American listener![104]

American composers could make little headway against musical journalists' adulation of glamorous foreign conductors who kept aloof from native music. When, for example, complaints arose in 1931 over Toscanini's unimaginative and repetitious programming of only European works, Lawrence Gilman, critic of the *Herald Tribune*, replied that he "would rather hear Mr. Toscanini conduct a performance of the C Major scale, than hear" any other conductor direct anything whatsoever. To cite another example, in 1933 the editors of *Musical America* were irked at composers' claims that they were discriminated against. No amount of pushing, the editors countered, would get American works approved if they lacked "sound merit." Moreover, these editors added, conductors were the final and most capable arbiters of what should receive performance: "Our conductors will, we hope, exercise the right of choosing such new works by foreign and American composers to which their exalted musicianship entitles them. To assail these conductors as ignorant of what our composers have written because they themselves are foreigners seems petty and unworthy of workers in so lofty a field as creative music."[105]

American composers also made little headway against the propensity of music journalists to judge native works by inappropriate criteria. Composers inveighed against "the critics' racket" of constantly faulting "similarities" between the music in a new

American work and that in some well-known and preferably European work, implying that absolute originality was a *sine qua non* for Americans, without applying a similar standard to Europeans. In any case, Randall Thompson maintained that absolute originality was an impossibility, whatever the circumstances. Moreover, the critics' "cult of individuality" discouraged the efforts of several composers to create a viable American musical style.[106]

When an American composer incorporated elements of popular musical style into his compositions, he had compromised his claim to artistry, according to several critics. (The previous chapter noted how the overall concept of the composer as an artist might be attacked if he proved popular; here we deal with how individual works were torn apart.) To give an instance, George Gershwin's *Porgy and Bess* was considered anything but artistic by some reviewers who attended the first performances in Boston and New York City in 1935. Reviewing the Boston premiere for *Musical America*, Grace May Stutsman said the work was insignificant and had only "rhythmic cleverness" to sustain it. Reluctantly, she admitted that "it has called forth tremendous enthusiasm from its Boston audiences." Another reviewer, Olin Downes of the *Times*, said the piece was neither fish nor fowl, since its style vacillated between opera, operetta, and "sheer Broadway entertainment." William Henderson of the *New York Sun* observed that the work contained several "song hits," but also contended "it was miles from opera." Lawrence Gilman of the *Tribune* wrote that its popular melodies were "cardinal weaknesses" and "blemishes upon its musical integrity," and he made this still more curious pronouncement: "How trite and feeble and conventional the tunes are, how sentimental and vapid the harmonic treatment under its disguise of fussy and futile counterpoint! . . . Weep over the lifelessness of the melody and harmony, so derivative, so stale, so inexpressive."[107]

Such censure from important reviewers, as well as weak approval or refusal to take any notice at all of new compositions, could easily have relegated new music of the time to the dustbin of forgotten opuses, since what the reviewers had to say was avidly read and heeded by the public. It was therefore most unfortunate that only rarely did a critic find an American composition to be outstanding. Frank Rossiter writes that the first real recognition for Charles Ives came when Kirkpatrick performed the *Concord Sonata* at Town Hall on 20 January 1939. Neither the *Times* nor the *Musical Courier* bothered to send reviewers, but Lawrence Gilman of the *Tribune* happened to attend. The sonata, Gilman announced, was "exceptionally great music." Immediately Olin Downes rushed to mount the bandwagon with a *Times* article on Ives. *Time Magazine* subsequently wrote up the composer in its issue for 30 January 1939. Even more surprising, the communistic *New Masses* took notice and decided Ives was important enough to discuss in its pages.[108] The work swiftly became much talked about and played. One cannot help but wonder what might have happened if Gilman had not attended the concert or had formed a personal dislike for the music. Would the *Concord Sonata* have attained the position of eminence it occupies today?

Olin Downes claimed that among new American works were many scores either clumsily written, experimental, or imitative of the latest European fashion, and said he would have been less than truthful if he praised them. Yet, he complained, the composers of these works felt he should encourage their creative efforts by discussing their music and interpreting it for the public, but on no account criticize its shortcomings.[109]

The pages of *Modern Music* afford more than a few examples of how American composers themselves, when reviewing contemporary music different in style from their own, failed to heed their own advice and savaged without pity music representative of a disapproved aesthetic. The problem of what was and was not pertinent or valid criticism rested on the question of whose ox was being gored. Hardly any of these composer–writers had the perspicacity of Virgil Thomson, certainly the greatest composer-journalist of the lot, despite the idiosyncrasies that appeared now and again in his judgment of others. During his incumbency as music critic for the *Herald Tribune* (1940–54), he served his fellow composers well by trying faithfully to review their music as sympathetically as he was able, knowing that he had his biases and that his word was not infallible.

Of his and others' criticisms, he wrote:

> Let none of us who think we belong to music fancy too highly our opinions about it, since in twenty-five years most of these will

have either gone down the drain or become every man's private
conviction. And please let none imagine, either, that his personal
tastes are unique, indissoluble, and free. Those who think themselves most individual in their likings are most easily trapped by
the appeal of chic, since chic is no more than the ability to accept
trends in fashion with grace, to vary them ever so slightly, to follow
a movement under the sincere illusion that one is being oneself.
And those who imagine themselves most independent as judges
make up the most predictable public in the world, that known
to managements as the university trade, since intellectuals will
always pay for the privilege of exercising their intellectual powers.
Rarities of any kind, ancient or modern, are merely stones to whet
their minds against. You can always sell to the world of learning
acquaintance with that which it does not know.[110]

Government as Patron

The Great Depression idled thousands of musicians. Like other
jobless workers, they clamored for financial assistance from the
federal government, but little would be done for them until after
Roosevelt's election.

In a couple of instances, a precedent for federal assistance had
been set by local governments. Baltimore had supported the
Baltimore Symphony since 1916 and had approved the orchestra's
enlargement from sixty-five to eighty members in 1932. San
Francisco, faced in 1930 with the dismantling of its orchestra,
rushed to assist the ensemble with a city tax. A variety of limited
emergency relief programs were being attempted in New York,
Chicago, Los Angeles, and a few other cities. To some extent the
example and experience of urban governments made possible the
nationwide response of the Roosevelt administration after it took
office. Initially the federal government moved cautiously. The first
action came in the form of limited grants to local units, in 1933
and 1934, through the Federal Emergency Relief Administration
and the Civil Works Administration.[111]

The moves were swiftly hailed as necessary and enlightened, both
by musicians and by influential citizens concerned over the
imminent demise of musical culture. The members of the National

Federation of Music Clubs, for example, praised Roosevelt's aid to music, asked him to increase that aid, and pledged themselves to cooperation with the NRA in "support of symphony orchestras, opera, concert series, and music in public schools and other educational institutions whose maintenance will engage the services of 1,000,000 workers and will conserve American cultural traditions now threatened with annihilation."[112]

Franklin Delano Roosevelt not only saw the practical need for assistance to music, but also believed strongly in music's necessity in a democratic society. A letter sent to C. M. Tremaine sets forth this belief:

> Music is the universal language of cheer and good-fellowship. It unquestionably aids in inculcating the spirit of good-will now so greatly needed among all peoples of the earth. Music, because of its ennobling influence, should be encouraged as a controlling force in the lives of men. Discord vanishes with music; hence, music-loving people are amongst the happiest people in the world. With the brighter outlook which comes from a happy spirit we can keep a saner view of life and its problems and see values more nearly in their true perspective.[113]

The direction of Roosevelt's thinking is further revealed in his conversations with men and women active in the arts. Several times during his first two terms of office he called in and questioned various musicians to learn how effective they thought governmental assistance was and how that assistance might be improved. One musician, Lehman Engel, writes that when Roosevelt sent for him, he asked Engel if formerly jobless musicians were receiving adequate employment under his administration, if the public was helped by artistic presentations, if federal administrators of arts programs were competent, if eventually the private sector would benefit from federal action, and if some permanent improvement in taste and art consciousness could be detected among the general public.[114]

Given such an attitude, it follows that Roosevelt would not hesitate to increase substantially the government's patronage of the arts. In the summer of 1935 was begun the ambitious Four Arts Project of the WPA, with an appropriation of twenty-seven million dollars to art, theater, writing, and music. The Federal Music Project was that part of the undertaking meant to employ composers, conductors, instrumentalists, and singers—first, in the presentation of the finest music, foreign and American, at little or no cost to the public; second, in the conducting of instructional classes in singing, instrumental playing, and music appreciation; third, in research aimed at broadening knowledge about music in America. Harry Hopkins, head of the WPA, announced in August that Nikolai Sokoloff, former conductor of the Cleveland Orchestra, would direct the Music Project and shape it into a potent tool for bringing artistic music to a citizenry which, owing to lack of education or means, did not turn out for concerts. Thus began "the most extensive program for artists' rehabilitation ever undertaken by a government" and a "broad cultural awakening" which embraced symphonic, choral, and chamber music, as well as dance, musical theater, and opera.[115]

Most significant of all would be the constant performance of American music and the sponsorship of new compositions by native composers. Because the making of a profit was not essential, musicians were free to experiment with innovative programs that made room for fresh works in every conceivable style. In 1938, Deems Taylor would write: "It is safe to say that during the past two years the W.P.A. orchestras alone have probably performed more American music than our other symphony orchestras combined, during the past ten."[116]

Conceivably, this uncustomary support of American music encouraged composers to direct their styles in the more populistic direction discussed earlier. One supposes they were only human if, once they had discovered a potential patron (the government) and audience, they cultivated both to some extent.

Six months after Sokoloff began his tenure with the Federal Music Project, he reported that ten regional directors were in place overseeing 270 projects, which employed 13,000 musicians. Symphony and concert orchestras numbered 107, and included 5442 instrumentalists. Thirty-three bands employed 4042 musicians, eight chamber-music ensembles, 158 musicians; seventeen choruses and vocal quartets, 499 musicians; thirty-four teaching projects, 1248 musicians; four light-opera projects, 303 musicians; various projects for soloists; and 18 projects for 361 copyists, librarians, tuners, and music-binders. To give an instance of the democratic orientation of the WPA music projects, the Vermont WPA Project, headed by Paul Pelton, the associate conductor of the Vermont State Symphony, was directed in a town-meeting tradition. Otto Luening, who was teaching at Bennington College, says that local advisory committees set up in seventeen towns had as members housewives, farmers' wives, a teacher, a bookkeeper, and an overseer of the poor. Questionnaires sent to fifty-eight villages and towns requested information on their musical needs. School instruction on instruments, folk-music groups, theory and orchestration workshops, adult appreciation classes, and various performing groups were the result. When public buildings were unavailable, particularly in rural districts, classes and rehearsals were held in private homes. Interest in music—making it, learning about it, and hearing it—grew tremendously.[117]

Free concerts attracted vast numbers of musically inexperienced Americans curious about art music and eager to try to understand it. Early on, it became obvious that these concerts also attracted a disreputable minority hostile to musical culture and intent on disrupting performances and disturbing listeners. Toward the end of the summer of 1935, Sokoloff was already protesting the rowdiness of adolescents and young men at the Prospect Park (Brooklyn) concerts of the Brooklyn Symphony and the Forest Park (Queens) concerts of the New York Civic Orchestra. "The audience, for the most part," he claimed, "were serious and well-mannered. There were quite a few youths, however, who did their utmost to compete with the musicians and merely succeeded in discomforting the people near them."[118]

He and his advisors then thought that in some instances a small admission fee might help keep the offenders away. This would especially be effective in those large urban areas that contained a disproportionate number of unruly people. It was also hoped that this action would funnel more money into the projects and, perhaps, encourage local governments and private sponsors to come forward with assistance. Two-thirds of all performances, nevertheless, would continue to cost nothing to attend. Though over the next two or three years some concerts did have admission prices added, tickets were never expensive. The best concerts could be attended for 25 cents. Over the months, a few went to 55 cents, then to 83 cents or $1.10.[119]

The concept behind joint federal and local sponsorship was for the federal government to assume all labor costs, and the state, county, or city to assume the remaining costs. This the administrators of the Federal Music Project encouraged. Soon several localities were experimenting with the idea. San Diego sponsored both opera and symphony concerts though such a partnership; Manchester, New Hampshire, a teaching center; New York City, its own station to broadcast good music; and several cities, retraining programs for musicians and music teachers. One or two municipalities, Cincinnati and New York City among them, took a further step and granted tax exemptions to an already established symphony orchestra or opera company. Assuredly, its exemption from real estate taxes, made final in 1943, helped the Metropolitan Opera Association stay solvent during a trying time.[120]

The performances of the WPA instrumental and vocal ensembles were not always as perfectly rendered as connoisseurs might have wished. Moreover, the management of several music groups could be characterized as inefficient and misdirected. Yet the music-making of WPA ensembles did immeasurably enrich the cultural life of the nation by widening the aesthetic horizons of countless Americans. It also helped preserve people's mental health by making less onerous the effort to cope with daily life. Thousands of men and women attended concerts for the first time, and a large percentage of those who attended kept on coming back for more.[121] The increasing number of Americans interested in art music emboldened Nikolai Sokoloff to assert in 1938 that growing public opinion demanded a larger place for music in community life. "There is abundant reason to believe," he said, "there is now a desire for music commanding a greater audience than the nation has ever known before, and this brings us to a proposition of whether music in the United States shall be a luxury available only to persons of the higher-income levels, or whether music will take its place in the cultural program and pattern of this country side by side with the free public library, the public museum, and the educational system."[122]

New York's government-sponsored groups played wherever they could find space (Randalls Island Stadium, Central Park, Jones Beach, Lewisohn Stadium), to large crowds of attendees.

The *New York Times* of 21 August 1936 printed an editorial commenting on the huge increase in popularity of the WPA art-music concerts. On the other side of the country, Alexander Fried, in the *San Francisco Examiner* of 31 August 1938, wrote about Antonia Brico conducting the one-hundred-member WPA Bay Region Symphony and a 120-voice federal chorus, in a "Dime Symphony" program, where eight thousand persons paid the ten cents admission charge and filled the seats. A Boston respondent describes her aunt, a coloratura soprano, as belonging to a performing group that engaged in concert tours for the WPA. The group brought music to communities throughout New England during the late thirties. One concert, given in the Boston Red Sox's Fenway Park, "filled all the seats to overflowing."

Equally well-attended were the 250 music-teaching centers, served by four hundred music teachers, giving free class instruction on any music instrument and in singing, history, theory, and composition. Encouraged by the local enthusiasm for music instruction, New York City in 1936 started the Art and Music High School as an educational experiment. It was the first public school in the United States intended for artistically gifted young people.[123]

The government's sustained effort at educating the public and making easier its access to art music acted like leavening in the music world. Not only the regional WPA groups but, as never before, new civic symphony and opera associations formed, at a time when it made better economic sense to political and economic conservatives to see such groups dismantled. Increasing numbers of musical instruments and disc recordings were sold to a public whom the government had persuaded into amateur music-making and into enjoying fine music. A previously untapped audience, from every walk of life, showed a growing interest in artistic productions. It seemed that the dream of liberal planners to bring qualitative excellence into a democratic culture was about to be realized.

For American art composers, the federal government's intervention on behalf of the arts proved a godsend. After having been ignored by the established musical organizations and their conductors, managers, and trustees, after having made next to no progress with radio executives, movie producers, disc-record manufacturers, and music publishers, all of a sudden they were receiving serious attention from WPA organizations. Contemporary native works were performed with amazing frequency. Consensus grew among WPA music directors that their groups should avoid competition with the non-governmental music forces, should cultivate a distinct repertoire of their own, and should, as a matter of duty, nurture an American music with the American tax dollars they received. Izler Solomon, who during his six years as conductor of the WPA's Illinois Symphony Orchestra gave first performances to 150 American works, sums up the reasons why the Federal Music Project's conductors mined the neglected field of American music. Speaking of what led him to feature Americans, he explains:

> I realized that with the artistic and financial limitations of the WPA it would be suicide to try to compete with the Chicago Symphony, that I had to do something different. Besides, since it was the American people's money that I used, I felt it was my duty to foster new music, particularly to give new American compositions a break. Public performance was impossible for all the compositions submitted. So once a week we'd hold reading rehearsals—to let the composer hear his work and spot the weaknesses in material or orchestration.[124]

Composers were encouraged to submit compositions to regional boards for audition. If in rehearsal a work sounded competently made, it was given a public performance. If the work was well received in one city, it was played by other WPA units in other cities. Thaddeus Rich, regional assistant in the Pennsylvania–New Jersey District, said in 1937 that this policy heartened composers, provided "refreshment and stimulation for unbelievably vast audiences," and was laden with "significance for the future."[125]

The San Francisco Project was headed by the composer Ernst Bacon. Concerts were free and given in libraries, museums, and public schools. When "less than three months old," the project had "already featured close to a score of local composers, conductors, singers, and instrumental soloists," and elicited an "eager response" from the audience, which voiced requests for more such entertainment. As further evidence of the WPA's widespread activities, it should be pointed out that the information on Bacon is taken from *An Anthology of Music Criticism*, which is volume seven of "The History of Music in San Francisco," a part of the North California Writers' Project, published in 1942.

A grateful Virgil Thomson assuredly was speaking for a majority of American composers when he said in May 1941 that the Federal Music Project "picture . . . is one of healthiness and vigor." Its "contribution to musical culture and its tradition is a real one and far more important, I suspect, than is currently imagined. The W.P.A. groups, in particular, are indefatigable at playing and replaying the music of our own time, especially that composed in the United States. The major orchestras play comparatively little of this"; instead they play the same fifty pieces over and over again.[126]

The WPA also worked toward uncovering America's rich cultural past. A *Bio-bibliographical Index of Musicians in the United States of America Since Colonial Times* was compiled. A music index of hundreds of forgotten musical works led to the revival of many compositions from the past by the WPA ensembles. WPA folksong collectors searched Appalachia, the Creole bayou country, the cowboy's West, and the various habitations of black Americans for the singers of ballads, blues, spirituals, dance-songs, worksongs, and other traditional musics, and recorded their performances on disc recordings. Every project "became a sort of road map for the cultural rediscovery of America from within. There seemed to be, on the part of project planners, a common realization" that music native to America "had been too long neglected," that music of foreign lands had been "too long preferred, and that the time had come at last for a national cultural stock taking."[127]

Of major importance to composers were the innovative Composers' Forum Laboratories, which began to be set up in the fall of 1935 as a part of the Federal Music Project. Reporting on the first forum laboratory, organized in New York City, *Musical America* in the issue for 10 October 1935 told its readers:

A series of Wednesday evening meetings is planned at which a lecturer will introduce the composers and state their musical views, when the composers do not wish to do so for themselves, and soloists and ensembles from the local concert unit of the W.P.A. will perform the music. The purpose of the venture is to provide an opportunity for serious composers in this country to hear their own works, get the reaction of listeners, voice their musical views, and profit by public discussion of their music.

Other forums, meeting semi-monthly, were established in cities harboring colonies of composers, as in Boston and Chicago. Where serious composers were less numerous, as in Detroit, Milwaukee, and Indianapolis, forums took place at less frequent intervals. Wherever the forum might be held, new and often experimental compositions were giving a hearing in the instrumentation called for, and then underwent "appraisal and suggestions from a critical and musically enlightened audience," according to Grace Overmeyer.[128]

On occasion, composers did attempt to explain fully their aesthetic concerns and to educate the audience, as did Lazare Saminsky in the fall of 1936:

> During the forum that followed the concert, Mr. Saminsky very aptly explained, with Hegel's terse formula, Thesis, Antithesis, and Synthesis, that a composer goes through three distinct periods of development: the thesis stage, where he absorbs everything that he comes in contact with; the antithesis stage, where he revolts against the strictures of his earlier training, mostly because he finds that the materials at his command fetter him. In revolt he strikes out into new paths and writes what may be sincere, but is nevertheless voluble and vociferous music of protest rather than music of ripened conviction. The last period, the synthesis stage, is when the composer, mellowed by time and experience, finds a language that is expressive, restrained, subtle, and personal.[129]

The audience rarely hesitated to straighten out any composer it thought in error. In early 1938, *Denmark Vesey*, an opera by Paul Bowles and Charles-Henri Ford on a slave revolt in Charleston, had its first act given in concert form. Virgil Thomson, who attended the performance, thought the call for a black American cast was a mistake, since a "non-Negro point of view about Negroes" was presented. The questions and criticisms "from Negroes in the audience" were sharp and bitter.[130]

Generally, composers like Roy Harris, Virgil Thomson, and William Schuman gratefully listened to and learned from the performances of their music, carefully considered and answered the audience's questions, and manfully defended their right to follow their own aesthetic pathways on those occasions when they felt their questioners were mistaken. To them, the forum experience was one of utmost value. A dialogue at least had been started between contemporary composers and some members of the larger audience.

A few composers would have been happier if the audience had been muzzled. Paul Bowles, for one, disliked the brisk and biting question-and-answer period. He claimed it to be "strictly a heckling session by 'leftists.'" This he said about the post-concert exchange in 1936, after the audience had listened to an all-Bowles program. A second composer, Elliott Carter, admitted in 1938 that the New York Composers' Forum Laboratory had performed works from the "ultra-dissonant" to the "ultra-consonant," and noted some changes in the organization of the series (among them a decrease in the number of concerts, particularly of orchestral music). He felt the changes would improve the standard of performance. "But," Carter asked, "what of the public who asks such pitiless questions of the composer?" He, like Bowles, balked at the price he had to pay for a hearing of his music.[131]

Now and again a composer would display little of the live-and-let-live tolerance appropriate to the formulators of the forum programs. The twenty-seven-year-old Arthur Cohn noted in 1938 that the Philadelphia Forum Laboratory had "a truly first-rate orchestra on hand to do well by any work." Yet, as far as he was concerned, it devoted altogether too many evenings to "third-rate men"—that is to say, "composers of a past generation" or "those who have nothing more to offer than academic twaddle" (in short, composers not of Cohn's own generation or aesthetic persuasion!)[132]

The six years before America entered World War II were heady times for composers who, unlike the young Bowles and Cohn, had known the neglect of the twenties and early thirties. A few had learned to feel compassion for all composers of serious purpose, whatever their age and stylistic bent. A bemused Aaron Copland, the encourager of composers of every ilk, was surprised to discover "even our own government needed us," when the State Department sponsored visits of American composers and performers to foreign countries. He himself was sent to tour South America in 1941 by the Office of the Coordinator of Inter-American Affairs.[133]

Virgil Thomson was pleased to join Pare Lorentz in 1936, and write music for a documentary film requested by the U.S. Resettlement Administration, *The Plough that Broke the Plains.*

The government needed him, as it did Copland. He was also pleased to work with Orson Welles and John Houseman, composing music for the Federal Theater. How different he sounds from Bowles and Carter, when he observes that the standard wage paid to all WPA employees, $23.86 weekly, enabled him to survive and made him want to keep up his end in bringing modern theater to an "audience, poor, part intellectual, part professional, not stylish at all but not easily fooled either."[134]

From its inception the WPA, and in particular its Four Arts Project, came under relentless attack from conservative Republicans and Southern Democrats. They saw the government agency as a negation of private enterprise and the capitalistic system, and a disturbing move toward complete state control of American society. In addition, they had a deep-seated suspicion of painters and musicians, viewing them as effete, shiftless, parasitic, and immoral. To support the arts and their temperamental practitioners with taxpayers' money struck them as offensive in the extreme. Behind these politicians were millions of farmers and small-town residents who disesteemed and derived no benefits from the arts projects. Congressmen, state legislators, and editors of rural newspapers took strength from this opposition to public subsidy of artists. Through speeches in Washington and the state capitals, and through news items and editorials in conservative newspapers, the denounciation of the Four Arts Project built up relentlessly and ominously.[135]

The musicians were acutely aware of this hostility. Almost daily, reports came to them of the imminent termination of their government-supported undertaking. As Lehman Engel said: "We were never free of rumors about discontinuance of the W.P.A., which had become a hot political football, and I think all of us knew that sooner or later this would be more than a rumor."[136]

Conservative fears about the leftist leanings of artists seemed vindicated in June 1937 when Marc Blitzstein, employed by the Four Acts Project, completed his musical stage work *The Cradle Will Rock*, a no-holds-barred satire of America's powerful industrialists. *The Cradle* immediately was perceived as the creation of a political extremist, if not a Communist. Influential businessmen and politicians pressured Washington into barring its production in a federal theater. But, assisted materially by Orson

Welles and John Houseman, Blitzstein got hold of a privately owned theater and had the work performed without costumes, scenery, or orchestra, and with the actor-singers scattered throughout the auditorium in order to circumvent a WPA rule that kept them from appearing on any stage other than a federal one. The work was a hit, and its continuing performance provoked conservatives into intensifying their assaults on the "dangerously radical" Four Arts Project, which had paid the composer to write the work.

The WPA sponsorship of music came under attack from another direction—the private music sector. As early as November 1935, Arthur Judson, manager of the New York Philharmonic, was complaining to Sokoloff that the Philharmonic's ticket sales had suddenly decreased with the commencement of the Federal Music Project and its policy of free concerts. The competition was unfair, he claimed, and contrary to the spirit of free enterprise. He asked Sokoloff to start charging admission.[137]

Jacob Rosenberg, secretary of Local 802, rebutted Judson by insisting free admission should continue, since the whole idea "was to give employment to as many unemployed as possible and to provide cultural entertainment for the unemployed." An admission charge would keep the WPA's audience away from all concerts.[138]

Unfortunately, Judson's complaint was followed by similar complaints from others. These, in turn, provided new ammunition to the politicians diligently working to abolish all Four Arts activities. Soon private music teachers were complaining. Representative Joseph Martin, director of the Eastern Division of the Republican Party, for example, seconded a statement by Hilda Grace Gelling, head of the Music Teachers' Defense Committee, which described the WPA's activities "as a menace to private instructors in the musical arts." She warned that all private teachers would be forced "to abandon their practices and take federal jobs."[139]

Protests like those of Judson and Gelling fed into conservative prejudices. Not surprisingly, the fear that WPA musical activities would force independent music teachers and organizations out of existence took on exaggerated dimensions in the minds of those already vexed by governmental aid to artists and musicians.

The Federal Music Project possibly might still have survived, despite its enemies, if it were not for the certainty that a major war was about to break out. In May 1939, Germany and Italy bound themselves into a military alliance. In August 1939, Germany and Russian signed a non-aggression pact. With the concern of a two-front war eliminated, Germany invaded Poland on 1 September 1939. World War II had commenced.

Anticipating the war to come and deciding that governmental resources had to be concentrated on increased industrial production in the event of war, the Roosevelt administration terminated the Federal Arts Project on 31 August 1939. No longer would musicians need employment. If not in music, there would be plenty of work available elsewhere for all who needed it. WPA performing groups were disbanded, instructional classes closed down, and researchers into music in America dismissed.

In the four years of its existence, the Federal Music Project had disbursed some fifty million dollars, and presented 225,000 performances to an audience of 150 million people. Another 15 million people had enrolled in its music-instruction classes. At least six thousand works by sixteen hundred American composers had received public performances.[140]

Some directors tried desperately to keep their ensembles together. Lehman Engel says he "ran around frantically to concert managers in a death-throe effort to establish" his choral group "on a commercial footing, but it was to no avail."[141] A former Boston violinist says that after his orchestra was dissolved, he and other idled musicians tried to form a "cooperative orchestra," but no one would hire them. The musicians, including himself, had to give up music, never to return to it. The violinist also speaks about his own bitterness: "What a waste after all that study, starting at eight years of age."

On a more positive note, Harry Ellis Dickson, director of the WPA Music Project in Massachusetts, states: "At one point, there were about five hundred musicians on my 'payroll.' We had a State Symphony Orchestra, a Commonwealth Symphony, a whole opera company. I'd say that forty percent of the current BSO players came out of those W.P.A. orchestras."[142]

A few orchestras managed to survive. In Oklahoma City, an audience of five thousand people had been developed by the WPA orchestra and its conductor, Victor Alessandro. When federal support was withdrawn, the city's civic pride was aroused and a campaign for funds was begun, which eventually made possible the continuance of the Oklahoma orchestra. A similar action was taken in Buffalo. Franco Autori and the Buffalo WPA Orchestra proved so popular that a Buffalo Philharmonic Orchestra Society was formed to sponsor the ensemble.[143]

The musicians who lost out the most were the composers. They no longer had performing groups eager for their compositions. The American audience, which for over four years had been developing an interest in and a knowledge of American music now was forced to pay (if it wished to continue listening to art music) ever-increasing admission prices to hear music that was infrequently either innovative or American.

The Four Arts Project was one of the highest points in American cultural history. For the first and only time in its existence, the Federal government took a profound interest in the arts and felt it had a democratic responsibility to bring the finest music, including that of its own people, before a wide public. It gave heart to composers, who had rarely received encouragement for their creative activities, by supporting them financially, playing their music, and fostering a growing audience that was taking an interest in what they had to say. For four years composers were regarded as useful members of society. Yet at the same time they were almost always allowed to maintain their artistic integrity by writing what they, not the government, wished.

It was a cultural tragedy that just when American composer, performer, and more than an extremely tiny segment of the American society seemed about to consolidate into a lasting partnership, the noble experiment of relating art to daily life was given up.

3

The General
Audience for Art
Music

The twentieth-century composer tends, especially if his music is of difficult cast, to define the truly musical audience in terms of his own requirements. At the same time, indifferences to the general listener's viewpoint, and even criticism of it, are found in most twentieth-century books and articles on music written by authors concerned with post-World-War-II musical trends. Oftentimes the listener is either ignored for his irrelevance to, scolded for his lack of sophistication about, or instructed on his proper posture vis-a-vis the artistic process.

What have a few of America's most prominent composers from between the two wars said about the listener—Sessions, Copland, and Harris, to name three? In 1949, the composer Roger Sessions delivered a series of lectures at the Juilliard School of Music, later published in book form under the title *The Musical Experience*. Since Sessions has been one of the most serious of America's art composers, and a musician constantly praised in the highest terms by writers on music and by other American art composers both for his compositions and his thoughts about music, it is instructive to begin this chapter with his comments on the relation of the listener to the composer.

121

Sessions states: "The question . . . is what we [the listeners] demand of the composer. Do we demand always what is easiest, music that is primarily and invariably entertainment, or do we seriously want from him the best that he has to give? In the latter case, are we willing to come to meet him, to make whatever effort is demanded of us as listeners, in order to get from his music what it has to give us?"[1] He then dismisses everyone who wishes entertainment and asserts that the genuinely musical person demands only the best and will make every effort to understand whatever the best is that the composer has to offer.

Regrettably, this talk of "the best" is vague and never clearly explained. In addition, it does seem to contradict what most listeners may mean by the term. Perhaps they do desire fine construction and deep significance, but certainly for them "the best" also means some degree of entertainment. Composers in the past have responded to this stimulus. For example, Haydn's operas and works for baryton were written to please Prince Esterházy; his late symphonies, to please the London audience; much of his chamber music, to please amateur performers; and his oratorios *The Creation* and *The Seasons,* to please the Viennese audience. These works became no less serious or noteworthy because they addressed listeners' needs and at the same time succeeded in entertaining.

Sessions takes several things for granted. One, that the serious composer does give of his best. Two, that his best is important and worthy enough for others to make an effort to understand. And three, that the sincere music lover has the time, willingness, experience, and attention span to devote to an art work in the way the composer desires.

How should the listener understand an art work, according to Sessions? Sessions replies that before hearing any music, the listener must get thorough education in musical matters and leave "no stone unturned in the effort to prepare" himself "fully for the strenuous [sic!] task of listening to music." Only then is he equipped to begin listening. The next step is really to hear the work, "with no other preoccupation than that of hearing." After that, the listener must grow aware of "a sense of communication between him and the composer: "Only then does the listener move on to a higher stage—understanding the music," which translates into "the ability to receive its full message . . . not in merely hearing it, but in inwardly reproducing it . . . in his imagination." The composer explains:

> What the layman needs is not to acquire facts but to cultivate senses: the sense of rhythm, of articulation, of contrast, of accent. He needs to be aware of the progression of the bass as well as the treble line; of a return to the principal or to a subsidiary key, of a farflung tonal span. He needs to be aware of all these things as events which his ear witnesses and appreciates as a composition unfolds. . . . His main source of understanding will be through hearing music in general, and specific works in particular, repeatedly, and making them his own through familiarity, through memory, and through inner re-elaboration.[2]

Sessions's requirements are impossible to meet; his listener has metamorphosed into a supernatural being. In truth, no mere human can concentrate on listening alone, and ignore what the eye sees, the body feels, and the wandering mind images. Also necessary to include in the equation is the reality of the listener's usual bias against most dissonant music like that of Sessions as well as his unfamiliarity with new works owing to their rare performance.

Who truly listens as Sessions asks? Some years ago a first local performance of a major Sessions work, *When Lilacs Last in the Dooryard Bloom'd,* took place in Sanders Theater, Harvard University. Several prominent musicians, presumably those who could be numbered among Sessions's ideal listeners, were present. As the work unfolded, this author witnessed one of these musicians surveying the rows of people around him, and two others occasionally whispering to each other. Another kept on glancing at her watch, obviously wishing the music would come to an end. Still another fell asleep five minutes into the performance. If these musical performers, musicologists, and composers failed to come up to Sessions's expectations, what then can be asked of the general listener?

In this context, an informative story is told by Luening in *Odyssey* (p. 385). Luening states that in 1935 Franco Autori and the Brooklyn Symphony Orchestra played his *First Symphonic Fantasia,* which had been played in Rochester in 1926. "A well-known composer" wrote to Luening complimenting him as follows: "How you have grown in your mastery of the medium since that early work of yours I heard in Rochester in 1926." Luening was shocked by the letter and never fully recovered from its effect. He laments: "If professionals cannot tell after an interval of a few years whether they are hearing the same piece or a new one, how can we expect critics and untrained listeners to follow carefully composed music in detail after one hearing?"

Aaron Copland has not been adamantly on the side of the artist, as we have seen; but he does vacillate between what he knows is the reality of the listening situation and what he wishes it might be. In addition to his great musical accomplishments he has been widely read and respected; everything he has said must be examined seriously.

In Copland's lectures delivered at Harvard University during 1951 and 1952 (later published as *Music and Imagination*) he entertains Sessions's fantasy of the ideal listener. Copland speaks about "the gifted listener," the amateur music lover, and not "the professional musician as listener," since the latter "is an initiate" and has "an inner understanding of music's mysteries."[3] He, like Sessions, makes a distinction between two kinds of listening experience—"the interesting question . . . is not whether he is deriving pleasure, but rather, whether he is understanding the import of the music."[4] To understand, the listener must "distinguish subtle nuances of feeling" in the music, be familiar with the work's stylistic characteristics, and be able "to see all around the structural framework," however extended the piece. These requirements met, the listener apprehends "a unified and total image of the work's essence." "What has the listener understood?" Copland asks, and answers: "If anything was understood, then it must have been whatever it was the composer tried to communicate."[5]

Copland discounts pleasure and sets up criteria for listening that many members of the concert audience must fail to meet. Most doubtful of all is his notion that the composer clearly knows what he means to communicate, and that the listener's and composer's understanding must coincide. His view, moreover, is contradicted by what was said in chapter 2 about performers' and managers' certainty that, in their experience, listeners insisted on pleasure first and showed far less concern about what a composer was trying to say.

The composer may in fact not be the ultimate authority on what his music actually means. Note the composer Ned Rorem's comment that when an artist explains his music, "he doesn't know quite what he's talking about." He can only "clarify his method to others, but not his esthetic. . . . He explains what you're supposed to hear rather than what you do hear."[6] In other words, there is no assurance that what the composer wants to accomplish and what the listener thinks has been accomplished will be the same.

Today we may enjoy Machaut's fourteenth-century Missa *Notre Dame*, Monteverdi's seventeenth-century *Lamento d'Arianna*, and Vivaldi's eighteenth-century *Il Cimento dell'Armonia e dell'Inventione*. But we have no certainty that the performances heard are authentic—and it sometimes seems that the more authentic a performance is claimed to be, the less our enjoyment. Assuredly, our understanding and that of these composers does not coincide; yet our pleasure may be intense. Like all listeners, we do grasp the music's meaning after our own fashion. It is unrealistic to expect more. So it must be with contemporary composers and their compositions.

Copland admitted as much in an article in the *New York Times.* He realized listeners and modern composers might not see eye to eye. At the same time, regrettably, he indicated that he washed his hands of such listeners:

> If you hear this music and fail to realize that it has added a new dimension to Western musical art, that it has a power and tension and expressiveness typically twentieth-century in quality, that it has overcome the rhythmic inhibitions of the nineteenth century and added complexes of chordal progressions never before conceived, that it has invented subtle or brash combinations of hitherto unheard timbres, that it offers new structural principles that open up vistas far into the future—I say, if your pulse remains steady at the contemplation of all this and if listening to it does not add up to a fresh and different musical experience for you, then any defense of mine, or of anybody else, can be of no use whatsoever.[7]

Elliott Carter, who was to become one of the leading post-World-War-II composers, was scornful of a public addicted to "easy" music and to sentiment. To Carter, listening was a strenuous undertaking, since the most worthwhile art music, he stated, took the shape of a complicated statement. His prescription for honestly experiencing music called for a listener who was "objective" yet "enthusiastic." Writing in *Modern Music* (March–April 1938), he delineates this listener:

> . . . eager for new ideas and new feelings. When hearing familiar works he always re-evaluates his previous impressions. The style, no matter how difficult or unusual, does not prevent him from trying to find what the music is all about. He follows it attentively for he knows that it is a living message to him from another living man, a serious thought or experience worth considering, one that will help him to understand the people about him. To him, dead, worn-out formulas or non-communicative styles are anathema. Serious composers and musicians have always aimed at this listener and he in turn has shown that he could take his listener's share of responsibility by keeping his mind actively fixed on the music he was hearing.

Musical history proves again and again that difficult styles have usually put off listeners in every age. Carter's statement deals more with his wishes, less with things as they are. Only a negligible number of concertgoers try to learn what the music is all about. Nor do most listeners, even experienced ones, always follow music as attentively as Carter desires them to do. Nor do they gain, or necessarily want to gain, greater insight into their fellow beings through listening to difficult music. At best, only a minority of a minority of the concert-going public seems to come up to Carter's expectations. Assuredly, this was the state of things between 1925 and 1945. Excellent as some of the more advanced works certainly are, they were heard (if they were performed at all) by most listeners in a manner that Carter could never have condoned.

Doubtful, also, is the belief that serious composers have always aimed at Carter's ideal listener. For the most part, composers have been practical realists who knew they had to entertain and, through a variety of means, keep the listener interested in what they had to say—since in no other way could they be certain that the listener's mind would remain "actively fixed" on the music. Carter's fictional listener joins that of Copland and Sessions.

Even when purporting to be interested in writing an identifiably American music intended for the American listener, a native composer might succeed in communicating more by happenstance than by considered reflection on what his listener is like. With one major composer of the thirties and forties, Roy Harris, the potential lack of correspondence between his and the audience's perceptions was quite disconcerting. Roy Harris demanded that listeners accept his music's vision of America and its conclusions about what they—the Americans who heard his works—were like.

As he says in his prefatory remarks to the *American Overture* (1935), he believes he is expressing "a gamut of emotions particularly American and in an American manner." He tries to capture the predominant characteristics of Americans: "noisy ribaldry," "sadness," "groping earnestness," and a struggle for "sheer power in itself." "There is little grace and mellowness in our midst," he concludes, and insists that Americans really do conform to his valuation of them. Harris leaves no room for variant opinions. That Americans might think differently and hear other things in his music than what he says is there does not perturb him.

All too often, the public spurned the contemporary composer's view of its role. If it found little in new music to hold its attention, the public turned contrarily to the tried and true sounds of an earlier music and hardened itself against every contemporary artistic censure.

Of course, composers existed who were anxious to write music that pleased a general audience. And Copland, in much of the music he wrote in the late thirties and forties, was one of these. Moreover, the sort of exchange made possible in the Composers' Forums during the WPA years unquestionably helped bridge the gap between artist and audience. Composers began to hope that they would eventually win over a broad audience for their music, one that would set aside its customary abhorrence of the new. And the broad audience began to show a growing curiosity about native contemporary music that sought to meet the listener halfway. But the dialogue had hardly begun when World War II abruptly ended it. Then ensued more decades of divorcement between art composers and the general music public.

The sad cross-purposes at work in the musical era between the two world wars may be explained in terms of political-economic, societal, and technological trends. Nevertheless, a more immediate barrier was the conflicting perception of what con-

stituted quality in music and what constituted a proper relationship
between composer and listener. The general public chose to hear
mostly works written before World War I because it had difficulty
keeping its attention fixed upon a modern work's performance,
let alone comprehending the music. If a composition sounded
like one damned thing after another, it became an annoyance;
if an elite group pronounced the work to be a masterpiece intended
only for gifted listeners, it became a downright provocation. One
far-reaching consequence was a large body of listeners militantly
against hearing any new music and indifferent to anything the
contemporary composer and his partisans had to say about artistic aims.

The Uncultured Majority

The art composer cannot afford to alienate any listeners who profess
to value art music for whatever reason, because so few of them
exist in relation to the total population. This principle held
especially true in the twenties, when the first real public for art
music began to develop, in the early thirties, when economic
conditions discouraged attendance at concerts, and in the forties,
when war monopolized everybody's attention and energy.

In July 1936 an editorial in *Musical America* estimated that
a few years before, only sixteen thousand persons had supplied
the basic audience for all of Manhattan's musical events. The editor
suggested that in the mid-thirties, smaller cities had serious
problems supporting music in the same way as New York City,
not because New Yorkers were more musical, but because they
comprised a huge population concentrated in one spot.

If it was difficult in the smaller cities, it was next to impossible
to foster a love for music in the thousands of modest towns and
villages. A WPA survey of the musical situation in Michigan was
published in *Musical America*, 25 December 1937. The survey found
that of the more rural schools, 54 percent taught no music at
all; 29 percent gave some mark in music; and 95 percent had no
active music society in their area. Only 11 percent of the students
who said they would like musical instruction were able to get
any. The children and their parents could develop a taste for art
music only on their own.

Throughout the thirties and early forties, various estimates were published about the number of Americans interested in art music. The highest of these estimates rarely exceeded 6 percent of the total population. In 1974, Ned Rorem could still point out: "That Classical music seems irrelevant to most young people of today is a truism: it's always been irrelevant to most young people as to most people, not because it doesn't obtain to the moment, but because it obtains only for certain sensibilities, and even for such sensibilities it's hard."[8]

In 1934 the National Recreation Association questioned Americans on what they did in their leisure time. Men and women cited, in order of importance, reading newspapers and magazines, listening to the radio, attending the movies, visiting and entertaining, and reading novels. When asked what they would rather have done, they cited tennis, swimming, boating, golfing, camping, gardening, and playing a musical instrument. Listening to art music was not significant enough to list among the ten activities preferred. The survey takers concluded that Americans liked action and were not a contemplative people.[9]

Americans who might otherwise have made the effort to sample some form of art music were discomfited by the artist's and aesthete's differentiation between a higher art requiring deep understanding and a lower popular music meant only to amuse. Some also were aware of the claims that the audience for artistic works must always remain small and that the attempt to win over more listeners would serve to cheapen art music. This view, among others, helped to make the majority of people hostile to everyone with elevated cultural interests, and opposed to governmental aid to the arts.[10]

The public found discouragement in the accusation that the audience is "always about twenty-five years in lag behind the composer," and that nothing worthwhile was ever appreciated when new.[11] While the criticism contained a great deal of truth and made the modern composer feel better, it unfortunately also convinced many people that they could happily ignore new music and leave its appreciation to the elect or to a future generation.

An example of such criticism is found in Madeleine Goss's *Modern Music-Makers*, a book on contemporary American composers, published in 1952. The purported object of the author is to inform the general reader about the significant composers in their midst. Unfortunately, she falls into the fashionable intellectual trap of denigrating the general audience for music. In censorious tone she describes how listeners booed and hissed Ruggles's *Portals,* and how Eugene Goossens, the conductor, announced to them, "I consider it a very important work" and, despite the hostility, played *Portals* a second time. As if talking about reprimanded children, Goss observes: "This time" the orchestra performed "to a more respectful audience." Next she describes the first performance of Ruggles's *Men and Mountains* and a women who kept muttering: "Terrible, horrible!" until a friend of Ruggles told her to shut up. With malicious intent, Goss goes on to say that when the Dvorak *New World* Symphony followed, the woman sighed in relief, saying: "Now—I can enjoy myself," and immediately fell asleep. Then Goss quotes Ruggles himself, who said that on hearing one of his works, a man exclaimed: "I could write a better piece than that"; to which the critic Gilbert Gabriel replied, "Why don't you go home and do it, then?"[12]

Whether such anecdotes are apocryphal or not is unimportant. That Goss pounced on tales portraying the audience as stupid, imbecilic, and crass is most significant. Goss and other critics of the American concertgoer forgot a simple truth—if you tongue-lash the public continuously, accuse it of philistinism, and assert that art music is forever beyond its scope, then the multitude has no desire to listen, dismisses you, and assumes an adversarial role.

The painter Thomas Hart Benton, writing about the elitist criticism of the American public in the twenties and thirties, says that a great deal of anti-artistic feeling was generated in New Mexico and other Western states, since ordinary citizens found "nothing quite so offensive as a clique or colony which . . . takes superior or patronizing airs toward them." The offending talk, "borrowed from the jargon of Parisian aesthetes, was outrageous." He felt saddened that people "should have been inflicted with all the artistic drolleries just when western American was ready to take some interest in the social place of the arts. Art to function healthily must have some significance for a whole society."[13]

Benton might be accused by some of cantankerousness owing to his strong bias pro–American folk and anti-French culture. However, interviews with ordinary citizens living in the Northeast during the thirties and forties bear him out. One person told the author that he had been an actor in New York City during the early thirties, but had had an "inferior education" in the arts. Before long, he "found" himself "in sophisticated and bohemian circles," which regularly put down Americans as "uneducated boors." He decided he was not intellectual enough to continue seeing his "new 'arty' friends." Since he could not carry a tune, he was now convinced he had no aptitude for music. Thinking himself innately insensitive to nuances that others perceived, he left off listening to music. This man's son states that in the sixties, he kept on urging his father to "give himself a chance and expose himself to music" but found him "simply incapable of" motivating himself "to enter these higher esthetic realms." The son angrily adds: "I know my father to be a vital and sensitive man, and this dimension of him confuses me and makes me resentful of the pretentious 'intellectuals' whose scorn of his inferior education has produced this defense mechanism in him and severed him from some beautiful things that I know he is peculiarly capable of appreciating."[14]

A young woman says her mother reached adulthood in the thirties while living in a town close to Boston. As her mother grew up, she "learned one had to be perfect and show a real and obvious musical talent" in order to "have an initiation into and grasp intellectually art music [sic], to understand and enjoy it." Therefore, her mother thought it "useless" to try taking an interest in good music.[15]

In December 1968, an interviewee asked the author: "Can a person be tone-deaf and completely uneducated in music and still appreciate music?" As a youth in the forties, the interviewee "couldn't sing" or "distinguish Composer Number One's Symphony from Composer Number Two's Symphony." At the same time, he "winced under the verbal arrows which have been fired" at people like him "for many years." Fortunately, he was certain he had "a vivid appreciation for music." Even more fortunately, he obtained a summer job as gate-keeper at Tanglewood and got to hear the Boston Symphony regularly. The result was that he slowly learned to distinguish between and enjoy symphonies. He was sorry to think that few other people had this sort of determination.

It was only natural that the public would react by forming its own firmly held prejudices concerning the entire art-music world, whether contemporary or otherwise. Jane Feuer, in 1978, wrote an informative exposition of these prejudices as revealed in the motion picture *It Happened in Brooklyn* (1946). She points to the oppositions between the popular and elite spheres delineated in the picture, which conform the oppositions in the minds of thousands of viewers:[16]

Movie: *It Happened in Brooklyn*
Oppositions

POPULAR	CLASSICAL
1. Brooklyn	1. Europe
2. the folk	2. upper classes
3. Sinatra, Durante	3. Lawford, Grayson
4. amateurs	4. trained musicians
5. spontaneous	5. studied
6. youth	6. tradition
7. friendly	7. snobbish
8. "comes from the heart"	8. intellectual
9. melody, plus rhythm	9. melody without rhythm
10. sexual potency	10. castration

Not only instrumental music but also operatic works, old and new, met with disparagement from the public. Many Americans felt no meaningful aesthetic relationship to opera. The editors of *Musical America,* the singer Lawrence Tibbett, the opera–stage director Herbert Graf, and the composer–writer Deems Taylor were in agreement on this point.[17] Opera was usually an importation, sung in a foreign language. Even when sung in English, operatic words sounded stilted and were unintelligibly mouthed, for the sake of rounded vocal execution. The plot and stage action remained a mystery to most auditors. Acting was poor; characterization, artificial. As often as not newspapers reported on operatic performances less as a musical event than as a social gathering for high society and as a showcase for trendsetters and eccentrics. The man in the street could never fit himself comfortably into that kind of environment.

Some Necessary Considerations

Musical creation presupposes an audience of some sort and anticipates intelligible communication with that audience— eventually, if not immediately. Unfortunately for the art composer, the new general music public of the years following World War I attended performances with the primary expectation of present enjoyment. We may be certain that if a work was found unpalatable on first contact, and equally unpalatable on second and third contact, it was thereafter avoided; if possible, no further listening in concert or on recording ensued. A key of some sort to comprehending contemporary music, that is to say writing that the laity could digest, was not usually provided by either educator, composer, or performer. If forced to listen again and again, the public seemed not to benefit from prolonged contemplation of complex sound; instead, their displeasure grew, and all like works were damned out of hand.

Before the Great Depression, so long as music was a recreation for a wealthy class willing to give the artist his head, the composer could afford indifference to the general public. Yet, even from this class, support was rare and what little there was existed mostly in and around New York City. Some grants, prizes, and subsidies came to him from private and business sources. Yet the total amount of money available to the composer was limited, and even that small amount shrank owing to the economic crisis. Beginning in the thirties, government was looked to for help; but since government had to take notice of the wishes of taxpayers and voters, it expected reciprocity for aid given to composers—reciprocity in the form of compositions of wide appeal and also of composers' willingness to defend their works when questioned by an audience. Underlying these expectations was the belief that the concurrence of the composer and listener might give rise to a masterpiece. In order to be accepted as great, art was expected to demonstrate its ability to engage the affections of a large number of listeners. It could never become a masterpiece in absence of an audience or because a limited group of people approved it. This explains the thrust of the WPA Music Project, and discloses a viewpoint not easily dismissed in a democracy.

In the same decade, with fewer affluent patrons and growing deficits to worry about, symphony orchestras and opera companies had to turn more and more to the public for assistance and to accommodate its preferences, preferences which rarely included contemporary works couched in problematic idioms. By the end of the forties, John Mueller, writing about the American symphony orchestra, could state that artistic supremacy was fine in the days of "unfettered wealth," when music was the "plaything of the rich"; but that those days were gone: "Today, when the 'guarantors' consist of thousands of little men, from whom subsidies are coaxed in chicken-feed lots, reckless expenditures may not be practical. They may desire a *quid pro quo* in musical entertainment, as well as an increment of prestige." Mueller goes on to say: "It is a question whether strong *popular* support would be forthcoming for the financially weak *aristocratic* taste. By a program that is too esoteric, the orchestra may 'aesthetisize' itself out of the market and endanger its existence more fatally than if it made some concessions to public taste."[18]

Esoterica included all works whose meaning consistently eluded the listener. The conductor Eugene Goossens, who did more than his share to promote contemporary American works during the thirties, concluded in 1943:

> I have known audiences to strive with all their might to find the key to a work which the composer has so effectively hidden that he might have spared himself the trouble of writing the work at all. This is not a matter of 'idiom.' The opus can be contrapuntally, harmonically, and rhythmically 'advanced' as you like. (The public will probably like it all the more for that.) But there comes a psychological moment in any piece of music when, unless the composer has already established some kind of 'rapport' with at least a fraction of his audience, the conductor might as well stop and proceed to the next item on the program. There is here no question of 'compromise', but rather a question of the composer having something interesting to say, and knowing how to project it to the listener.[19]

As director of the Cincinnati Symphony Orchestra since 1931, Goossens had taken a great interest in the interaction of contemporary composer and audience. He wanted to encourage the creation of viable modern compositions. For this reason, he maintained that the composer's idea must be convincing; he must exploit the idea in a congenital format; and he must give the audience satisfaction, whatever the manner in which it chooses to be gratified.

Goossens and most other performers recognized that ultimately the audience itself placed its imprimatur on a work, pronouncing the music worthy of survival. No composition continued long in the repertoire without its sanction. This was assuredly true in the thirties and forties. Virgil Thomson, a composer-writer knowledgeable in the ways of both composers and audiences during these decades, stresses that "it is the ignorantly formed and categorically expressed opinions of the amateur, in fact, that make the music world companionable." The "personal likings" of professional musicians

> . . . are eclectic; they imply no agreement of any kind. It is laymen who like to like together. Musicians' opinions influence nothing; they simply recognize, with a certain delay but correctly, the history of music. Lay opinion influences everything—even, at times, creation. And at all times it is the pronouncements of persons who know something about music, but not too much, that end by creating those modes or fashions in consumption that make up the history of taste.

Furthermore, Thomson adds, while lay opinion may be influenced by "knowledgeable people—by critics, college instructors, conductors, publishers' employees, and leaders of fashion," it is not wholly controlled by them. "The leaders of taste can no more create deliberately a mode of music than advertising campaigns can make popular a product that the public doesn't want."[20]

Unsuccessful in gaining wide acceptance for their music, the composers of difficult works frequently reproached the general music lover for preferring music they declared to be simple, obvious, trite, and without merit. Defenders of the larger audience countered by insisting that, though less complex and more familiarly featured, the music sponsored by these music lovers had excellences not recognized by the criticizing composers and had undergone a real trial period before achieving any sort of status. The composers of ultra-modern works, because they aroused positive response within a tiny sophisticated circle, erred in thinking that such approval mandated an extensive endorsement. The defenders of the general audience argued along these lines: Excellence is not absolute. An audience of millions exhibits an overwhelming diversity of backgrounds, attitudes, and tastes. All love different musics in different ways. One person's flawless masterpiece is another's dull dog, and both persons may be right. Too frequently the artist knows only a small group, whose values he reflects in his works. Instead of feeling satisfied with the accolades of his own circle, he demands recognition from listeners whose values have not been considered. However, when both the composer's and the public's values are encompassed in a single work, and that work has an appeal superior to its fellows—which was true of Barber's *Adagio for Strings* (1936) and Copland's *El Salón México* (1936)—then the greater recognition ensues.[21]

These arguments were amply borne out by events. When values diverged and the work failed to have broad approval, which was true of Ruggles's *Sun-Treader* (1932), Riegger's *Dichotomy* (1932), and Copland's *Short Symphony* (1933), then recognition rarely grew. This is not to say that such works were inferior, but that the recognition of their excellences might elude most listeners for a very long time, if not forever.

Save for the few years after 1935, it was not chic for composers to show concern over the needs of the non-specialized listener. Inevitably, the composers were the losers. Works approved by advisory boards of the League of Composers, the International Society for Contemporary Music, and the New School, writes Lehman Engel, "attracted only a scant group of listeners—mostly those of us, so to speak, 'in the family.' . . . Even the prestige gained from such programs was *en famille* prestige, about which the general public could not have cared less." This small audience was a "tight" New York-centered group, claimed George Antheil. It aped the Paris salon and "was not America." The somewhat conservative Olin Downes described it as "a minority pressure group in this country, highly vociferous and harboring a persecution complex."[22]

A humorous Oscar Levant describes his Piano Concerto, performed early in 1942, as dramatic and dissonant but a luxury he could not afford: "It won attentive approval" in particular musical circles, "but most audiences were shocked and found it disagreeable." When Eugene Goossens asked to do it in Cincinnati, Levant replied: "I can't afford to lose any more of my audience."[23]

Levant would have agreed with the conclusion about audiences reached by William Grant Still. Still insisted that audiences willingly listened to contemporary music at concerts, whether of the American Composers' Festival in Rochester, or of the International Composers' Guild in New York City, and reacted quickly and sharply, pro and con. However, when the same music of which audiences disapproved kept on being offered, interest fell off and people ceased attending. It was then the turn of "unrepresentative" small groups to call the public "unsophisticated," "old fashioned," or "ignorant."[24]

A Hodgepodge of Audiences

What was the nature of the audience that Levant and Still wrote about? Without question, it did not include the coteries, each with an identity of its own, that were concentrated principally in the New York City area, and whose members usually came prepared to accept whatever was offered them. When Copland spoke nostalgically in 1939 of the special audience that had attended the Copland–Sessions Concerts and the Yaddo Festival, he meant one containing a large number of liberated art composers and devoted supporters of innovative forms of musical expression, most of them from around New York City. This audience was variously described by the press as "the inner brotherhood," "youthful highbrows," "scholars of extremely modern music," and was called by one composer "the elite of America's modern-music circles."[25]

When Vernon Duke reflected in 1955 on the special audience once attracted by the controversial works performed by the International Composers' Guild about twenty-five years before, he remembered the "extroverted young people" of New York, who reacted "violently and noisily to whatever novelties were served up by the Guild. The hissing and booing in counterpoint with shouts of approval that accompanied the premiere of Carl Ruggles's harsher pieces was . . . thrilling to me."[26]

Copland's and Duke's type of audience did not readily transplant to other areas of America. Thomas Benton, for one, noted that the music this sort of group approved was difficult "to reconcile with the dust-blown realities of Oklahoma." Furthermore, Benton said, when one of its representatives appeared in the West to denounce "the low cultural status of the community," and praise "some kind of higher life," he made no impression on the local inhabitants, since his words were those of an "aesthetic Europe" and "sounded like something to be read out of the back of the *New Republic* in a Greenwich Village tearoom."[27]

Irving Kolodin and Virgil Thomson have discussed another special audience, the one that turned out in the thirties to hear the anti-capitalist *Cradle Will Rock* by Marc Blitzstein, and *The Strange Funeral in Braddock* by Elie Siegmeister. They noted that this audience consisted of New York's leftist front—communists, radical intellectuals, workers' groups, and strong anti-fascists. It was a novice audience, "with its own brand of yeasty youthful ferment," according to Kolodin; but "welded into about the most formidable army of ticket buyers in the world, according to Thomson.[28] However, the music that fired this audience did not always export well to other parts of America. Hiram Sherman, a performer in *The Cradle Will Rock*, says that in the summer of 1938 or 1939 Blitzstein rounded up most of the original cast in order to give a performance in Bethlehem, Pennsylvania. "I thought this was marvelous. Because we were now going to take *Cradle Will Rock* to the workers, to the people for whom he wrote this piece." To the company's dismay, nobody showed up for the performance. In desperation, the performers invited a gathering of women at a church picnic to see the musical stage work. But when the ladies learned that a whore was to be portrayed, they "got up and picked up their picnic baskets and left us."[29]

Another special audience endemic in New York City was the smart set of au courant sensation-mongers, which bayed the latest aesthetic trend. When an artistically novel composer or composition came to its attention, it gave enthusiastic support until the newness wore off and some different novelty came to its notice. Claire Reis says "an ultra program" of the League of Composers, or of the Composers' Guild, inevitably attracted "members of café society and other sensation seekers ever on the lookout not just for the new but for the newest." When Thomson's astonishing *Four Saints* was scheduled for performance, with its black performers, cellophane decor, and nonsensical libretto, the opera's fame went before it. Those knowledgeable about avant-garde matters crowded the Forty-fourth Street Theater, and proclaimed the work a masterpiece whose originality equaled that of Debussy's *Pelléas et Mélisande*.[30]

When John Kirkpatrick first championed the music of Charles Ives, his audience was thin and most critics absented themselves. But in time the influential music critic Lawrence Gilman heard the "Concord" Sonata and made much ado about it; at once the alert antennae of the smart set trembled with Gilman's message, and its members jammed into Town Hall to hear Ives's music. Olin Downes, a critic who had neglected to attend Kirkpatrick's initial presentation of Ives, now did attend and reviewed not only the music but the audience, which included large numbers of the "literati and cognoscenti." Downes writes:

> This knowing audience had turned out largely because of the special publicity which had followed Mr. Kirkpatrick's courageous introduction of Mr. Ives's "Concord" Sonata in the same hall on January 20.
>
> If snobbism was present, it was not the fault of a ruggedly individual composer. Articles acclaiming the sonata itself and other articles recounting the strange and interesting career of the man . . . had prepared the public for a sensation. Therefore, many people who, before it had received critical approval, would have passed by the "Concord" Sonata without the flicker of an eyelash were now present, audibly and visually to be counted among those who really understood and appreciated the singular music of Mr. Ives.[31]

After the performance of his acclaimed Third Symphony (1939), Roy Harris was touted as the most authentic American voice of the time. He became the fashion among an intellectual group that intensely championed him and uncritically enthused over his music. John Tasker Howard, however, wondered how real was the cult's appreciation and to what extent it took Harris up simply because he was being widely discussed.[32]

One special audience of sorts comprised affluent Americans whose sense of *noblesse oblige* caused them to sponsor public and private concerts that included American works. An understanding of contemporary music was not part of the deal; only that some wealthy persons found it incumbent upon them to show a little interest in living composers. Owing to their chronic state of penury, especially in the thirties, composers could scarcely afford the luxury of accepting the aid of only the more musically informed patrons. They welcomed handouts from whatever source. Paul Bowles describes an amusing episode that took place around 1936, wherein the ignorance of a wealthy woman was as great as the poverty of the composers she hired to amuse her affluent guests. Bowles writes:

> Another time, and . . . at Virgil's instigation Mrs. Murray Crane hired a foursome consisting of Virgil [Thomson], Aaron [Copland], Marc Blitzstein, and me to entertain her guests. A week or so before the occasion we spent an afternoon at her house arranging the program with her. Everything went easily until Marc sang an aria from *The Cradle Will Rock*, which he was just completing. The song's title and repeated punch line was: "There's Something So Damned Low About the Rich." While he delivered it with all the precise venom of which he was capable, Aaron, Virgil, and I stole rapid glances at one another and at Mrs. Crane. Apparently she had discovered the words to be in Aramaic, a language which she did not understand. However, she also let one see that she was following the music with polite interest. When Marc had finished, she leaned forward and said placidly: "Yes, it's fascinating. But I always feel that for a song to be meaningful, one must hear the words. But of course there's no reason why you *should* be able to sing. Perhaps you have something purely instrumental?" Marc then played selections from his ballet *Cain*, which Mrs. Crane found suitable. The evening went off smoothly, and we were given our checks before leaving. I felt horribly ashamed at that moment; it seemed a bit like accepting payment for moving one's hostess' chair for her. But Virgil's indoctrination asserted itself: a composer is a professional man, and professionals get paid. I hoped there might be other such musical evenings. It was the Depression, and Mrs. Crane's check seemed extremely generous. But there were no more.[33]

That there were no more checks could, in part, be attributed to the affluent music crowd's greater allegiance to time-honored music, written by proven composers and performed by the foremost musicians in settings that demonstrated the prestigious status of the rich.

Most of the general audience, to some measure, shared high society's conservatism, but of course not its wealth or certainty of place. In the decades following World War I, a decided change took place in the composition of the concert- and opera-going public, from one comprising a prominent upper class, to an undefined middle class, and, with the late thirties, shifting to some of the working class.[34] Many elements contributed to this transformation: the democratic conviction that all Americans should have the opportunity and means to enjoy good music, the rapid proliferation of performing ensembles, effective merchandising by concert-management enterprises, the furnishing of low-priced or free tickets for admission to concerts through private and public subsidization, the educational programs and concerts, open to all, that were sponsored by the Federal Music Project, and the cultural broadcasts by the radio networks. Furthermore, the total aggregate of concert-going Americans, which once numbered only a few thousands, soon numbered in the millions. (It should always be kept in mind that this audience probably numbered, at most, about 8 or 9 million out of a total population in the thirties of around 140 million Americans.) Less educated, musically inexperienced, and green in taste, the newfound public for art music groped after the most elemental principles by which to evaluate what it heard. Its deficiencies made for unease and for a diffidence upon which both authoritarian critics and colorful performers battened. Whether rightly or wrongly, this public cast aside the works it found persistently displeasing and clung tenaciously to the music it genuinely enjoyed. Moreover nobody, however exalted his position—whether a Leopold Stokowski, an Aaron Copland, a John Kirkpatrick, or a Paul Rosenfeld—could convince it otherwise.

As early as 1929, various observers of the American cultural scene were mentioning this new public with approval. In January 1929, Ernest Fowles, representing British musicians at the convention of the Music Teachers' National Association, expressed surprise and delight at the progress of music in the United States, saying: "I expected to find that we in England could teach you in America something musically, but I must be honest. Your audiences in America are better, far better, than ours in England. . . . It is like everything else we hear about America—all fairy tales."[35]

A month later, Sergei Rachmaninoff commented on the fact that American concert audiences had grown larger and more appreciative of good music: "Year by year, the thing that impresses me more and more about America is the wonderful improvement in public taste and appreciation that has taken place within an astonishingly short period of time. When I first went to America, in 1909, audiences were not one-tenth as large or as discriminating as they are now."[36]

About the same time that Rachmaninoff was making his evaluation, George Engles, a concert manager, told a *New York Times* reporter about the huge increase in concert audiences throughout the country. Engles, discussing a survey on the support given to good music, said that LaPorte, Indiana (population 15,158), was the most musical community in the United States, with 9 percent of its population attending concerts regularly, as contrasted to the total population, of which fewer than 4 percent attended regularly. Newark, Ohio, was second, with 6 percent attendance; and Portsmouth, Ohio, and Aurora, Illinois, tied for third place, with 5 percent. On the other hand, he claimed, metropolitan centers, like New York City and Chicago, numbered less than 1 percent regular concertgoers.[37] (Not given by Engles, however, are the criteria underlying the survey).

Nine years later, radio was making its influence felt among American audiences. NBC had put on the New York Symphony, the Boston Symphony, and the Philadelphia Orchestra. CBS was now regularly broadcasting the concerts of the New York Philharmonic; NBC, the productions of the Metropolitan Opera and the concerts of Toscanini and the NBC Symphony. The estimated combined audience of the Metropolitan Opera, the New York Philharmonic, and the NBC Symphony numbered around 10,230,000 families each week. In addition, the NBC Music Appreciation Hour, directed by Walter Damrosch, was reaching more than seven million children, in seventy thousand schools, and about four million adults as well. The accuracy of these figures remains unproven and may well be inflated.[38] On the other hand, the figures do testify to the huge increase in the number of Americans willing at least to sample art music—though it was mostly not contemporary music they heard. Whether they would continue to listen even to this music depended on the continuation of such broadcasts, the programming of music that the radio audience could comprehend, and the encouragement given neophyte listeners by musicians, educators, and radio's policymakers.

Contrary to what some composers claimed, the audience for serious music was not entirely stuck on a limited repertoire. Ordinary music lovers from time to time wrote letters to newspapers complaining about hearing the same few works repeatedly; this woud seem to contradict what many conductors and concert-circuit managers maintained. On the other hand, most of these letters suggested the revival of lesser-known works from the classical and romantic eras, and next to none requested modern works. A Chicago radio fan, Victor Yarros, wrote to protest the programs of the New York Philharmonic that he heard over the air. He asked, why so much Tchaikovsky, Wagner, and Franck? Why not a composition of Mahler, Elgar, or d'Indy?

A letter from Eva J. Welcher, in 1931, made an interesting suggestion. (Other writers would make similar suggestions over the years.) She thought that the contents of too many programs were the whims of conductors or the end result of cultural politics. "At the close of the concert season," she advised, "a questionnaire should be issued, seeking information as to the tastes, preferences, and suggestions of the audience. This service should be extended to the enormous radio audiences by means of the same blanks to be mailed by request . . . to the listener. By this method, I feel, we are assured of ascertaining the musical pulse of the nation, thereby insuring the balance of our future symphonic programs."[39]

The larger music public consisted principally of urbanites, who (according to several writers of the thirties) still retained a belief in humankind's dignity and worth, and in every person's right to freedom and happiness. Music that pictured this dignity and worth and that contributed to enjoyment they would prize. These men and women subscribed to the myth of the city as the grim antithesis of the country, and saw rural Americans as having a oneness with their environment and a sense of social order and their place within that order which was absent in the cities.[40] Hence the potential attractiveness of compositions directly or indirectly utilizing folk melody and myths centered in the traditions of an older America. They also wanted to feel deeply, since by feeling deeply they came alive again; hence, the search for emotion-provoking music, the more perceptibly melodious the better.

But, as already pointed out in this and earlier chapters, various obstacles to their enjoyment remained. Art music to the general public had long meant a high culture that was foreign, costly, undemocratic, and necessitating considerable leisure and special education to appreciate. They were indoctrinated with a belief that music was hopelessly divided into an evanescent popular type of entertainment and a long-lasting serious art demanding thought and expert listening skills. The gulf between popular and artistic music seemed deep. At one time, contemporary expressions of popular and artistic music had shared the same styles and were often written by the same composers. Or, at least, the serious composer wrote both artistic and semi-artistic music, thus bridging the gap for the listener. What existed in the twenties and early thirties was a decided separation between the two, which produced *two* musical cultures, not two aspects of the same musical culture.

Not surprisingly, ordinary men and women wondered if they might be stepping out of their class if they aspired to opera and symphony.[41] Yet aspire they did, once they had repudiated the false division separating what they already enjoyed from what they might possibly learn to enjoy. And frequently the accounts describing how their desire for music was realized are quite moving. Regrettably few writers on music have actually bothered to investigate what motivated these new music lovers or to chronicle the pilgrims' progress to attaining their goal.

Over the past twenty years, the author has succeeded in discovering some, though admittedly not all, of these motivations by means of an ongoing series of interviews and the acquisition of written cultural biographies contributed by over five hundred individuals. Many of the results have appeared in a previously published book, *A Sound of Strangers* (1982); some appear here. It should be kept in mind that Americans living in the Northeast, and Massachusetts in particular, are the principal informants. Nevertheless, there is every reason to believe, in light of accounts given by people from other areas (San Francisco, Chicago, St. Louis, Houston, and Atlanta, to name several), that the views expressed in one part of the country held also for the general public in another part of the country.

In an interview that took place in 1970, a young man told the author that his father had been a poor factory worker in the thirties, with a pittance for wages, but that in spite of his difficulties he had always been "interested in learning about the unknown." Encouraged by the free concerts and instruction of the Roosevelt years, he "began to read and learn about the so-called great composers." In time, he was enjoying "symphonies, especially Beethoven's, whom he admired so dearly." He told his son that the music helped him get away from, and cope with, the harshness of his existence. "After a long day's work he would come home and listen to good music played on the radio."

An elderly woman said to the author in 1977 that her husband, after passing seven years in a seminary, had left it to marry her and work as a carpenter. He brought with him a love for literature, especially Irish (he was of Irish extraction), and Latin, and for Gregorian chant. In the thirties, he learned to play the violin and cornet, and acquired a taste for "classical and operatic music." She recalled a weekend ritual that commenced in the thirties: "On Saturday we'd all [she and her six children] go out and Dad would listen to that opera all afternoon. Dad would listen to the Saturday afternoon opera program and through the pre-show explanations, the performance, and whatever commentary followed, would allow no noise at all. To avoid tempting fate, the family would leave for the duration of the show."

Another interviewee described her parents in the thirties as enjoying Bing Crosby, Al Jolson, and Broadway musicals, as well as attending performances and buying recordings when they had the spare money. Soon free concerts and radio broadcasts of good music caught their attention. For no reasons her parents could advance, they began to listen to composers like Tchaikovsky, Chopin, and Ravel. Later, they learned to enjoy ballet. Indeed, "it soon got to be that they were dismal if they couldn't hear or see the performances they loved."

One must always remember that to this audience of recent converts to art music, the compositions of Schubert, Tchaikovsky, Verdi, Brahms, and Beethoven were heard as *new music*, which made its own demands on the audience's understanding. But once a few works were understood, they were guides to the enjoyment of a host of other compositions written in a similar style.

The General Audience's Music Values

In discussing the values of the general public concerning music, it is wise to look beyond what composers, performers, and music critics have said on the subject and to consult directly with men and women from other walks of life, who profess a love for art music. What did music mean to a few of these listeners? In 1972, one woman, describing herself as "a mediocre piano player" and a faithful attender of the Boston Symphony Orchestra's concerts since the beginning of the forties, said:

> It's a marvelous thing to have music inside you—to grow up with an orchestra in your head continually playing symphonies, rags, and pop tunes. Sometimes it'll drive you crazy if one theme gets caught in your head . . . because your orchestra doesn't know the rest of the melody! I walk down the street in step with a Sousa march, if I'm feeling spritely; a Hungarian Rhapsody, if I'm in a hurry; or a mournful hymn if I'm down. Sometimes my musical mind spills over into my mouth, and, much to the chagrin of those within earshot, I sing joyfully along with my orchestra.

In 1971, an interviewee said he learned to like art music through his uncle and mother. They had introduced him to composers "from Beethoven to Tchaikovsky." Why his fascination with music? He states:

> It is difficult for me to . . . try to describe why I am interested in music as my reasons are romantic, idealistic, and personal, not rational and concrete. I think of music as being my way of understanding God. He's there, and so is his message, but it cannot be defined nor fully understood. He can only be felt in one's heart and sought after as the Eternal Truth. For me, it's the same with music as it is with God; I don't know fully why I believe in it; I only know that it is good and that it's in my heart.

Music enlarged the emotional lives and gave insight into the essential humanity of these two listeners. This observation should be made to stand beside the unsympathetic views of several modern composers. It partly refutes, for example, Elliott Carter's claim, stated in 1938, that people listen in order to give themselves up to an evening of reminiscence or revery, with nothing deeper intended. They think, according to Carter, of their childhood and adolescence, or the condition of their bank balance or love life; or they worry about their future.[42]

The findings of psychologists also contradict these composers' views. A study by C. W. Valentine discusses the testing of hundreds of persons in order to determine what meaning music had for them. After saying that most people first started off by describing objectively what they heard—loudness and softness, the prominence of one sound over another, and so forth—he found the largest number reacting subjectively to the sounds, describing in general terms what feelings were aroused—as melancholy, creepiness, elation, and so on. A far smaller number read something akin to personality into musical sounds—such as forceful music, sullen sound, and so forth. A slightly lesser number associated sound with something else—church bells, birds singing, a walk by a resonant sea, and other images. Listeners were less inclined to attribute emotion to the music itself, more to what the sound produced in them. When, instead of selections, they heard complete musical works, the "low aesthetic value" of associative judgments was further confirmed. Another significant result of the testing was to find a strong "imagery of movement," with music inclining listeners to tap their feet, or sway their bodies, or, in some instances, get up and move about. If no regular beat was perceived, enjoyment lessened considerably.[43]

However much writers on music, such as Eduard Hanslick, August Halm, and Ernst Kurth (most of them German and Austrian theoreticians), claim that music can have only a self-contained meaning devoid of any emotion, associative, or personality-related characteristics, the general audience, according to several recent writers, such as Susanne Langer, Percy Buck, and John Booth Davies, who have made some study of it, never believes music to be a pure sensation with its meaning limited to itself. A composition is beautiful—that is to say, takes on meaning—when it elicits a positive subjective response in the listener. Let one listener speak for the many. A man born and brought up in Chicago told the author that by the end of high school his "relationship to music . . . was one of passionate enthusiasm, undisciplined but far from casual. Music was an emotional experience. Listening to a Beethoven or a Mahler symphony was a religious, profound experience, a catharsis."

After studying the growth of American symphony orchestras in the first half of the present century, John Mueller concluded: "Beauty is not a transcendental entity waiting . . . to be incorporated into a composition by a sensitive composer; nor is it a quality resident *in* the object . . . waiting to be discovered and enjoyed. . . . Beauty in music is not a fact but rather a human *experience,* a judgment that results from the *contact* between the particular arrangement of sounds and the particular background of the auditor. . . . If there were no observer, there would be no beauty."[44]

Both Carroll Pratt, in *The Meaning of Music* (1931), and Morris Weitz, in *Philosophy of the Arts* (1964), say much the same thing. They write that music can have no definite meaning. Listeners, however, associate certain sounds with certain symbolic references. The greater the audience's agreement on the symbolization, the more uniform its comprehension.

When hearing music within the framework of common practice, Western listeners have learned to associate a minor triad with sadness, a diminished-seventh chord with unease, persistent melodic leaps upward of a fourth or octave with elation, and a long appoggiatura descending a half step with poignancy. Slow harmonic rhythms can lull; fast harmonic rhythms excite. Note Valentine's observation elsewhere in the above-cited study: "We may suppose that the custom of setting sad songs to minor keys originated without any felt suitability of the key to the ideas, but that gradually by repetition of the association, we have come to connect the two, so that a piece of music in the minor key now usually appears to us sad or plaintive."[45]

When pressed, a listener may say a work makes him feel joyous or melancholic. The explanation calls for cautious acceptance because it involves the translation of a sound symbol to a verbal symbol, which imprisons, and delimits, and even falsifies the true response. At best, terms like joyous and melancholic but vaguely designate the rich and limitless significations that the musical symbol can summons from the depths of one's being.

Yet no two people hear the same work in exactly the same way. Each is governed by his or her own unique psychological, sociological, educational, and experiential background. The mix can never be identical in any two people. As a case in point, in the fall of 1941 the author took part in a rehearsal of Beethoven's Quartet for Strings, opus 18, no. 1, held in a home in West Roxbury, Massachusetts. All the players were young amateurs, aged eighteen to twenty years. A discussion ensued over coffee and cake on the meaning of the D-minor *adagio* movement. Beethoven had marked it "affettuoso ed appassionato," to be played tenderly and in impassioned style. The movement is supposed to have been inspired by Shakespeare's *Romeo and Juliet.*

The violist, a devout Catholic, said it evoked in him feelings similar to those he experienced when he thought of Christ's travail in the Garden of Gethsemane. The cellist, the oldest person in the quartet, disagreed; to him, the music sounded intoxicating. The placid mother of the cellist was one of the listeners. She found most of the movement restful, in an elegiac sort of way.[46] They all loved the piece but verbalized their understanding of it in different fashion. The common denominators among them were the entirely subjective response to the sound, and the sense of inadequacy in trying to communicate a profoundly personal experience to others.

Among general audiences of this period, a common denominator on yet another plane was their desire for entertainment. Relaxation, recreation, and a hunger for distraction for besetting worries brought people into concert halls and opera houses. As an unidentified writer in the *New York Times,* said about the Lewisohn Stadium concerts held in the summer of 1932, only a small part of the audience comprised trained and critical listeners. By far the largest number had "no intellectual pretensions to musical knowledge," and were attracted to the New York Philharmonic's concerts by the "popular prices." The writer continues: "These people doubtless come for a variety of reasons. They live near by; they rather like music; they feel that an evening outdoors listening to an orchestra would be an enjoyable way to pass the time. They seek entertainment, relaxation, pleasure." Furthermore, says the writer, they have "no predilections of taste" or "preconceptions of what should be liked." They are honestly "ready to respond but as ready to be discouraged."[47]

What the above writer states is confirmed by a young man interviewed in 1969. He said that his father's love for music grew slowly but steadily during the thirties and early forties. "He began to attend the outdoor concerts in New York [Lewisohn Stadium] and found classical music to be extremely relaxing, although he never studied it."

Respondents again and again have pointed out music's therapeutic value. In 1970, an interviewee said that her mother, "half-Cherokee Indian, half-Dutch in descent," had grown up in extreme poverty in Oklahoma during the thirties. The radio introduced her to art music. Before long, music was playing "a very important role in her life in a relaxing almost therapeutic sense; where she can sit down and listen to music and forget her problems."

Also in 1970 another interviewee, Armenian in descent, said that during the thirties classical music "began to play an even more important part in my grandparents' and parents' lives, because of the Depression." They "found music helpful and unifying in meeting the problems besetting them. Though they lacked the money for concerts, the radio provided them with music." We have here another confirmation of the important role that radio played in bringing art music to the public, who might otherwise have never heard it.

Several orchestra conductors were very aware of the public's need for diversion. After Eugene Ormandy was appointed to share the conductorship of the Philadelphia Orchestra with Leopold Stokowski in 1936, he received many letters from subscribers asking to be entertained and not educated, as had been Stokowski's intent.[48]

Several years later, Goossens claimed that the prime reason people attended concerts was for diversion, not "uplift and culture." He was certain that "the sooner composers and conductors acknowledge the possibility of a person being at one and the same time deeply moved and likewise *entertained* by music, the sooner will both discover the secret way to the hearts of their audience." Furthermore, "composers can no longer afford to preserve that attitude of subjective isolation which results in long, sententious symphonic works filled with morbid self-contemplation, and devoid of the one element which puts them in sympathy with their audience. The public, in short, insists on adopting a very realistic attitude about the whole business, and there is little one can do about it."[49]

The Preferred Music

What kind of sound was it that moved the public pleasurably? Unquestionably, almost all of the serious music that listeners requested and musicians programmed after 1920 was composed before World War I. General audiences took a lively interest in the art of the contemporary performer and no interest in the originative talents of the contemporary composer. A large body of musical literature already existed that they could love wholeheartedly. Why should they, then, put it aside for twentieth-century works of elusive comprehensibility and offensive sound? No, they were not adventurous. The new music of conservative composers often sounded like tired examples of the rich, colorful, emotionally satisfying works of the romantic era. The new music of venturesome composers, though intended for performance before a large audience, embodied no aesthetic they recognized.

Nineteenth-century composers, on the whole, seemed best to address the needs of the commonality of twentieth-century concertgoers. Their musical values and those of audiences between the two world wars had major points of correspondence. The dramatic symphony, the spectacular or intensely lyric opera, the heroic concerto, the colorful tone poem, the expressive art song, and the sentiment-laden character piece for piano delighted the general listener.

This music that the public most enjoyed was set in a clear tonality and had melodies to which the vocal chords responded sympathetically. Indeed, such melodies, supported by tangible rhythms, triadic harmonies, perceptible structures, and striking instrumental colors, were the prime sources for musical pleasure.[50] Thus the more advanced composers, in making vast changes in the very nature of music, had downgraded the sounds that listeners wanted. At the same time, audiences persisted in listening for what was no longer meant to be there. Because modern music failed to touch them, they remained with the older music that met their expectations.[51] In addition, the older music had withstood the test of time and won the approval of countless authorities. It left listeners secure in their aesthetic judgments of what was and was not beautiful.

Not surprisingly, then, however much contemporary composers criticized the policies of hidebound institutions like the Metropolitan Opera, they won little support from the majority of the music public—for the Met espoused mostly the dependable masterpieces on which the public doted. Radio broadcasts, recordings, and proselyting by the Metropolitan Opera Guild increased the audience for traditional opera over tenfold. In 1939, when the original stockholders were forced to relinquish ownership of the Met's building, a nationwide effort was made to raise a million dollars to buy the property. About 170,000 people, one-third of them from the radio audience, donated the needed money.[52] These men and women would never have done the same for an institution dedicated to the kind of modernity just described.

The audience's acceptance of contemporary American works was disadvantaged in several other ways. For one, the names and faces of art composers, even the most prominent, were unknown or of no great importance. Koussevitzky, during an out-of-town concert with the Boston Symphony, happened to look behind him at somebody the audience thought was Charlie Chaplin. The look-a-like at whom the conductor was looking was, however, the composer of one of the programmed works. The local newspaper reported the incident with a prominent headline: "No, Not Charlie: Only a Composer."[53]

An obvious concomitant of the lack of familiarity with the composer's person was the lack of familiarity with his music. Audiences heard hardly any contemporary works (save in the concerts sponsored by the Federal Music Project, during the few years of its existence), and those few modern works they heard were normally presented only once or twice. As Virgil Thomson rightly observes, the general audience leaned "toward a timid conservatism with regard to unfamiliar music." While "the lay public will try anything . . . it will be disappointed, on first hearing, in anything it has no method for remembering."[54] Without several presentations of the same work to the same audience, no clear verdict of approval or disapproval could be given. If an opinion was ventured, it was founded on ignorance. Furthermore, regular performance of contemporary music outside the environs of the largest cities, and sponsored by organizations other than those specializing in presenting modern works to select groups, was essential to win a reliable consensus on any work's worth.[55]

Another handicap was the audience's distaste for discordant sounds meant to "express the spirit of today." Typical listeners wanted no such representation of the realities about them, especially during the Great Depression. To cite one from many examples, an interviewee told the author that there was in her family during this troubled time "a distinct adult dislike of some modern music." Her aunt in particular wondered if it was "old-fashioned to expect beautiful voices, chords, and melodies." She felt that too much emphasis was placed "on the dissatisfaction of the individual with his surroundings and the consequent urge to tear down what is and has been, and the result in our music is discord and harsh sounds to fit the modern thought."[56]

Deems Taylor says that in his radio talks he tried to play it fair and explain "ultra-modern music" to the Americans of the thirties and forties. But his radio audience criticized him for trying to gain acceptance for it. He writes that later, when he confessed on the air to finding much of it dull and sterile, he received "several hundred letters and postcards—a heavy mail for a symphony broadcast. I was dumbfounded at the unanimity of the writers' opinion. Out of the lot, there were just four who sharply disagreed with me. The rest said that they hated most ultra-modern music and were glad to find somebody who agreed with them."[57]

Listen to what one listener had to say about modern American music. The *New York Times* in 1935 printed a letter from Robert Courneen, of Lyons, New York, who wrote: "I love music—the classics, I mean—opera, symphony, voice, etc. But for some unexplained reason, I cannot begin to fathom American music about which we are hearing so much today. I attend concerts of American composers at the Eastman School, in Rochester, and I listen to them via radio. Yet I cannot decipher it. To me it sounds like a grand convention with implements of the boilermakers, riveters . . . all together in a building that reeks with echoes."[58]

Two points in the letter should be noticed. One, that Mr. Courneen did go to hear American compositions; two, that he was puzzled by what he heard. He did not say he wanted never to hear it again. Indeed, like a significant number of other listeners, he showed at least some tolerance toward new music.

A similar tolerance is shown by E. B. Hough, of Haddonfield, New Jersey, in a letter written to the *Times* in 1940. He says he is tired of Olin Downes and other critics who wondered what was the "American essence" and what kind of music Americans should write. His advice is to "lay off the American composer, stop pestering the poor guy! Why get so all het up over what is American music? The American composer will write music and

if he's interested in America and soaks it up, the music will be
American music. . . . Let him compose what he feels and what
the spark inside tells him to compose. . . . If he has something
to say, people will listen; until then, let's keep the ants out of
the pants of the American composer."[59]

A musical preference poll among subscribers to the Indianapolis
Symphony Orchestra was made public in 1950. True, most of the
subscribers preferred music from Haydn to Debussy. But an
astonishing one-quarter of the audience said it would not mind
if half the playing time was given over to American works, while
45 percent would accept programs 10 percent of whose playing
time was given over to American compositions. Virgil Thomson,
who reported the results of the poll, says the same tolerance existed
elsewhere. For example, the Boston Symphony Orchestra did
perform many contemporary American works; yet it regularly sold
out on season subscriptions and had received no serious complaints
about the practice. One further comment by Thomson is that those
who were "really receptive to modernism are almost all under
forty and mostly under thirty"[60] Tolerance and the growing
receptivity of the young were good signs; might they yield in time
to genuine enthusiasm?

To build a radio audience for new music, advised Alfred
Frankenstein, do not play too much of it on any one program,
nor frighten listeners by warning them it is modern—and never
forget that listeners make up a "broad, heterogeneous, catch-as-
catch-can audience." When Frankenstein's San Francisco radio
station, KSFO, programmed the broadcast of music at the same
time as the New York Philharmonic concerts, the Hooper
measurement of listeners tuned in to radio broadcasts showed the
Philharmonic to have the larger audience at first. However, when
Deems Taylor began his commentary during the intermission of
the concert, then KSFO had twice the Philharmonic audience.
When polled, the radio audience expressed a primary interest in
works from the previous century. It had definite ideas on what
it liked in the older music and the vaguest of ideas about what
the new music was all about. Nevertheless, one-third of all requests
were for music of the twentieth century: "Modern music goes does
particularly well," Frankenstein writes, "when it is simply given
as a matter of course, when it is contrasted with the 'classics,'

when the 'classics' have preceded it and made the hearer comfortably receptive to the whole program, and when it is not hedged about with 'explanations' and excuses which tend to make the hearer suspicious."[61] (One wonders to what extent Taylor's commentaries contributed to the anti-new music attitude that he writes about.) Around the end of the forties, Frankenstein taught at a Harvard summer session, during which the author assisted him with the transcription of American folk music. The author spoke about the article on radio listeners Frankenstein had written and asked if "modern music" had included many American compositions. "Of course," was his reply.

The possibility always existed that members of the audience might gradually learn to accept, if not to enjoy, a non-conservative composition. As a case in point, when Copland's First Symphony was premiered in New York City in 1925, it was greeted with both applause and a great deal of hissing. Some listeners were shocked, others insulted. Ten years later, the Boston Symphony programmed it. Grace May Stutsman, a critic normally unsympathetic to any kind of advanced music, wrote: "Bostonians, for the most part, took the work quite calmly: a few evinced downright enthusiasm for it. The piece is unquestionably pagan, undeniably exciting."[62]

The same year that the Boston Symphony played the Copland work, Howard Hanson wrote to the *Times,* describing the success of the American Music Festivals at Rochester, now in their tenth year. The number of people desiring admission had increased so much that additional police were needed to control the crowds. The listeners were "intensely interested" and "curious" about American modernism. He found that they "did not take kindly to formlessness. A work which meandered through yards of score-paper without, as they expressed it, 'getting anywhere,' received scant applause. They showed admiration for a good time, infectious rhythm, and for musical vitality, and a work such as Randall Thompson's Second Symphony, . . . which has all three of these qualities, earned their immediate affection and had to be repeated at later concerts."[63] (It should be observed that the work did not transgress many of the general music public's values.)

When the Federal Music Project of the Roosevelt years got into full swing, the possibility of acceptance was thought to have become a probability. American music was played as never before by performing groups in every part of the United States. Men and women, most of them recent converts to art music, came to listen. They were unskilled listeners fearful of outré sound and puzzled by the advanced concepts in modern compositions. But tastes were in a formative stage. Attitudes had not yet hardened. Continual exposure to new sounds and encouragement to listen, given time, might have won much of this large audience over. Unfortunately, as already noted, the project was closed off four years or so after its inception.

The lesson to be learned from the federal experiment is that nobody should prefigure how large or small the audience for contemporary American music might be. Except during the last half of the thirties, the larger audience was little cultivated for new music. From the fifties on, proponents of the newest music wrote this audience off, finding its cultivation an impediment to artistic experimentation. The schism between general listener and modern composer has widened into a formidable breach. Not to mend it means the conversion of the former into a dedicated musical museum-goer, and the latter into a totally redundant member of American society.

4

Music of Two Decades

A monolithic high musical culture free of admixture and free of stylistic diversity is an impossibility. All art musics contain traits reflective of present and past sounds from diverse sources, national and international. When we consider the music of Americans, we must admit that, for the most part, it adhered to no one mode of expression and belonged to no clearly defined American school, where composers thought and wrote similarly. Ruggles, Riegger, Sessions, Moore, Copland, Barber, Thomson, and Blitzstein, for example, had individual attitudes about the composition of music and individual styles.[1]

Nor can we say that a composer necessarily keeps his style consistent throughout his lifetime. Copland, Antheil, Cowell, and Blitzstein, to name four composers, each produced works during their maturity based on different aesthetic principles. Immediately coming to mind are the contrasts between Copland's *Symphonic Ode* and *Rodeo*, Antheil's *Ballet Mécanique* and Second Symphony, Cowell's Piano Concerto and *Hymn and Fuguing Tune*, Numbers 1 to 8, and Blitzstein's *Percussion Music for Piano* and *The Cradle Will Rock*.

The only period, during the years under consideration, when music suggesting a united approach was evident was that of the middle thirties through the forties, when several significant composers reached out to a common citizenry through their music. They deliberately simplified their styles, employed greater consonance and melodiousness, and introduced American themes and traditional American sounds into their works. Likenesses may be detected in compositions like Copland's *Billy the Kid,* Thomson's *The Plow that Broke the Plains,* Gould's *Fall River Legend,* Harris's *Folk Song Symphony,* Siegmeister's *Western Suite,* and Schuman's *American Festival Overture.* On the other hand, these works usually revealed only likenesses, nothing more deeply conjoined in musical style.

In this chapter, the author has selected representative examples of musical compositions written in a variety of contemporary styles, in order to discuss them in relation to their audiences. No attempt is made to examine every composer active from the twenties through the forties or to list every composition created in these decades.

Difficult Music

As was previously mentioned, the United States in the 1920s had barely completed the establishment of its first permanent symphony orchestras and opera companies, and had just begun to see more than a handful of the public recognizing the value of art music. Then suddenly maverick American composers took an unorthodox stand against established musical practice, sharing in the radical innovations pioneered by Igor Stravinsky or Arnold Schoenberg.[2]

"A native band of young Turks," Elie Siegmeister calls these composers, who "had introduced such daring devices as tone clusters, polychords, quarter tones, polytonality, tone rows, and percussion music." He continues, "Modernism galvanized the young composers, but was royally rejected by major orchestras and the broad musical public, and survived in those tiny concerts attended by 100—always the same 100—people."[3]

Apologists for the new music pointed to the meticulous care taken to plan each work and the logical reasoning which guided every sound. Audiences found the sound chaotic.

Modernists like Ruggles and Sessions aimed to create lasting compositions uncompromisingly serious in purpose, however tense, relentlessly somber, and oppressively heavy general audiences found them.

Carl Ruggles (1876–1971) wrote compositions showing affinities with Arnold Schoenberg's twelve-tonalism. Lengthy, uninterrupted horizontal lines that avoided tonal repetition until after the sounding of six to ten different tones characterized his melodic writing. Melody was non-vocal, antilyric, and moved in wide chromatic sweeps with little articulation of phrase and no clear reference to any regular meter. For contrast, Ruggles introduced brief, eccentrically moving passages which, though quiet, were based on unstable intervals.[4] Harmony, the result of clashing counterpointal parts, consisted of seconds, sevenths, and augmented fourths, unmeliorated by even an occasional consonance.

His early *Men and Angels,* a suite for five trumpets and bass trumpet, was first performed in New York City in 1922. It already demonstrated Ruggles's intense, boldy discordant linear style. The composition was later revised, given a different instrumentation, and reissued as *Angels.*

Men and Mountains, a three-movement symphonic suite, was premiered in New York City in 1924. Nicolas Slonimsky says it tried to depict "his country's stern landscapes," in music "entangled in Schoenbergian formulas." Slonimsky mentions "powerful strings in unison for striding men and bulky discords for marching mountains."[5] Lazare Saminsky asserts that Ruggles's technique was "crude and clumsy"; yet, he detects "New England spirituality" in *Men and Mountains.* In 1936, the work was rescored for a larger orchestra and played by Hans Lange and the New York Philharmonic. The reviewer for *Musical America,* identified only as "O", found in it a "whole-hearted example of the harmonic revolt of the now dimming era of post-war experimentation." At the same time, the work had dated, was no longer shocking, and won no affection from the audience. "The applause," the reviewer writes, "was negligible. A few half-hearted hisses were equally indicative of the indifferent reception of the once controversial score."[6]

In 1926, *Portals* for string orchestra was heard in New York City. By this year Ruggles had become sensitive to the repetition of tones; now no tone is repeated until merely four to six other tones intervene.[7] Although the composition is individual in expression, the clumsiness Saminsky speaks of is evident, as the composer continues to have trouble finding a mode of expression congenial to him.

Then came *Sun-Treader* for full orchestra and lasting a little over seventeen minutes, a lengthy work for Ruggles. Premiered in Paris in 1932, it remained unperformed in the United States until 1966. This knotty chromatic piece opens with a persistent thud of the kettledrum. Above, strident brasses declaim apocalyptically. Now and again the loud prophetic voice is interrupted by softer sounds which involve the contrapuntal permutations of a brief motive. The doubling of parts by different choirs of the orchestra fills out an otherwise thin texture and makes for a sameness in instrumental coloration. Normally, nine or ten different tones occur before tonal repetition. Elliott Carter hears in *Sun-Treader* "a very thin but intense texture, contrapuntally speaking." "The music," Carter says, "is extremely sophisticated for its time in its use of dissonances but very primitive in its textual layout. This dissociation makes the piece seem un-European," not fitting the European concept of balance. "Of course," Carter adds, "this kind of thing is symptomatic of the free attitude that American composers have often brought to the writing of music—an interest in trying things that in Europe would be considered dangerously out of line with proven esthetic standards. American composers have felt free to do this, partly because they have not been able to write for a ready-made audience for new music. . . . In a way, American works have been of necessity 'private works.'"[8]

Later, Ruggles wrote *Evocations* (1945) for piano, and *Organum* (1949) for orchestra. These, too, failed to interest anyone beyond a narrow circle of admirers.

Various specialists in modern music agree that Ruggles's music embodies a private vision at once sublime and ecstatic. Paul Rosenfeld qualifies his praise, saying he can see no benefit in avoiding tonal repetition. Moreover, he sometimes senses "a restrained quality" in certain musical passages that strike him as too mathematical.[9]

Conventional critics and the general musical public remained totally unsympathetic. But Ruggles stubbornly refused to compromise what he saw as his creative integrity. The result was that few performances of his music occurred. Wearied by the ceaseless opposition, the composer isolated himself on a Vermont farm,

THOMAS HART BENTON, *The Sun Treader—Portrait of Carl Ruggles.* The Nelson–Atkins Museum of Art, Kansas City, Missouri. Gift of the Friends of Art. Reproduced with permission.

took up painting, and ceased to have much to do with the world of music. Though interest in his music revived in the seventies, it was limited to a small group. While there is much to admire in a work like *Sun-Treader,* with its overwhelming climaxes and delicately textured interludes, most listeners still resist Ruggles's music.

Wallingford Riegger (1885–1961) studied music with the German-trained Percy Goetschius, in New York City, then continued his musical education at Berlin's Hochschule für Musik. His early Trio in B minor (1920) sounds as if written by a conservative Middle-European romanticist. But over the next six years, Riegger shed his conservatism. With his *Study in Sonority* for ten violins or any multiple of ten, written in 1927 and first performed by Stokowski and the Philadelphia Orchestra in 1929, Riegger emerged as a modernist sympathetic to the innovations of Arnold Schoenberg (at that time, a teacher in Berlin's Prussian Academy of Arts).

The work is atonal, though not twelve-tone. Dissonant harmonies, usually made up of eight to twelve different tones, result from random choice sanctioned by the composer's ear. Unison melody is contrasted with a complex web of contrapuntal activity. Oscar Thompson thought it to be "just . . . a study," and "its merits . . . essentially technical." Virgil Thomson declared it "airy," "animated," and "witty all at the same time." Nevertheless, general audiences have never accepted the work. Richard Goldman, for example, writes: "Stokowski, to his great credit, had the courage to present the *Study* to a subscription audience. This work had a sensationally abusive reception." Listeners were "horrified and angry" at having to sit through its performance.[10]

Then, in 1932, Riegger's *Dichotomy* for chamber orchestra was performed in Berlin, and a few months later, in New York City. The dissonance and atonality are now built on two contrasting tone rows, one of eleven tones, and other of ten tones. Melody is given a rhythmic propulsion certainly not Schoenbergian in derivation. Richard Goldman claims Riegger at this time lacked a thorough knowledge of Schoenberg's music and took many liberties with his two rows, and that the influence of Stravinsky is noticeable in the rhythm.[11] Israel Citkowitz, a young composer trained by Boulanger, wrote an unsympathetic review of the New York performance, calling the themes "flaccid," the development of ideas "banal," and the dissonances "excruciating . . . unwarranted by any musical or emotional necessity."[12]

Riegger did get to know Schoenberg's music well. By 1938, in his String Quartet No. 1, he was able to demonstrate a thorough acquaintance with serialism. Conlon Nancarrow, a young composer from Arkansas, heard the composition in a radio broadcast

CHARLES SHEELER, *Fugue*. Courtesy of the Museum of Fine Arts, Boston. Arthur Mason Knapp Fund.

and described the music as "forbidding," and in "the twelve-tone system," a technique not then popular with American composers. "Development," Nancarrow states, is "carried through in all voices with the use of a large array of contrapuntal devices."[13]

The composer had to wait until 1948 for his first important critical recognition. That year, his Symphony No. 3 was performed by Dean Dixon and the CBS Symphony. It won the New York Critics' Circle Award as the best new American orchestral work of the season. The two aspects of Riegger's mature style—the twelve-tone serialism and the strong rhythms—are quite evident in the symphony.

Riegger also had a penchant for set contrapuntal forms— witness his *Three Canons* for four woodwinds (1931), *Fantasy and Fugue* for organ and orchestra (1931), *Passacaglia and Fugue* for band or orchestra (1944), and *Preamble and Fugue* for orchestra

(1956). These compositions can sound attractive owing both to their sometimes Americanized, though unconventional, themes, to the skillful manipulation of these themes, and at the same time to a variety of bold rhythms that drive the music onward. Ray Brown, after he heard Hans Kindler and the National Symphony Orchestra perform the *Passacaglia and Fugue,* writes that it "met with the kind of spontaneous response that delights a composer. Anything but a dull and pedantic essay in traditional forms, the work begins with a snare-drum roll that would have startled Bach or Handel as would the biting dissonances in the brassy clamorous introduction." He speaks of the passacaglia as having a "staccato theme announced by the 'celli and basses with a syncopation suggestive of a Negro funeral procession." The counterpoint abounds with "ironic humor." The fugue is lively, jazzy, and "expertly instrumented for color contrasts and has besides an engaging quality of frank emotion."[14]

Then there are the pieces composed for various dance companies, like *Frenetic Rhythms* (1933), *New Dance* (1935), *Machine Ballet* (1938), and *Dance Rhythms* (1955). They sport strong percussive beats, terse reiterated rhythmic patterns, and snippets of staccato melody.

Every now and then Riegger would write a tonal composition replete with recognizable melody, acceptable harmony, and pungent humor. One such work, the Concerto for Piano and Woodwind Quintet (1953), has pleased more than a few people.

Riegger's more ambitious and less conciliatory *Study in Sonority, Dichotomy,* four symphonies, and two string quartets have had a hard time winning a wider following. They are, on balance, potentially more attractive than the works of Ruggles. They suffer, however, the usual malady of most American art works—neglect.

Roger Sessions (b. 1896) shows the influence of his teacher, Ernest Bloch, in his first major composition, *The Black Maskers* (1923), incidental music for the Leonid Andreiev play which he later refashioned into an orchestral suite. More than any of his subsequent works, it exploits orchestral colors, appeals directly to listeners' feelings, and images both atmosphere and drama. It also continues as his most liked and performed composition. This is not to say that *The Black Maskers* was ever really popular.

For example, when performed on 11 January 1936, at a League of Composers concert, the greater part of the audience remained apathetic. The reviewer who reports the reaction adds: "A certain willfulness mars much that would otherwise be first-rate writing. The composer bowed from his box, while his admirers kept applauding."[15] Indifferent audiences, unyielding composer, and approving devotees have been the hallmarks of Sessions's career.

Sessions's First Symphony, performed by Koussevitzky and the Boston Symphony in 1927, is already well along the road toward the abstract style of his maturity. The music, with its Stravinskian rhythms and Schoenbergian chromaticism, makes few concessions to listeners' sensibilities. At the 1927 performance an admiring Roy Welch listened to the three short movements and put Sessions among the "most compelling figures in modern music." (Roy Welch, it should be stated, was chairman of the music department at Smith College, where Sessions had taught theory from 1917 to 1921.)

With a sneer behind his words, Welch sets down "solely for historical purposes" that the audience hissed the symphony. Then follow several paragraphs of lavish praise that, ironically, suggests why this symphony and all other works of the composer have failed to engage listeners' interest. "The symphony," he writes, "is pure music. It has no commerce with the externals or inconsequentials that so frequently intrude upon modern music. . . . The only relevant matter is the musical thoughts and the living shape their composer has given them." The audience's prerogatives are quite ignored: "The score is never sensuous; the composer is never diverted from his purpose either by the enticements of sonority or by facile effectiveness." Welch comments on Sessions's "ascetic restraint," and is delighted that the composer is not seduced "into luxurious richness of color," nor into "the familiar clichés of sequence and extension and of rhetorical emphasis."[16]

After establishing the composer's technical competence, partisans found it difficult to prove the symphony had any profound meaning. Welch, for one, had applauded primarily what was not in the symphony. A few years later, Lazare Saminsky struggled to speak positively and drowned his sense in a silly purple patch of a sentence: "In the opening *Giusto* of his *Symphony,* an obstinate force with deep glints of emotion clearly racial, yet personal and centrifugal, streams through the cyclopean lines of its structure. And, one must add, this force is coupled with a stark innate rigidity that allows for only well defined, limited, and predictable swings of creation."[17]

The composer traveled further and further along the road toward a music typified by complex, chromatic polyphony, resolute dissonance, and opaque sound.

His First Piano Sonata (1930), Copland says, is problematical for the listener and written in a universal style, "without any of the earmarks of obvious nationalism." Rosenfeld hears "the deeply inward expression of an aristocratic musicianship." For Carter, it is strong, concentrated, intellectualized music that shuns easy effect and immediate appeal.[18] All three writers show, in their praise, why a limited audience alone could appreciate the work.

Randall Thompson was far more frank in his appraisal of the sonata's effect. He finds the piece enormously difficult to play. Dissonant counterpoint is excessive; the upper register of the piano, overly exploited. Scarcely any textural or coloristic contrast is introduced. Thompson continues:

> The work is, if anything, overcharged with thought, tightened beyond the point of freedom in its own expression, condensed in its incisiveness to a point where its communicativeness is hampered rather than helped. If a short story is condensed to a day letter, the day letter may contain all the essentials but the short story is bound to contain something—perhaps even an irrepressible irrelevancy—that makes it better reading and heightens its powers of communication.[19]

Listened to more than fifty years after its composition, the First Piano Sonata sounds oddly attractive and expressive. Yet most listeners still refuse to be persuaded that it is enjoyable.

Sessions's First String Quartet, premiered in a year (1936) when many composers were attempting some reconciliation with the larger musical public, explores the same musical vein as the sonata. Its prevalent chromaticism and unfocused tonality pose insurmountable problems for the listener.[20]

Of the Violin Concerto (1940), Copland has much to say that parallels the words of Thompson on the sonata. It makes "extraordinary demands" on "even the best-disposed listener and interpreter." Sessions has given the audience "more than you can reasonably expect it to be able to digest." Texture is "too continuously complex;" melody, "too frequently involved;" and structure, "on too gargantuan a scale."[21]

When the Second Piano Sonata (1946) was first performed, Virgil Thomson admired the composer's learned inventiveness and seriousness, but also sounded a litany similar to that of Thompson and Copland about the music's difficulty and lack of "melodic and harmonic appeal."[22] Other critics spoke in like manner of the Second Symphony (1947) and the "bloodless" opera *Montezuma* (1962).

Complaints have been voiced about the music never smiling, never giving the impression of spontaneity. Musically skilled auditors respect Sessions's music; few of them admit to loving it. The consensus of the general audience is neither to respect nor to love it. Even those inured to dissonance call Sessions's compositions monotonous, boring, and lacking in charm.

This is unfortunate. A great deal does go on in his music, and his ideas, though complex, are fitted into absolutely logical structures. To follow the thought, however, minds must not ever wander. But wander they do. Much as Sessions's defenders wish otherwise, the impediments to more than desultory performance seem too great to overcome. He has been described as the composer's composer. He may never be the American people's composer.

Walter Piston (1894–1976), though he has written music unassimilable at first hearing, is not nearly as hard to enjoy as Ruggles, Riegger, and Sessions. After attending Harvard, he continued his musical education in Paris with Nadia Boulanger and Paul Dukas. When he returned home, Koussevitzky and the Boston Symphony Orchestra give his work public exposure by performing his *Symphonic Piece* (1928), Suite for Orchestra (1930), and Concerto for Orchestra (1934). He soon established a reputation as an extraordinarily skilled craftsman, in whom emotion subserved intellect. He also won wide recognition as a teacher, with the publication of his books on *Harmony* (1941), *Counterpoint* (1947), and *Orchestration* (1955).

Piston valued tonality. He integrated melody, rhythm, and harmony into balanced classical structures. To music commentators, his melody tended to sound cool and prickly; his harmony, discordant and austere; his rhythm, ingeniously varied and syncopated. Some contemporary critics prasied the logicality of the music but faulted its absence of beauty, warmth, and inspiration.[23]

His mastery of counterpoint, though manifest in his early works, adds great power to the *Prelude and Fugue* for orchestra (1936). His ability to leaven seriousness with wit enlivens the Concertino for Piano and Chamber Orchestra (1937). And his flair, when he wanted to do so, for creating genuinely entertaining works with delicious tunes and catchy rhythms is demonstrated in his ballet, *The Incredible Flutist* (1938).

The First Symphony (1938) sums up his early style in its controlled melody, sharply defined polyphonic lines, expanded harmonic relations to a tonic, and recurring rhythmic figures. Dispassionate discourse rules.[24] Yet, hearing this symphony, the music public remained unexcited.

Around 1940, Piston did modify his style, electing to use less complex and dissonant textures, warmer lyricism, and rhythms akin to jazz or American country dance (though he always rejected the idea of musical nationalism). This new sound is heard in the Violin Concerto (1940), Second Symphony (1944), and Fourth Symphony (1951). These works may yet win a respectable following and achieve the status of American classics.

Piston composed eight symphonies altogether, the last (1965) employing serial techniques. He also wrote a great deal of chamber music, including five string quartets, a piano quartet, and a string sextet. In the same way that his carefully thought-out pedagogical writings have instructed thousands of music students, his many compositions have served as models on how logically to organize large structures within a non-tertain but tone-centered harmonic system—structures that can satisfy not only the eye but the ear.

Aaron Copland (b. 1900) has been the most important musician in twentieth-century American music, active as a composer, as an organizer of concerts, musical organizations, and composers' alliances, and as a lecturer on—and author of—books and articles explaining modern music. After completing his study with Nadia Boulanger in Paris, he returned to America in 1924 to try his hand at writing jazz and blues-oriented compositions.

Five years later, chafing at the restricted expressive possibilities of the idiom, he started to cultivate a more austere style, one replete with jagged melodies, unpredictable accents, polyrhythms, and clashing chords. Between 1929 and 1935, five somber compositions embodied this new departure: the *Vitebsk* Trio (1929), Piano Variations (1930), *Symphonic Ode* (1929–31), *Short Symphony* (1934), and *Statements* (1935).

These compositions, according to Julia Smith, a biographer of Copland, represent a synthesis of French, Stravinskian, jazz, and Jewish elements—plus polytonality and some dodecaphony. They mirrored "the spirit and mood" of "the disillusion-filled depression years of the early Thirties," according to Smith. However, they were not easy to perform or listen to. Save for the Piano Variations, writes Smith, works from this period were rarely performed.[25] An unsympathetic Hugo Leichtentritt, in his biography of Koussevitzky, describes them as the products of "a sophisticated, highly pretentious, *l'art pour l'art* point of view . . . ambitious to impress the exacting connoisseur with the intrinsic values of a distinguished musical art."

The Piano Variations, a composition representative of that period in his life, has often been declared to be a gaunt, fragmented piece, dry and brittle in sound, thin in texture, percussive in rhythm, and without emotion. The same few tones are taken apart, shuffled, and repeatedly recombined. Copland himself played the work with a hard staccato touch, "driving home to the evidently unwilling listeners his uncompromising truths," according to Moses Smith.[26] Henry Boys states: "Copland's hardness of touch made the listeners' difficulty more acute," and produced irritation.[27] It was played on several occasions, not because of public demand, but because only one performer was required. Sitting through it was a problem for listeners, writes Marc Blitzstein: "Its color is dead gray"; "pain is the whole keynote"; "the summary impression" is "monotony." For "too many moments . . . the same thing happens," concludes Blitzstein.[28]

From time to time in later years, Copland wrote compositions to demonstrate he still kept faith with the abstract manner of the early thirties. Four works come to mind: the rather accessible Piano Sonata (1941), the quasi-dodecaphonic Piano Quartet (1950), and the clearly serialistic *Connotations* (1962) and *Inscape* (1967).

Almost fifty years after the completion of the *Short Symphony*, Seiji Ozawa and the Boston Symphony Orchestra revived it. The extraordinary technical difficulties which the conductor and his players had to surmount were obvious. Yet, the driving pulsations, eccentric accents, and quirky wisps of melody had an electric effect on the audience, which cheered the performance. If only it is played with some regularity, acceptance may be in the offing. And such acceptance could give hope that still other ultra-modern works from between the wars will gain approval.

Certainly, the most puzzling compositions for listeners have come from experimenters who have made trial of radically novel ways of representing sound. Henry Cowell (1897–1965), for example, pioneered the use of tone clusters, the simultaneous sounding of several closely grouped tones. In several of his early compositions for piano, the keyboard is struck with the forearm or palm of the hand. At times, a ruler laid across the keys must be punched. Or the pianist reaches under the lid to strum the strings or bang them with a variety of hardware. In 1911, *Adventure in Harmony* incorporated the first tone clusters. A year later, *The Tides of Manaunaun* tried to locate their *raison d'être* in Irish folklore. They were unpleasantly obtrusive in *Advertisement* (1915). *The Aeolian Harp* requires the fingers to brush the piano's strings; *The Banshee* (1925) produces eerie sounds when metal coils resting on the strings are rubbed. Tone clusters abound in Cowell's Piano Concerto (1930), described by Hugo Weisgall as "a fiendishly difficult piece with secundal chords for the orchestra and a finale of great rhythmic complexity,"[29] and in *Synchrony* for orchestra (1931).

Cowell also cooperated with Leon Theremin to develop the Rhythmicon, a device capable of simultaneously and precisely reproducing up to sixteen different rhythms, each on a different tone. *Rhythmicana* (1931) was written for this innovative instrument.

Intricate rhythms, explosive sound effects, and sheer noise assaulted the ear when the *Ballet Mećanique* of George Antheil (1900–59) was first produced in Paris on 19 June 1926. New York City heard it on 10 April 1927. Eight pianos, airplane propellers, and an astonishing array of percussion instruments comprised the orchestra. The work exemplified the aesthetic of musical futurism, which Francesco Pratella said called for music meant to represent the modern industrial age, through the use of sirens, anvils, factory whistles, guns, and so forth. Henry Cowell thought Antheil designed the work to "out-Stravinsky Stravinsky" of the *Sacre du Printemps*. Antheil said: "My idea was to warn the age in which I am living of simultaneous beauty and danger of its own unconscious mechanistic philosophy." The New York audience was scandalized, for the ballyhoo that proceeded and accompanied the performance was great, and the composer was suspected more than a little of being a sensation-monger and publicity-seeker.

Cowell and Antheil prepared the way for the arrival of John Cage (b. 1912), who would explore unusual means for creating sound—prepared pianos, electronic tones, everyday noises, and "chance" happenings. Most of Cage's fame came in the years following World War II. However, in the late thirties he was already giving indications of the direction he was heading. In 1937, he said: "I believe that the use of noise to make music will continue and increase until we reach a music produced through the aid of electronic instruments. . . . Whereas in the past, the point of disagreement has been between dissonance and consonance, it will be in the immediate future between noise and so-called musical sounds."[30]

On occasion, Cage was a twelve-tone composer; *Metamorphosis* (1938) for piano employs strict serialism. In 1939, *Construction in Metal* called for gongs, bells, anvils, brake-drums, and other metal "instruments." His first work for prepared piano—that is to say, one whose strings are doctored with metal, rubber, and leather objects so as to alter the sound—was composed in 1938, and entitled the *Bacchanale*. The jingling and plunking of the piano's strings when the keys are depressed has a little resemblance to the gamelan music of southeastern Asia. Two years before, Colin McPhee (1901-64), after a residence in Bali, had written *Tabuh-Tabuhan* for orchestra, which more directly captures the colorful sounds and rhythms of gamelan music.

By mid-century, American avant-gardists had pushed the Western major–minor system to its limit and had tried out several radical compositional techniques which supplanted musical tones with noise. The road they traveled gradually became a lonely one as they left behind them more and more of their audience. What they were trying to communicate confused many people. Listeners commenced wondering if these composers wanted to communicate at all.

At best, the pathway to wider acceptance of works like Ruggles's *Men and Mountains*, Riegger's *Dichotomy*, and Sessions's Second Symphony is strewn with every conceivable obstacle—lack of verbal communication between composer and public, lack of sympathy from performers, lack of support from many younger composers working in divergent styles, lack of representation in concert hall and opera house, and lack of demand. The older these works become, the more they dim in people's memories. Nevertheless, however much they remain unloved by the general public, these compositions took considerable time, effort, and thought to write. They are a part of our musical heritage and represent America's best endeavor to come abreast of the more radical cultural movements then afoot in the Western world. For these reasons, they deserve more than a now-and-again hearing. They should most probably be heard in an urban center like New York City, where there is available for this music as large an audience as is possible anywhere in the country.

Evolutionary Music

Evolution, not revolution, was the pained cry of traditional composers caught in the maelstrom of modernism. They believed that triadic harmony, unambiguous tonal relationships, and recognizable repetition neither constituted "bondage," nor "sullied the immediacy and purity of experience" (the claims of Wilfred Mellers, in a discussion praising Carl Ruggles's music).[31] They believed that composers should build on the past. Only gradual changes could preserve that delicate and vital link relating composer to audience.

These composers wanted to reach not the few but the multitude of music lovers. They maintained that members of the general music public wanted music that communicated hope, nobility, and those other basic feelings that made men and women believe they were one with angels and not with savages. To hold firm to widely acknowledged precepts of aesthetic law and to attempt their orderly expression were imperative in a chaotic world, where values were becoming self-directed, tentative, or disturbingly spurious. Assuredly, this was part of the tenet of the older traditional composers, who in mid-career were confronted by a radically different way of hearing music.

While traditionalists might make little impression on younger composers and would continue to think in terms related to the previous century, at the same time they did write solid works in the decades following World War I. Among the more noteworthy were Henry Hadley (1871-1937), Arthur Farwell (1872-1952), Edward Burlingame Hill (1872-1960), Daniel Gregory Mason (1873-1953), John Alden Carpenter (1876-1951), Mabel Wheeler Daniels (1878-1971), Arthur Sheperd (1880-1958), Charles Wakefield Cadman (1881-1946), John Powell (1882-1963), and Deems Taylor (1885-1966). What they composed was not outstanding original and mostly contained elements derived from the style of late middle-European romanticism, somewhat spiced with French impressionism. Here and there was a tentative try at jazz, American folk melody, exotic color, or restrained primitivism. Their compositions, nevertheless, were well crafted and at one time gave genuine pleasure.

To maintain that subsequent experiences have made this music obsolete, or that it exhibits shopworn characteristics of former musical styles no longer esteemed begs the question of its real worth. Since composers tend to disparage the immediate past, and conductors in the United States show a European bias and happily forgo performing any native works if given the excuse, a final verdict on the merits of this music is still in the future.

More germane to the subject of this study are the compositions of younger composers, who grew up amidst the creative furore of the early twentieth century, and who deliberately chose to conserve major portions of the older triadic system. Three composers immediately come to mind: Howard Hanson (1896-1981), Samuel Barber (1910-1981), and Paul Creston (b. 1906).

In the music Howard Hanson chose to write, he employed what he found most congenial from the panoply of late-nineteenth-century practices. His strong spiritual affinity with his Scandinavian ancestry set his music apart from that composed by Americans of national or international bent. His espousal of heart over intellect and the writing of agreeable works to gladden the majority of music lovers left him out of favor with those advocating creative boldness and innovation. An unabashed romantic, he opted for spacious or tenderly lyrical melody and dark instrumental colors. His harmonies are opulent; his rhythms, strong, persistent, and oftentimes irregular; and his climaxes, powerful.

After winning the Prix de Rome in 1921, Hanson went to live in Italy for three years. While abroad, he composed his *Nordic Symphony*, which was performed in Rome in 1923. This, his first symphony, already reveals two major strengths running through much of his music: the ability to integrate a profusion of musical ideas within a unified and convincing formal structure, and the ability to balance uninhibited emotional expression against the need for musical cogency. Hanson himself states that the symphony "sings of the solemnity, austerity, and grandeur of the North, of its restless surging and strife, of its somberness and melancholy." The sound reminds some people of Sibelius, Borodin, or Tchaikovsky. Yet it is Hanson's own voice that predominates in the impassioned modal tunes, the asymmetrical ostinatos, the blare of brasses succeeded by gentle strings, and the striking climactic points that are tense but attractive. This composition has remained a distinguished contribution to symphonic literature.

The Lament for Beowolf, for chorus and orchestra, was premiered in 1926, and it too shows Hanson's temperamental connection to Scandinavia. "Romanticism at its best"; a work "that has worn singularly well"—these are Robert Sabin's evaluations of the piece. Sabin praises "its powerful, insistent rhythm, its sombre masses of sonority, and its cumulative excitement." He finds similar fine qualities in *Drum Taps* (1935), also for chorus and orchestra, with text drawn from the writings of Walt Whitman.[32]

The *Romantic Symphony* (1930), Hanson's second symphony, was frequently performed to enthusiastic audiences during the thirties. Hanson expressed the belief that with works like this symphony, "Romanticism will find in this country rich soil for a new, young, and vigorous growth." No, he had not returned to an older outmoded style. His object in this symphony was "to create a work young in spirit, romantic in temperament, and simple and direct in expression.[33]

HOWARD HANSON. Photo: U.S. Information Service. Courtesy of the Boston Symphony Orchestra.

Regrettable to say, the harmonies in this symphony are a bit too sumptuous and ripe, owing to the employment of the suspended appoggiaturas and the ninth- to eleventh-chord constructions of late Germanic romanticism. Melody, while attractive, teeters between sentiment and sentimentality. The incessant repetition of short motives, and the constant introduction of sequential passages with no resultant development of ideas give a choppy effect to the music and induce boredom, if not impatience, in the listener.

Colin McPhee found the orchestration to be rich and brilliant, the expression pathetic and noble. In contrast, Virgil Thomson found the orchestration bombastic, the expression poverty-stricken. To Thomson, everything sounded too familiar and unsurprising.[34]

Hanson composed five more symphonies, the seventh in 1977; also, several symphonic poems, a string quartet (1923), an organ concerto (1926), a concerto for organ, strings, and harp (1943), and a piano concerto (1948). The music is pleasant at its weakest, moving in its elevated moments. Missing is a strength to match that found in the *Nordic Symphony, Beowulf,* and *Drum Taps.*

Last to be mentioned is the opera *Merry Mount,* which Hanson based on a story of Puritan New England; it was completed in 1933, and produced by the Metropolitan Opera Association in 1934. Hanson describes it as "essentially a lyrical work" which

> makes use of broad melodic lines as often as possible. . . . The form of each small scene within the larger scene is considered as an entity in itself, a series of small forms within a large form, almost as in symphonic structure. Both harmonically and rhythmically, the listener will hear certain Americanisms. In orchestration, too, use has been made of certain orchestral colors and devices which were born on this side of the Atlantic.[35]

Most critics who reviewed one of the nine performances given by the Metropolitan were agreed on the excellence of the choral writing, in contrast to the miscalculations in the music sung by the soloists, who often were covered up by too weighty an accompaniment. In addition, most of the singers were foreign-born, and understanding their English pronunciation frequently was an impossibility. Moreover, though the overall sound was beautiful, it was not always suited to the dramatic situations.[36]

Other weaknesses were apparent. Too many scenes lacked action and drama; the characters failed to become human. Melody required more animation; harmony, a greater sense of movement; and motives, a convincing reason for their many repetitions.

Yet, Donald Grout praises "the beautiful sensuous love music of Bradford's aria 'Rise up, my love' and the duet which is its continuation." He speaks of the contrast between "the psalmlike choruses of the Puritans" and "the bacchanalian strains for the evil spirits of the 'Walpurgisnacht' ballet in Act II," and declares Hanson's music to be "able, serious, and sincere," with "no compromise of principle, no writing down to a supposed lower taste of an opera audience." It is Grout's opinion that "the whole is good enough to make one sad at the thought of what American composers might do in opera" given "more incentive to produce" and "opportunity to try out their works in actual performance."[37]

Grout's opinion is well founded. During the second half of the twentieth century, all sorts of third-rate European romantic works have been performed and recorded. Hanson's compositions are so far and away superior to them that no excuse can be accepted for the non-performance of his music.

The twentieth-century American composer of art music who has shown the greatest genius for expressive melody has been Samuel Barber (1910–81).[38] He is also one of the most noteworthy creative artists that the United States has yet produced. Though some critics praise his careful and superior craftsmanship, audiences value more his attractive lyricism couched in a language it well understands. Barber's eloquent *Dover Beach* (1931) for voice and string quartet, his now elegiac, now passionate Cello Sonata (1932), his perky *Overture to the School for Scandal* (1933), and his deeply felt *Music for a Scene from Shelley* (1935) arrived on the American scene in the period when most prominent composers were trying to forge distinctive styles that abjured romantic expression.[39] Though his tunes show a vocal orientation, they seem to have scarcely any discernable antecedents in operatic aria, art song, folk ballad, or popular ditty.[40] Nor can one say that sudden inspiration prompts the writing of an entire work. As Broder explains: "Barber works slowly. He attaches great importance to his thematic material, and the search for the right themes is often painful and long drawn out, with many discarded along the way."[41]

Barber's harmony, though traditional, can turn pungent, even acid, when the mood or emotional content of a piece requires a harsher sound. Moreover, he experimented with non-triadic, dissonant harmony, Viennese serialism, and post-Stravinskian rhythms. However, whether cautious or bold with melody, harmony, and rhythm, Barber always is surehanded in his choice of voices and instruments; he gives them music that is idiomatic, and vividly presented.

John Gruen, in his biography of Barber's close friend Gian-Carlo Menotti, says Barber's music sounds more astringent than Menotti's. He continues: "Like the man, the music is diffident,

Samuel Barber, 1940. Photo: Rembrandt Studios, Inc., Philadelphia. Courtesy of the Boston Symphony Orchestra.

although beneath the diffidence there exists a vast storehouse of strong emotions. A brilliant orchestrator and a fertile melodist, Barber conveys feeling through understatement and subtlety. Like the man, however, the music can become too witty, or plunge into glowing romanticism. But . . . Barber tends to be a lean and judicious composer. There is a noble symmetry, which often eschews the temptation of easy accessibility."[42]

Barber's First Symphony, completed in 1936 and revised six years later, was a major composition that quickly won over the music lovers who heard it. Ostensibly in one movement, it divides into four sections corresponding to the four movements of a traditional symphony. It opens in E minor, on a trenchant first theme set forth fortissimo in the grand rhetorical manner of romanticism. Next comes a lovely and quiet second theme, played by violas and English horn supported by a delicate accompaniment. The third and final theme of the first section, ardent and restless, is heard first in the massed high strings and woodwinds, then in the low violins in unison with the cellos and English horn. After the development (mainly of the first theme) reaches a point of great tension, the second section of the symphony begins—a deft scherzo in 6/8 time, based on a variation of the first theme. This, in turn, is followed by the third section, an *andante tranquillo*, employing an augmented version of the second theme, first played softly by the oboe against a shimmering background of strings, then repeated with expressive eloquence by the strings. Finally, the fourth section, in E minor, is heard in the shape of a gigantic passacaglia on the first theme. Especially striking is the *allargando*, where the third theme at last is recapitulated, but as a counter-melody above the passacaglia bass. Shortly thereafter, the symphony ends as impressively as it began.

In 1938, Toscanini and the NBC Orchestra gave first performances to two works, Barber's *Essay for Orchestra, No. 1,* and the *Adagio for Strings,* the last a string-orchestra version of the slow movement from the String Quartet, completed in 1936. The extraordinary melody of the *Adagio* spins out in long lines that are at the same time artless and elegant. Slowly the strings achieve a peak of intensity, then die away to nothing.

The *Adagio* swiftly became the most popular art work by any American composer. "The work of a young musician of true talent," wrote Olin Downes in 1938. Downes found the piece unpretentious, honest, and clearly structured.

What did the ordinary music lover think? In 1969, a woman told the author that she and her mothers had always disliked twelve-tone compositions because it seemed to them that such music was the result of "pure brain work without a real inspiration." She went on: "My taste is rather on the romantic side. I enjoy music which is melodic, emotional, and stimulating. I prefer music which moves me. . . . Samuel Barber and his *Adagio for Strings* moves me as if I would be floating on clouds. Every time it would come on the radio, I'd have to stop whatever I was doing."

After completing the Violin Concerto (1941), Barber made a trial of writing less lyrical, more angular melody; less sonorous, more strident harmony; and less circumspect, more forceful rhythm—in the *Capricorn Concerto*, for flute, oboe, trumpet, and strings (1944), the Cello Concerto (1946), the *Medea* Suite (1947), the Piano Sonata (1949), and the Piano Concerto (1962). Yet, Barber's individuality is perceptible throughout. Despite some awkwardness (as if the experimentation went against the grain), these pieces are attractive, even to some extent fresh-sounding, and pose no great problem for listeners.

Barber's writing for voices is almost invariably appealing to music lovers who find the advanced approach to vocal writing aesthetically displeasing. *Dover Beach* has already been mentioned. Add to the list of admirable vocal compositions the *Prayers of Kierkegaard* for soprano, chorus, and orchestra (1947), *Andromache's Farewell,* for voice and orchestra (1962), *The Lovers,* for baritone, chorus, and orchestra (1971), and the superb set of ten songs for voice and piano, *Hermit Songs* (1953).

Two operas, *Vanessa* (1958) and *Anthony and Cleopatra* (1966), were mounted by the Metropolitan. They have not been performed enough to permit an opinion on their effectiveness as musico-dramatic works. They both came out during the years when avante-gardism was ascendent in American art music. Neither received a decent press. And the talk persists that the latter's stage work was sabotaged at its initial presentation. Without question, the acoustics were terrible, the stagehands' efficiency low, and the singing not entirely sympathetic to the music. Pitiless reviewers, blaming all the mishaps on the composer, damned the operatic writing. History may prove the reviewers wrong. At a minimum, both operas contain much music worth hearing.

The last work to be mentioned is *Knoxville: Summer of 1915* (1948), for soprano and orchestra, its text from James Agee's novel *A Death in the Family.* Only a brief section, the description of a racketing street car, resorts to musical modernism. The remainder of the composition follows traditional procedures and stresses vocal lyricism. At the end of the work, when the poignant description of a long-gone childhood centers on remembered parents, who once gave love and security, *Knoxville* manages to stir the emotion-laden memories in most listeners.

Gilbert Chase is wrong in his claim, in *America's Music* (1966), that the reason for the wide acceptability of Barber's music is simply its "conventional quality." If this were so, then a host of traditional works by other twentieth-century composers would have found a place in people's affections. Hanson's music, for example, holds no such exalted position. What makes Barber's compositions special is the genuine gift of the composer for writing music that sounds alive, delights the ear, and elicits a marked emotional response from ordinary men and women.

The discussion of Barber's music ends on two sentences of summary, written by Walter Simmons: "I have no doubt about the extraordinary value of Barber's achievement, considered *in toto*. Fully half of his entire output, including works in all the media in which he worked . . . stand among the most universally communicative, deeply moving music our century has produced."[43] An imposing number of listeners agree.

Paul Creston (born Joseph Guttoveggio, in 1906), like Hanson and Barber, is a composer who wrote vital music in a traditional style during the first half of the twentieth century. Five symphonies, at least fifteen concertos, many dances for chamber ensembles or orchestra, and several chamber suites are numbered among his works. His music, which seems constantly embedded in dance rhythms and song melody or plainchant, usually commences with an idea in embryo. This idea is then developed through extended, smoothly unfolding lines that testify to Creston's inventive resourcefulness and strong sense of structure. Rich harmony, sonorous orchestration, and homophonic texture also distinguish his style.[44]

Creston's *Threnody* (1938), an orchestral composition, opens *con sordino*, with strings playing a theme reminiscent of Gregorian chant. Little by little, a drive toward climax gathers momentum until a moment of high intensity is reached. The piece ends as it began, in quiet melancholy, a flute recapitulating the opening melody over muted strings. The arrangement of the piece is somewhat similar to that of Barber's *Adagio;* the sound is entirely different.

Creston's piece entitled *Two Choric Dances* for chamber

orchestra (1938), later rescored for full orchestra, conjures up scenes of dancers in an ancient setting, who respond with a studied ceremoniousness to the several changes in tempo, dynamic, accented rhythm, and instrumental color. Infectious sound encourages listeners to respond physically.

Creston's statement that his Second Symphony (1944) was "conceived as an apotheosis of the two foundations of all music: song and dance" underlines the significance of this base for his creativity. The work is in two long movements, a slow *Introduction and Song* and an *Interlude and Dance*, which goes from moderately slow to moderately fast. The Third Symphony (1950), entitled *Three Mysteries*, shows Creston's religiosity and love of plainsong. The first movement, "The Nativity," employs two Gregorian melodies: *Puer natus est nobis* and *Gloria in excelsis Deo*. The second movement, "The Crucifixion," opens on *Pater, si non potest*, which takes on the characteristics of a recurring ground, and turns later to elements of the *Stabat Mater*. The last movement, "The Resurrection," uses three more chants: *Angelus Domini descendit de caelo, Christus resurgens ex mortuis*, and *Victimae paschali laudes*.

Regrettably, this bare description of the two symphonies cannot convey the magnetic attractiveness of the actual sound, nor the individuality of the style. Howard Mitchell, a conductor who championed the two symphonies with the National Symphony Orchestra, speaks of conducting Creston's music in America and Europe, before highly enthusiastic audiences.[45] New generations of music lovers have come along since the two symphonies were written, yet few of them are aware that an excellent composer named Paul Creston exists. The fault lies neither in the composer or his music.

Although their compositions are not discussed here, three other traditional composers active between the wars should be mentioned: Bernard Rogers (1893–1968), Leo Sowerby (1895–1968), and Vittorio Giannini (1903–66). All three composers have left behind impressive compositions worthy of revival.

If, as I said earlier, the music of our difficult composers deserves further performance, how much more deserving is the music of composers like Hanson, Creston, and Barber! These men did sympathize with the audience's concerns and did attempt to write pieces that pleased contemporary listeners. Unfortunately, American culture today provides no follow-through for any of its native music. Accessible as they are, works like Hanson's *Nordic Symphony* and Creston's *Third Symphony* are now kept in limbo owing to the biases of Europophiles, modernists, and fashion-mongers. Of the three, Barber alone continues having hearings, to some extent owing to the advocacy of his friend Gian-Carlo Menotti. There should be no need for such special advocacy. If any sounds can appeal to an audience whose affections are still directed toward the romantic style, those of these three composers are most likely to win out, provided their music is given anything like fair treatment.

I do not mean to claim that this music will definitely prove a success. The general music public may find too much me-too-ism in a style already liberally represented by nineteenth-century compositions. Or a new generation may find its own values and the values mirrored in this music altogether foreign to each other. But this last possibility is a danger all music faces.

Out of Jazz

The various antecedents of American jazz include the music and dance of backwoodsmen, rivermen, and sailors, Afro-American gospel song, blues, and dance, coon song, rag, and elements of Latin-American rhythm. In the second and third decades of the twentieth century, black performers principally were credited with synthesizing these several American expressions into a unique body of sound glaringly different from European music. Jazz sounded as if spontaneously improvised. Syncopated melodies in individual rhythmic patterns freely unfolded against an insistently steady beat. Intonation of tones was subtly altered. On trumpet, trombone, clarinet, saxophone, and percussion, performers created sounds unlike anything produced by orthodoxly trained musicians.

Several important European composers were fascinated by jazz and tried to incorporate its style into some of their compositions. Thus, in 1918, Igor Stravinsky created *Ragtime,* for eleven instruments, and *Histoire du Soldat,* for narrator and seven instruments; in 1922, Paul Hindemith wrote the *1922 Suite*, for piano; and in 1923, Darius Milhaud, *La Création du Monde*. One older American composer, John Alder Carpenter, had rather diffidently introduced jazz-like sounds into his Concertino for Piano and Orchestra (1916), the "jazz pantomime" *Krazy Kat* (1921), and the ballet *Skyscrapers* (1926). It remained for the younger composers, who started their careers in the mid-twenties, to make bolder use of jazz.

When Aaron Copland returned to the United States from Paris, he put himself forth as a native composer of jazz-suffused art works, first in the Symphony for Organ and Orchestra (1925), but more especially in the *Music for the Theater* (1925), and the Concerto for Piano and Orchestra (1927).

The *Music for the Theater* is in five movements: Prologue, Dance, Interlude, Burlesque, and Epilogue. Clean, pungent, and jittery music, with no hint of romantic eloquence, is kept in motion by mechanized rhythms. Every now and then a bluesy tune prevails—melancholic, meditative, and lingering in the ear. Pitts Sanborn, reviewing an early 1926 performance by Koussevitzky and the Boston Symphony Orchestra, commended the enthusiasm of the conductor and the sureness of touch of the composer. He detected a "keen feeling for rhythm and an extraordinarily fine sense of instrumental color" in the composition. It contains, he said, "irony," delightful "burlesque," and "a vein of wistful haunting melody."[46] Some of the general music public liked the composition; others were uncomfortable with the thought that jazz had its origin in low-down bars and brothels, and so they rejected *Music for the Theater* as trivial, barbarous, or tainted with corruption.

Copland's Piano Concerto is, if anything, more dissonant and grating in its fast sections, more tellingly haunting in its slow sections. Young listeners liked it; older ones did not. Composer-reviewers had mixed feelings about it. Edward Burlingame Hill thought Copland had "overdone matters." Marc Blitzstein said that, though it was the best work he knew in the genre, the concerto showed that jazz resembled "the Machine; a single work or two" in the idiom had "real but isolated value, and the thing has been said completely."[47] Thomson said jazz was Copland's "one wild oat" and "not a very fertile one," because he had "never understood that sensuality of sentiment which is the force of American popular music, nor accepted the simple heart-beat that is the pulse of its rhythm."[48]

Copland himself became dissatisfied with his "experiments with symphonic jazz," feeling he had done all he could "with the idiom, considering its limited emotional scope" and its confinement to two dominant moods: "the 'blues' and the snappy number." After thus confessing his own limited understanding of jazz, Copland went on to write works in a forbidding abstract idiom.

Louis Gruenberg (1884–1964) was also an enthusiastic experimenter with jazz during the twenties. Works like *Daniel Jazz* (1925), for tenor and eight instruments, *Jazzettes* (1926), for violin and piano, and *Jazz Suite* (1929), for orchestra, demonstrate this predilection. Unfortunately, critics detected defects paralleling those in Copland's jazz compositions. A. Walter Kramer, for example, writes about the "striking cleverness" and "composer's skill" evident in the music. Yet, he finds the works "artificial" and like musical "essays propounding jazz theory, rather than emotionally felt utterances."[49]

In January 1933, the Metropolitan Opera Association mounted Gruenberg's *The Emperor Jones,* based on the O'Neill play. The jazz-oriented music was fashioned to fit the drama closely, point up the action, intensify the impact of the characters' emotions, and project the atmosphere of each scene. The score, writes Olin Downes, is "prodigiously sure, headlong, fantastical, brutal in its approach; yet masterly in contrast of mood and in its major proportions." Lyricism, save for one "spiritual" sung in the forest, is absent. Most of the singing is speech-like, or it consists of sudden outcries. With Lawrence Tibbett in the title role, the performances kept on selling out. Men and women were fascinated by the production's savage primitivism and melodramatic power. *The Emperor Jones* was proclaimed a sincere, imaginative opera unbeholden to Europe and belonging entirely "to a new country and a young people fully alive to the present day."[50]

With the first sensations ended and the novelty gone, however, the opera was found lacking in memorable melody. Away from the stage, nobody could clearly recall the score. In fact, the singing and orchestral sounds struck listeners as incidental to the drama, and so in popular opinion the production remained mostly O'Neill's achievement. Moveover the music did not translate well onto disc recordings or over the airwaves; it was too integrated with the sights and actions of the stage. When stage performance ceased, the opera was forgotten.

After 1933, Gruenberg noticeably modified his style toward simplicity, consonance, melodiousness, and use of traditional music and dance other than jazz. His second through fifth symphonies, two string quartets, second piano quintet, violin concerto, and several later operas harbor this changed style. Passages of great beauty, at times stately and grand, at times meltingly delicate, abound. Nevertheless, nobody plays his music any longer. And composer–writers, like Virgil Thomson, ignore him completely when writing about American music and composers of the twentieth century.[51] The conspiracy of silence is unjust; Gruenberg deserves better.

Several other composers tried to use jazz in their compositions. Some examples are George Antheil's operas *Transatlantic* (1930) and *Helen Retires* (1934), Jerome Moross's cantata *Those Everlasting Blues* (1933), and Morton Gould's *Chorale and Fugue in Jazz* (1936). However, for the most part, jazz proved a difficult idiom to incorporate into art music. Most American composers who used it were not to the idiom born. They usually fell into the habit of imitating the French–Stravinsky adaptations of jazz for art purposes, rather than trying to strike out on their own. They wanted an unquestionably American sound; but, once isolated in the medium of art music, jazz lacked the variety of the original. Gone was the swinging improvisational feeling of true jazz, and also the sensuality, emotionality, and primal lyricism. Jazz was very much a creative performer's on-the-spot language; when played by symphonic performers the notes were present but the necessary spontaneity was not. The impediments to the realization of a vital symphonic jazz were too many to overcome.

All in all, if any composer succeeded in effectively transferring the American vernacular idiom into art works, it was George Gershwin (1898–1937). He, however, was innocent of European training, unresponsive to musical avant-gardism, and annoyed with the aesthetic posturing of art composers. Because his background was popular song and Broadway musical shows,

Gershwin was fluent in the American vernacular idiom, whereas art composers had usually learned it secondhand and consciously layered it onto a European musical base. In addition, he felt instinctively that without striking melodies, the rhythms by themselves would fail to hold attention, whereas art composers were usually content to emphasize the rhythms and special colorations of vernacular music. What Gershwin called jazz was the music natural to him—blues and rag, tempered by the necessities imposed on Tin Pan Alley and the Broadway stage.

Beginning at the age of nineteen, with his song hit "Swanee," he wrote a number of extraordinarily popular songs which not only excited millions of contemporary Americans, but also won the status of genuine classics. Some sound fragile and gently affectionate; others, extravagantly impetuous; still others, satirical or wryly humorous. He explores a wide range of human experience. And his best songs all have memorable tunes.[52]

Popular song is the foundation of Gershwin's "serious" compositions: the *Rhapsody in Blue* (1924), Piano Concerto in F (1925), *An American in Paris* (1928), the Second Rhapsody (1932), *Cuban Overture* (1932), Variations for Piano and Orchestra (1934) on "I got rhythm," and *Porgy and Bess* (1935). What distinguishes them is "lively rhythm, graceful harmony, and a fine melodic gift," qualities that audiences appreciated in all their dimensions.[53] Whenever a Gershwin concert was announced, and especially if Gershwin was appearing as piano soloist, Americans flocked to attend. On 5 February 1932, Koussevitzky and the Boston Symphony Orchestra played the Second Rhapsody in New York City, after Toscanini had refused to perform it. Lawrence Gilman wrote in the *Herald Tribune,* the next day: "Only Mr. Paderewski, perhaps, could have drawn a gathering comparable in numbers if not in kind. . . . Mr. Koussevitzky cruelly delayed the appearance of George I by playing a couple of superfluous introductory numbers [Prokofiev's *Classical Symphony* and Vincent d'Indy's *Istar Variations*]."

All Gershwin's art compositions are loosely structured and all of them alternate lilting rhythms and perky tunes with sadly beautiful blues sections. Each work contains at least one "big tune," which members of the audience can go home humming or whistling.

Typically of Gershwin, the *Rhapsody in Blue* opens with an arresting idea meant to catch the listener's attention, a rising glissando yawp on the clarinet. A number of repetitions of brief but engaging rhythmo-melodic ideas follow, which gradually produce a hunger for a long uninterrupted melody. At last, at the appropriate psychological moment, an opulent melody arrives, and the listener is granted release. When the applause-encouraging finale ends, the listener can leave with the easily remembered tune or the rich array of lilting rhythms running through his mind.

The Piano Concerto also maintains a rhapsodic flow of ideas having few parallels in European music. A freewheeling first movement, which makes a slight obeisance to sonata-allegro form, begins with a striking percussive passage. Next, the piano enters with a syncopated theme against a subdued accompaniment. Later, a new theme, at first perky in character, gradually transforms itself into an immense melody, *á la* the *Rhapsody in Blue*. The slow movement, in ternary form, is an urban nocturne poetically evoking the mood of empty city streets at night. It acts as a foil to the somewhat rondo-like last movement, a finale of swirling confusion in its unrestrainable rhythms, sometimes jaunty and self-assured, sometimes furiously excited. It is not well-behaved music. But it speaks in an American dialect that general audiences can appreciate.

Of *An American in Paris,* Gershwin said: "As in my other orchestral compositions, I've not endeavored to present any delicate scene in music. The rhapsody is programmatic only in a general impressionistic way, so that the individual can read into the music such episodes as his imagination pictures for him."[54] The work was an immediate success, not because of the structure, which is rickety, but because of the winning ways of its six themes, three of them picturing a leisurely promenader on the streets of Paris. A fourth theme exploits the honking sounds of taxicabs; a fifth is cast as a blues; and a sixth thrives on a Charleston rhythm.

The opera *Porgy and Bess* uses a black cast and claims to depict a black subject. It may, as critics claim, do violence to the reality of the black experience. Nevertheless, the work endures, not simply because the tunes are marvelous ("Summertime," "I Got Plenty O' Nothin'," "It Ain't Necessarily So," "Bess, You Is My Woman Now"), but also because a multi-faceted exposition of what ordinary people yearn after, live through, and learn to bear is

GEORGIA O'KEEFFE, *New York, Night.* Sheldon
Memorial Art Gallery, Nebraska Art Association,
Lincoln, Nebraska. Thomas C. Woods Memorial
Collection. Reproduced with permission.

set forth in meaningful terms. The conflicts within Bess are our conflicts; the losses of Porgy are our losses.

Gershwin's serious works "have a solid place in American musical history," writes Sydney Finkelstein. Though structurally crude, "they live, sing, and hold together. They indicate that the material of American popular music, including jazz, can be used successfully for greater musical and artistic ends. . . . These works confirm the truth that for a writer of good symphonic music, it is a great help to be able to write a good song."[55]

Because he meant a great deal to a great many Americans, he was mourned like no other American composer when he died suddenly and prematurely, in the summer of 1937. Prominent musicians, artists, actors, writers, dancers, and politicians attended his funeral. Silent crowds stood patiently to await the passage of the cortege. Gershwin would have loved the attention.

He had wanted to write artistically excellent music. He had often spoken about his desire to reach out to the American masses and move them with beautiful sounds. And he had not wanted to be forgotten—the fate of most American composers. All three objectives were attained.

Music Populism

Seventy years before Gershwin's birth, another American composer–pianist was born, who was equally driven to compose music that could move the masses and equally annoyed that America's art composers and Europeans frequently disparaged democratically conceived American musical compositions, especially those smacking of popular song. The composer was Louis Moreau Gottschalk (1829–69), born in New Orleans and trained in Paris. Both North and South America, Gottschalk was certain, had produced unique songs and dances worthy of notice by connoisseurs, and of utilization by art composers. Once, during the darkest days of the Civil War, he attended a social gathering where upper-class New Yorkers were discussing the arts, and music in particular. When an English visitor began to discredit American music, Gottschalk grew furious:

> White as a sheet, and in his excited overwhelming eloquence, he [Gottschalk] told them of a melody then being sung by regiment

after regiment, marching down Broadway *en route* for the cars to Washington, of a melody they learned at home in the far West, and that they would carry with them, and sing it on the battlefield; of a melody that would sustain them in the thickest fight. And, on the spur of the moment, he sprang to the piano . . . and gave such an astounding rhapsody on George F. Root's well-known "We'll Rally 'Round the Flag," as is entirely beyond description. I never heard anything like it. . . . The effect was earthquackean almost.[56]

From 1845 until his death, Gottschalk wrote mainly piano compositions, some of them remarkable, which reflected his beliefs. For example, *Bamboula* is based on a black melody overheard in New Orlean's Place Congo; *La Savanne,* on the French-Creole song "Lolotte," which sounds like a minor-key version of "Skip to My Lou;" *Banjo,* on Stephen Foster's "Camptown Races;" *The Union,* on patriotic tunes like "Hail Columbia" and "Yankee Doodle." In addition, he composed a number of colorful works that contain the melodies and dance rhythms of Latin America.

Later, around the turn of the century, at least four composers were incorporating Americanisms into their works. Henry Gilbert (1868-1928) brought out several works that exploit American folk and popular tunes, among them *Humoresque on Negro-Minstrel Tunes* (1903), *Comedy Overture on Negro Themes* (1905), *The Dance in the Place Congo* (1906)—which utilizes the same tune heard in Gottschalk's *Bamboula*— and *American Dances* (1915). George Whitefield Chadwick (1854-1931) wrote a striking orchestral suite, *Symphonic Sketches* (1908), whose movements, entitled "Jubilee," "Noel," and "Hobgoblin," reflect the American milieu. By 1923, Arthur Farwell (1872-1952) had written several pieces based on American Indian music and had completed his *Symphony Song on "Old Black Joe".* By that year, also, John Powell (1882-1963) had immersed himself in Virginia's black and white folk songs and composed *Rhapsodie Nègre* (1918), for piano and orchestra, *Sonata Virginianesque* (1919), for violin and piano, and the overture *In Old Virginia* (1921).

Standing apart from everyone else was Charles Ives (1874-1954), assuredly one of America's most individual and notable composers, and famous for his distinctly national works. He studied at Yale under Horatio Parker and received a thorough but orthodox musical education. Until 1918, when a heart attack curtailed most of his activities, he composed extraordinary works showing bewildering stylistic variety, from sentimentally romantic lyricism to potent dissonance of the harshest sort. An inveterate experimenter, he tried using tone clusters, quarter tones, polytonality, atonality, tone rows, polyrhythms, and just plain noise. He drew constant inspiration from New England history and literature, and from every type of popular and traditional music, sacred and secular. Indeed, he poured into his compositions all the sounds that had affected him deeply: "Columbia, the Gem of the Ocean," "The Camptown Races," "Oh, What a Friend We Have in Jesus," the motto of Beethoven's Fifth Symphony, Revolutionary War and Civil War marches, Southern spirituals, and rag. However, a wondrous alchemy transformed everything borrowed into a novel musical entity that was purely Ivesian. Among America's greatest cultural assets are the Second Symphony (1902), the Third Symphony (1904), the Fourth Symphony (1916), the *Three Places in New England* (1914), for orchestra, The *Concord Sonata* (1915), for piano, and the *114 Songs* (1884–1921). Among America's greatest cultural mistakes must be included the virtual dismissal of Ives's music until after World War II. He had little influence on the music-makers of the twenties, thirties, and forties.

Not until 1924, when audiences first heard Gershwin's *Rhapsody in Blue,* was a real precedent set for composing American works in the spirit of contemporary popular music. Certainly the art composers (most of them French-trained) who commenced their careers in the mid-twenties were aware of most of these previous efforts at creating a national music. If they wished to experiment with sounds characteristic of America, they had several native musics to draw upon, besides jazz—past and present popular music, and folk music principally from four ethnic sources endemic in the United States: Afro-American, British-American, Indian-American, and Latin-American. On the other hand, owing to the multi-cultural nature of this native music and the varied backgrounds of the composers, a unified national utterance was almost an impossibility.

Unlike the securer and more integrated creative identities of composers in other countries, those of artists in the United States were subject to a complexity of influences: urban, rural, East, South, or West. Ancestry might be British, Italian, East European,

African, German, or French. The composer could be a Protestant
or Catholic, Christian, Jew, or agnostic; musical education might
have taken place in the United States, France, Italy, or Central
Europe. Therefore, when Aaron Copland composed *Appalachian
Spring*, based ostensibly on a Shaker melody and a rural American
mythology, he could not help but also include the viewpoint of
a Jew brought up in Brooklyn. One notes a strong sense of isolation,
of wanting to belong to something secure, of yearning for release
from the clashing complications of urban life, and of commitment
to the concept of a democratic society however idealized. *Appalachian Spring* illustrates a point that Nicolas Nabokov made, that
while folkloristic memories could still linger in the musical materials the Americanists used, the art works incorporating these
materials "in one way or another . . . served urban needs and
reflected urban life and urban outlooks."[57]

The clarity of texture, fastidiousness of the workmanship, and
emotional reticence betoken Paris and Nadia Boulanger. Copland
himself found nothing inherently pure in folk, cowboy, or hymn
tunes: "They can be successfully handled only by a composer who
is able to identify himself with, and re-express in his own terms,
the underlying emotional connotation of the material."[58]

American folk and popular music, like jazz, provided the means
for developing a native syntax independent of Europe. Moreover,
traditional song and dance embodied the aesthetic values of a broad
range of the New World's communities and was more a music
"of the people" and possibly "far nobler than the country-club-
oriented so-called 'jazz' that many had dallied with in the 1920s."
Combining native sounds with "a simplified harmonic palette"
became an important means for reaching large numbers of
Americans, especially during the depression years.[59]

Another inducement to giving art music a national identity
was the somewhat misplaced hope that such pieces would serve
to guide the American people. Paul Rosenfeld wrote, in 1940, of
the conditions motivating American nationalism. First, he points
to the desire to break away from the dominance of European styles.
Then, he states it was his observation that

> creative individuals from time to time unite with their commun-
> ities—and strive beautifully to shape them—through the production
> of symbols of certain spiritual values or ideal aspirations apparently

latent in these communities. These symbols to some degree, more or less involuntarily, couch themselves in the style and color of the community's traditional art. . . . The value of the efforts and interpretations to the world would seem to flow not from their motives but from the quality of the feeling they embody and the dignity, the probity and the austerity of the embodying means.[60]

A last reason for utilizing traditional music was that its familiarity gave structural cohesion to a work in the minds of listeners. They could remember the musical ideas and recognize their recurrences and permutations as the piece unfolded.

Douglas Moore (1893–1969), trained by Horatio Parker at Yale University and by Vincent d'Indy and Nadia Boulanger in Paris, was one of the first Americanists among the younger composers. In 1924, he completed, and two years later the Cleveland Orchestra premiered, his *Pageant of P. T. Barnum,* an orchestral suite which became quite popular owing to its musical colloquialisms and its conjuring up of an American ambience. Harmony is conservatively triadic. Melody seems the spinning out of natural feelings indigenous to Americans. Rhythm evokes country dances and marching bands. The first movement, "Boyhood," sounds with fiddle tunes and spirited marches. The second movement describes one of Barnum's hoaxes, the century-and-a-half-old colored nurse of George Washington, by means of the spiritual "Nobody Knows de Trouble I've Seen." Next comes the satirically jocular movement on Tom Thumb. The fourth section features the flute playing a graceful and agile soprano melody, in commemoration of Jenny Lind. And a final section turns into a circus parade, lively and at times boisterously undisciplined.

Discussing Moore's (and also Thomson's) music, Copland claims nothing in serious European music is like it—"nothing so downright plain and bare . . . with simple tunes and square rhythms and Sunday-school harmonies." Though a sophisticated musician, Copland continues, Moore (like Thomson) is "attracted by the unadorned charm of a revivalist hymn, or a sentimental ditty, or a country dance." He found the "frank acceptance of so limited a musical vocabulary" to be "a gesture of faith in" his "own heritage."[61]

In other compositions that followed, Moore mined a similar indigenous vein: the symphonic poem *Moby Dick* (1927), the

Overture on an American Tune (1932), the orchestral suite *Village Music* (1941), the chamber-orchestra composition *Farm Journal* (1948), and two outstanding "folk" operas, *The Devil and Daniel Webster* (1938) and *The Ballad of Baby Doe* (1955). Even his finely crafted abstract music has a strong American cast: the String Quartet (1933), the Clarinet Quintet (1946), the Symphony in A (1946), and the Piano Trio (1953).

Although no actual folk songs are inserted into the score of *The Devil and Daniel Webster,* the simple music does sound as if folk-derived, and the subject is a part of the American mythology, and also a part of mankind's mythology—relating as it does how a human comes to sell his soul to the devil, then later regrets the bargain. Because they are carefully set to melody that follows the natural speech accents, the English words are easily understood; so also is a plot stripped of the usual operatic complications. The infectious excitement of the square dance in the opening scene immediately captures the listener's attention. Soon thereafter comes the affectively beautiful duet between the bride and groom. Next, the devil is given tellingly cynical and baleful music. And at the peak of crisis, when an infernal jury is about to decide in the devil's favor, Daniel Webster orates eloquently about democracy (as orchestral sound frames his speech), and gets his client off.

Otto Luening says the opera "expresses the simple gaiety of the country square dance, the lusty qualities of New England, and the particular imagination, spirit, and courage that belong to America." And Alfred Frankenstein states it is "as artful, eloquent, and effective a statement of the principles of American democracy as has ever been written."[62]

William Grant Still (1895–1978), a black composer, had also tried his hand at national music in the twenties. His inspiration had come from Afro-American dance, blues, spirituals, shouts, work songs, and jazz. Though a couple of his early works reflect the ultra-modern dissonant viewpoint of one of his teachers, Edgard Varèse, Still settled on the advice given him by a second teacher, George Chadwick, and wrote tonal music of more conventional cast in order to do justice to themes generated by the black experience. Among his earliest compositions of this nature are *Darker America* (1924), *From the Black Belt* (1927), *Africa* (1930), and *Sahdji* (1930).

He came to national attention in 1931, when Howard Hanson and the Rochester orchestra gave his *Afro-American Symphony* a first performance. The melodic material is quite expressive. The orchestration is by a sure hand. The music's kinship is to blues, in the first movement ("Longing"); the spiritual, in the second ("Sorrows") and last movement ("Aspirations"); and the nineteenth-century black jig, in the third movement ("Humor"). Comparing it to another symphony by a black composer, the *Negro Folk Symphony* (1934) by William Dawson, it is less sentimental, less derivative of Dvorak's *New World Symphony*, and less heavily textured. Though neither daring or startlingly original, the music has a gravity and attractive warmth readily perceptible to the ears of the listening public.[63] The symphony had frequent performance during the thirties.

In many compositions that followed, Still continued along the lines laid down by the symphony: the ballet *Lenox Avenue* (1937), the operas *Blue Steel* (1935), *Troubled Island* (1938), and *A Bayou Legend* (1941), tone poems like *Dismal Swamp* (1936) and *Beyond Tomorrow* (1936), suites like *A Deserted Plantation* (1933) and *Pages from Negro History* (1943), and a symphony in G minor (1937).[64] On balance, the music of William Grant Still runs more to the picturesque than the profound, to the weaving of pleasing patterns of melody and rhythm than the exposition of inner conflict and jarring truths.

A similar summing up could be given of Randall Thompson's instrumental music. Thompson (1899–1984) studied composition with Edward Burlingame Hill and Ernest Bloch. In the late twenties, he wrote at least one work in the currently fashionable imitation-jazz style, the *Jazz Poem* (1925) for piano and orchestra. But he soon was putting stress on Appalachian folk sounds, with liberal hints of contemporary Broadway dance rhythms backed by conventional triadic harmonies. This easy-to-enjoy nationalism is evident in the First Symphony (1930), a captivating work.

In 1932, Thompson's Second Symphony came out. The composer found it no sin to wish to please an American audience with contagious tunes and rhythms alternating between folk and "pop," integrated within a beautifully fashioned structure.[65] The composition's success was immediate. A reviewer in *Musical America* wrote on 10 November 1933 of a performance by Bruno

Walter and the New York Philharmonic as follows: "Applause such as seldom greets new compositions, native or otherwise, was the portion of Randall Thompson's symphony, and the composer was summoned to the stage several times to receive it. The audience liked the symphony's freshness, vitality, humor, and clever orchestration. . . . But the work contains other qualities, too, although nothing profound, nothing groping for the soul of man in music was to be found."[66]

A *Suite* for oboe, clarinet, and viola, completed in 1940, a String Quartet, in 1941, and a Third Symphony, in 1949, are filled out with indigenous sounds and clear sonorities which delight listeners. After hearing the String Quartet on several occasions in 1941, Virgil Thomson said that every rehearing brought the work closer to his heart, "not only for its touching Appalachian Mountain Americanism but for its broader musical interest as well. It is one of the loveliest pieces our country has produced, that any country, indeed, has produced in our century."[67]

Thompson also is one of America's most outstanding composers for chorus. In 1932, he completed his humorous satire *Americana*, for chorus and orchestra or piano, based on texts from the *American Mercury*. In 1936, his lengthy *The Peaceable Kingdom*, for unaccompanied chorus, was performed. The title refers to a painting of Edward Hicks. The text, from *Isaiah*, warns the wicked of the eternal suffering to come, and promises the righteous a future happiness without end.

His most popular choral works are the *Alleluia* (1940), for a cappella chorus, and *The Testament of Freedom* (1943), set to words of Thomas Jefferson and written for men's voices and orchestra. While the music is traditional in sound, the two works sound fresh, eloquent, and sometimes quite powerful.[68] Choristers ask to sing these compositions, and choral-music devotees ask to hear them.

The next composer to be discussed, Virgil Thomson, was born in Kansas City in 1896, and later became a student of Nadia Boulanger in Paris during 1921–22. After a brief sojourn in the United States, Thomson returned to Paris in 1925, and for a few years was a part of a circle of sophisticated artists, musicians, and writers, including Gertrude Stein. From 1940 to 1954, he was the music critic of the New York *Herald Tribune*, and during those years was one of the most-read writers on music in America.

Thomson can be described as a composer with superb technical knowledge, who deliberately chose to function within delimited creative boundaries. He is preeminent in his ability to capture a solitary atmospheric or emotional feeling through the simplest of means. Ingenuous caprice, in particular, is his specialty. Sophisticated banality stated within novel contexts is his reply to grandisonant bombast. For whatever his creative objective, his manner of writing is delightfully appropriate. Admittedly, he did not wish to advance more than this, even when undertaking to depict the social and economic dislocations of the thirties. These last he transmuted into artistic forms best suited to his disposition and most calculated to win a positive reaction from his audience.

Hymns, popular music, folk songs, blues, and cowboy tunes endemic to Kansas City comprise the Americanisms finding their way into Thomson's compositions. They are treated unromantically, purged of sensuality, and presented in unexpected configurations. Harmony is lean and, while inclined toward the triadic, cautious in the inclusion of sevenths and ninths, which were so central to the heated styles of late-nineteenth-century European composers. The harshest dissonances may occasionally sound; but they are never necessary components of his mode of expression. The same is true of the post-tertian chordal combinations that appear. In most pieces, rhythm is straightforward and, if dancelike, veers toward tango, waltz, or foxtrot. The hollow sound of open fourths and fifths lightens the texture and produces a wide-spaced effect that has come to be associated with the American West.

In 1926, Thomson completed his *Sonata da Chiesa*, the title referring to the church sonata of the Italian Baroque. Scored for clarinet, trumpet, horn, trombone, and viola, it contains both a Chorale and a Fugue; however, plumb in the middle, a tango rhythm intrudes, to show that the work is not all that serious.

Thomson's *Symphony on a Hymn Tune* (1928) exploits the opposition of the solemn and irreverent. The main tune is the hymn "How Firm a Foundation," and a subordinate tune is "Yes, Jesus Loves Me." But one also hears incongruous snatches of "For He's a Jolly Good Fellow," and a couple of cowboy ditties. Parodic witticisms tear the listener away from sobriety. Now and again a portentous swelling of music and a crescendoing drum roll will promise a significant big-voiced climax, only to be followed by something frivolous—thus ending up not with a bang but a whimsy.

Glanville-Hicks says this symphony sounds with "the special eloquence that nostalgia assumes in the mind of an exile [Thomson wrote the work while resident in Paris]. . . . The idiom is the musical terminology of the man in the street, and the sophistication implicit in the objective arrangement of such materials is the sophistication that has travelled full circle—back to the utmost simplicity."[69]

Thomson's Second Symphony, actually an orchestral arrangement of his First Piano Sonata, followed in 1931. Again there is merriment, dancing rhythms, and "For He's a Jolly Good Fellow" thrusting in to deflect the references to hymns.

On 8 February 1934, *Four Saints in Three Acts* was performed in Hartford, Connecticut, and caused a sensation. Gertrude Stein, who wrote Thomson's libretto, wanted "to present the saints as figures who by their simple existence were magical, and they would be figures in a landscape, itself by simply existing, magical."[70] The sparkling cellophaney staging exhilarated the viewers. The nonsensical dialogue, the comically odd imitations of classical ballet and Spanish dance, and the utterly commonplace melody and harmony proved to be silly but imaginative, amusing but daring. Teasing caricatures of many types of music were heard: hymn and tavern song, elevated Handelian chorus and lowly music-hall refrain, operatic aria with recitative and "My Country, 'Tis of Thee," stately saraband and goofy waltz, sensitive soliloquy and stentorian proclamation. Thomson's key to success was his requiring of nothing from his audience save a suspension of reason. *Four Saints* had a winning roguishness that made its musical vulgarisms sound homespun and wonderfully quaint.[71]

In *Filling Station* (1937), written for Lincoln Kirstein and the Ballet Caravan, Thomson portrays "roadside America" by means of waltzes, tangos, a satirical fugue, the Big Apple, and jazz-derived rhythms. People gather at a filling station, which gangsters hold up to the sound of music. Elliott Carter describes the music as "like old-time pre-sound film piano-playing," since it "does not underline the action, move by move, but forms a running background that catches the simplicity of character and situation amusingly."[72]

Thomson also composed music for three documentary films:

FLORINE STETTHEIMER, *Portrait of Virgil Thomson.* Courtesy of The Art Institute of Chicago. Gift of Virgil Thomson. Reproduced with permission.

The Plough that Broke the Plains (1936), *The River* (1937), and *Louisiana Story* (1948). The suites based on this music, which he later put together, have become American classics. At the time *The Plough* was filmed, the Midwest was devastated with drought. It was really questionable whether the American promise of the full life was more than a chimera. Formerly productive farmlands were burnt dry, and the dusty soil was being blown all over a desolate landscape dotted with forsaken farmsteads. The music written for this documentary, commissioned by the Farm Security Administration, depicts movingly a slice of American life—sad, poignant, yet with an impressive grandeur. The "Prelude" sets the scene, with a mood of deep melancholy produced by dissonant strings astir under a lining out of the Doxology by the winds. The sadness increases with the wistful gentility of "Pastorale (Grass)," which tells, by means of a canon, about the serenity that once had existed. The next movement, entitled "Cattle," intensifies the longing for a lost past, using the traditional cowboy melodies "Laredo," "Git Along, Little Doggies," and "I Ride Old Paint." Then follows "Blues (Speculation)." Now a saxophone moans a jazz lament and produces a mood of suppressed restlessness. At last comes "Drought," a brief canon leading directly into "Devastation," which employs motifs drawn from the opening section of the suite, including the Doxology. The Coda achieves an extraordinary climax of intensity and beauty, as the melodic lines soar above a persistent tango beat.

Other compositions by Thomson are a second opera to a Stein libretto, *The Mother of Us All* (1947), on the life of the suffragist Susan B. Anthony, *Three Pictures for Orchestra* (1948–52), a Cello Concerto (1950), a Flute Concerto (1954), a Concerto for Flute, Harp, Strings, and Percussion (1954), and several fine contributions to chamber music literature, as well as to choral literature. Though one of America's most prominent composers between the two world wars, Thomson was a casualty of the decades following World War II, when simplicity, diatonicism, native melody and dance, and a demotic orientation went out of fashion.

Roy Harris, born in Oklahoma in 1898, took lessons in composition from Arthur Farwell and Nadia Boulanger. The music he wrote later is cast in a unique style characterized by long-drawn melodic lines, asymmetrical rhythms, modal harmonies (usually

Roy Harris. Photo: Copyright © George Maillard Kesslere,
B.P. Courtesy of the Boston Symphony Orchestra.

tertian, sometimes bichordal or bitonal), and a predilection for
contrapuntal formations, such as canon, fugue, and passacaglia.

At the beginning of the thirties, Harris was perceived as the
composer of a truly American music, especially music evocative
of the wide-ranging lands west of the Mississippi River. He was
proclaimed a genius in a *Musical Quarterly* article written by his
teacher, Arthur Farwell, which appeared in January 1932. At every
point of his career, Harris himself has been absolutely convinced
about the greatness of his music and has never hesitated to proclaim
its virtues publicly. By means of lengthy essays and program notes,

he tells audiences what his music is all about and how they should properly react to it.

Simultaneous with the praise of Harris's sterling American qualities has occurred criticism of the music itself. To several experienced listeners, for example, the *Symphony 1933* never seems to get anywhere. Inspiration seems sporadic, the writing undisciplined, and the structure rickety.[73] In 1935, a reviewer reported that the audience was very cool toward the overture *When Johnny Comes Marching Home*, and scarcely applauded at its conclusion. It sounded too noisy, too heavily orchestrated, and too artificial in form.[74]

Why, asked Charles Seeger in 1940, does Harris always want to play the role of giant? It gets in the way of "his announced attempt to achieve an American idiom." About Harris's String Quartet (1940), Seeger says that the music tends to get lost "in an amorphous kind of *durchführung* which he seems to think he has to write in order to be a great composer."[75] Four months later, Virgil Thomson heard Harris's *American Creed* for orchestra and complained of the absence of "colorful accent." Thomson adds: "He does not always get anywhere in his music, but it is serious music. . . . He is monotonous in his material and form." Every now and then, Thomson notices, "something really happens"; However, it has "as much to do with America as mountains or mosquitoes or childbirth have, none of which is anybody's property and none of which has any ethnic significance whatsoever."[76] In the same year, Copland summed up Harris, saying he always has problems holding a large work together, and his overblown spiritual explanations seldom correspond to a work's real "inner content." Moreover, Copland adds, a Harris work often has "no sense of real direction" and ends unexpectedly, for no apparent reason.[77]

In only a small number of works have the excellences of Harris's music been so great that they eclipse the weaknesses. One such composition is the Piano Quintet (1936). It is original, marked by an impression of strength and vigor, filled with fine melodies, and sufficiently varied in color and texture to sustain the listener's attention. The first movement has an excellent passacaglia theme and six variations. The second movement, "Cadenza," is a long rhapsody on a melody that spins itself out and grows over a lengthy time span. The third movement, a triple fugue, is the least interesting part of the piece, mostly because Harris goes on and on, not willing to let well enough alone.[78]

Without question, Harris's most successful composition is the Third Symphony. When first performed by Koussevitzky and the Boston Symphony Orchestra on 24 February 1939, it caused quite a stir. The work is in one movement, divided into five sections: the first, "Tragic," featuring the low strings; the second, "Lyric," and given to strings, horns, and winds; the third, "Pastoral," with winds accompanied by polytonal strings; the fourth, "Fugue," dramatic and with brass and percussion predominant; and the last, "Dramatic–Tragic," meant as a grand peroration, in which several themes heard earlier are reintroduced. The sections are clearly differentiated in material and mood. A high level of expressiveness is maintained. The fertility of invention is unfailing. Although folk melody is not directly quoted, the music sounds as if firmly rooted in the American countryside. Some miscalculations in instrumentation and harmonic spacing, and an abrupt, non sequitur sort of ending are defects made unimportant by the wealth of eloquent melodic ideas.[79]

Around 1935–36, when Aaron Copland began to have second thoughts about continuing along the austerely dissonant lines of his abstract period, he fortunately had the works of several composers to help suggest the new direction he might take. It is interesting to note that Virgil Thomson allots to himself much of the credit for Copland's conversion to what can be designated as his populist folk style. Thomson cites the "willful harmonic simplicities" in *Four Saints*, which fascinated Copland. There was the example of *The Plough that Broke the Plains*, where cowboy and other traditional American tunes appear: "Again the effect on Copland was electric; as a self-conscious modernist, he had not thought that one could do that either." *The Plough*, Thomson claims, was the guide for Copland's *Billy the Kid* and *Rodeo;* Thomson's *The River* and its pastoral use of "old Southern material," the guide for Copland's *Appalachian Spring*.[80]

The direction "away from complex experimentation, toward the broad musical audience" was widespread by the time Copland took note of it, writes Elie Siegmeister. Cited as examples of the altered direction are the engaging *Lieutenant Kije* (1933) and the singing Second Violin Concerto (1935). The same year the concerto appeared, Gershwin's *Porgy and Bess* and Shostakovich's "populist" Fifth Symphony were heard. Modern music, states Siegmeister, was leaving "its isolation ward" and "entering into the mainstream of musical—and human—life."[81]

Copland absorbed these various influences, domestic and foreign, and evolved his own people's music. His compositions became diatonic and tonal. He wrote expansive melodies organized into a number of short phrases, one growing from another. The melodies come directly from folk sources, or grow out of motives which seem inspired by them. Harmonies, whether tertian or post-tertian, change slowly and are vertically spaced to sound transparent, and also relatively free of the upsetting harshness that had invested his previous works. Orchestration is elegant and offers a kaleidoscope of changing colors. Quiet, static, pastoral-like passages hypnotize the listener at one moment; a sharp outburst of frenetic rhythms refreshes the listener's ear at another. The sound rarely registers as violent and impassioned. The composer's fastidious taste affects every measure. What is most significant is that this music was exactly right for its times. It stirred the feelings and imaginations of contemporary audiences and won Copland the large following he had dreamed of attracting.[82]

Summing up the effect of Copland's folk-period compositions on American audiences, Samuel Lipman writes:

> Copland's true achievement lies not in his use of rhythm, harmony, counterpoint, or original musical structures; it lies in his ability, through the use of melody, to evoke a mood—the mood of America of the period from the Civil War to World War II. There is in this period of American life a combination of leanness and grandeur that Copland manages to capture. He does more: he catches the emptiness of the city and the quiet of the land. Having done all this, he has succeeded in fixing in the mind of a large public an aural image of what America, and therefore American music, sounds like.[83]

Indicative of Copland's altered creative direction are the several works designed chiefly for performance by young people: "What Do We Plant" (1935), a chorus for high-school students; *Sunday Afternoon Music* and *The Young Pioneers* (both 1936), two

AARON COPLAND. Photo: John Ardoin. Reproduced with permission.

children's piano pieces; *The Second Hurricane* (1937), an opera for high school performers; and *An Outdoor Overture* (1938) and *John Henry* (1940), playable by high school instrumentalists. Works like these helped Copland resolve several stylistic problems: "I wished to be simple to the point of ordinariness," he says about the opera. "This was comparatively easy in relation to the more colloquial passages of the libretto where the music approaches musical operetta, but in the more dramatic moments it was rather difficult to make the distinction between grand opera and high school opera." Some elements of his earlier jazz style persist ("Jeff's Song" and the choral "Two Willow Hills"), but quite obvious is the new American folk sound ("The Capture of Burgoyne").[84]

In 1936, he completed the orchestral version of *El Salón México*, a tourist's imaginary recall of a popular Mexican dance hall. Music from Frances Toor's *Cancionero Méxicano* and Ruben Campo's *El Folk-lore y la Musica Méxicana* make up a major part of its melodic content. The work is simple, tonal, brilliantly orchestrated, folksy, readily understandable, and always attractive to the ear— one moment gay, the next sentimental or swaggeringly vulgar or impetuous or impulsive.[85]

Billy the Kid, a ballet Copland wrote for the Ballet Caravan in 1938, introduces a mythology of the United States that is clothed in economically stated sounds both warm, expressive, and at one with the American spirit of the thirties. Billy as a lone but heroic rebel against a straightjacketing, unfeeling society is the theme; not Billy as reprehensible outlaw committing acts of violence. A wealth of Western tunes are sewn firmly into the musical fabric. Not surprisingly, both the ballet and the suite that was later extracted from it pleased the public.[86] The success of *Billy the Kid* encouraged Copland to continue along similar lines. Four years later, commissioned to write a ballet for Agnes de Mille, he completed *Rodeo*. Again his music was received enthusiastically. The theme is one of loneliness, of yearning to be accepted by others. Western tunes, of course, are introduced; however, greater stretches of sound than in *Billy* are given over entirely to music of Copland's own invention. The lovely "Coral Nocturne" and the "Saturday Night Waltz," in particular, show that the composer has so deeply integrated the folk manner into his thinking that his original music is heard as identifiably American yet intimately personal, both at the same time.[87]

Then, in 1944, came Copland's *Appalachian Spring*, composed for the Martha Graham Dance Company. Much of the work is new-minted. The Shaker tune "Simple Gifts," introduced in a series of variations, is the only manifest quotation from folk sources. Warren Susman writes that Martha Graham appeared as "the Pioneer Woman, dominant, strong but loving, and dedicated to the future. The Bride is joyous and will not be put down by a hell-fire-and-brimstone sermon." The composition presents itself "as a special kind of American rite or series of rites—the sermon, the courtship, the marriage, the house-raising—which celebrates the American past and American character (especially the American

THOMAS HART BENTON, *Arts of the West.* The New Britain Museum of American Art, New Britain, Connecticut. Harriet R. Stanley Fund. Reproduced with permission.

woman) with humor, joy, and tenderness. . . . It was part of a body of music" that the times demanded.[88] *Appalachian Spring* has become one of the best-loved compositions written by an American art composer.

Copland also tried his hand at writing identifiably American music for motion pictures, from which he would later extract orchestral suites for concert performance. Among the most successful musically are *The City* (1939), *Our Town* (1940), and *The Red Pony* (1948).[89] For the Columbia Broadcasting System, he wrote *Music for Radio* (1937), also named *Saga of the Prairie*, in response to suggestions that CBS received after inviting its radio audience to retitle the composition.

Three other works are outstanding examples of Copland's musical Americanism. The *Lincoln Portrait* (1942), for narrator and orchestra, reminded wartime America of its roots in a democratic past—the words of Abraham Lincoln mingling with the tones of "Springfield Mountain." In the same year, the *Fanfare for Common Man*, for brass and percussion, was premiered and went on to become the music most symbolic of American ideals. It has been performed countless times to commemorate important public events. The *Fanfare* is the basic material for the Third Symphony (1946) and is quoted in its entirety in the last movement. This symphony incorporates most elements of Copland's Americanistic style into the sort of tuneful, formally balanced, and communicative work that made Copland the high priest of American music populism.

Finally, Copland issued two sets of *Old American Songs*, for voice and orchestra (1950, 1952), and completed a folk-inspired opera, *The Tender Land* (1954).

Several of the Copland compositions written between 1936 and 1954 number among the works that Americans most admire. And Aaron Copland himself is widely recognized as America's very own great artist.

Other composers, too, have contributed significant music in the name of American populism. Foremost is Marc Blitzstein's well-received proletarian opera, *The Cradle Will Rock*, written in 1937, after he had repudiated his avant-garde past. A superb libretto and acerbic songs "in idioms from Moussorgsky to boogie-woogie" catch fire and grip listeners, wrote Olin Downes in 1947.

MARCH, 1931

Otto Soglow

DRESS REHEARSAL

Cartoon by Otto Soglow from the *New Masses*, March 1931.

Union workers are the heroes; the capitalist boss and his cohorts are the villains. The opera sounds with "sweetness, a cutting wit, inexhaustible fancy, and faith," writes Thomson. It is a "fairy tale" that "is true because it makes you believe it."[90]

Attractive works in populist idioms have also been written by Robert Russell Bennett (*Abraham Lincoln Symphony*, 1931), Robert McBride (*Rhapsody on Mexican Themes*, 1936), William Schuman (*American Festival Overture*, 1939; and *William Billings Overture*, 1944), Morton Gould (*Spirituals* and *Latin American Symphonette*, both 1941; *Cowboy Rhapsody*, 1942; and *Fall River Legend*, 1948), and Elie Siegmeister (*Western Suite*, 1945).

Not surprisingly, after World War II this music was labelled excessively nationalistic and equated with cultural jingoism. The depreciation was unfair. This music, especially the best of it, had no extreme chauvinistic intent. It aimed to enshrine the ideals of American democracy and employ sounds that had fresh meaning for ordinary listeners. It was also an approach to composing that was not necessarily static, if but given a chance to build on a solid foundation of estimable works.

There can be no doubt that, by the fifties, the United States possessed many composers who were superbly competent at their craft, abreast of every contemporary trend in the art world, and sympathetic to the aesthetic needs of their own countrymen. They were imitators only so far as every composer who has ever lived must be beholden to one or more of the artists preceding him. More importantly, they were true to their native upbringing, and consciously or unconsciously mirrored that upbringing in their creative thinking. While some of their compositions, those that are most dissonant and anti-lyrical, have won acceptance within only a limited circle, a larger number has met with approval from general audiences, and a fortunate few with tremendous enthusiasm. Writers on music have characterized the years between 1925 and 1950 as the Golden Age of American music. Assuredly, during those years was put to rest the assumed incompatibility of democracy and excellence in high culture.

5

Lessons from Experience

The years 1925 to 1945 were a thriving period in the history of American musical culture, and an era of high achievement for American composers. One must reach this conclusion after surveying conditions before and after this time. For at least part of this period, the federal government and many city administrations liberally subsidized music and musicians. From 1935 to 1941, every sort of performing group, whether publicly or privately sponsored, was available for the presentation of new works. This is not to say that American composers were overwhelmed with a demand for their compositions, but rather that they were given a hearing as never before. Creative workshops and tryout rehearsals allowed the artist to test tentative but potentially exciting ideas, in order to discover if they were viable. Oftentimes these experiments were occasions for artist and attending music lovers to exchange views, discuss creative problems, and clarify creative purpose.

Especially during the lifetime of the Federal Music Project, more and more men and women listened willingly to a composer's new music and were grateful he had them in mind when he wrote. Indeed, a democratic and qualitatively excellent art was what many composers aimed to achieve. Their successful compositions gave immediate pleasure and comfort, and they also offered listeners deeply felt experiences upon which to meditate; at last, writing plainly was not equated with writing down to an audience.

Under the terms of the Federal Music Project no American, however poor, was denied entry to concerts and stage performances, or to classes giving instruction in singing, playing an instrument, and understanding art works. As never before there had grown an open-mindedness and even a curiosity about dissimilar opinions on what constituted a worthy contemporary expression. Composers of antithetical persuasions were provided with livings and opportunities to give full rein to their creative bent, whatever direction it took. People, however, did discriminate between the works they could give their hearts to and those that left them cold. A musical work, they felt, is estimable "only when it finds some way of dealing with a kind of experience which the objective sciences must dismiss as outside their provinence." Music succeeds "only when" the audience is "able to say, 'This is indeed what living feels like."[1] Barber's *Adagio for Strings* and Copland's *Rodeo* passed the test; but many other modern works failed.

During these years an endless discussion had taken place on the true nature of American art music, and a variety of works distinctly different from European ones had been written. If in these works an admixture existed of Stravinsky or Schoenberg or a French influence, it nevertheless had secondary importance; these were compositions no European could have created, whether *Sun-Treader, American in Paris,* or *The Plough that Broke the Plains.* For some composers merely being born in the United States was enough to put a native stamp on their music. For others, the infusion of characteristically American sounds was a conscious endeavor. But one way or the other, American compositions no longer slavishly followed foreign models.

Then arrived the post-war years, the disillusionment with humankind, and the abhorrence of nationalism. Anomie replaced the sense of connection between people; fear of atomic apocalypse replaced the faith in a better future. This disoriented perception of the world had a far-reaching influence on American art music. Walter Simmons, writing in 1981 about a contemporary-music conference that he had attended in New York, says that a recurring theme at the conference was introduced by the composer George Rochberg—"the recognition that the dominant emphasis since

World War II on structural manipulation at the expense of expressive, spiritual, or emotional content, and the concomitant renunciation by composers of their rich aesthetic heritage, have destroyed rapport between composer and performer and between composer and listener." Except for a few diehards, the majority of attendees at the conference agreed that their "inability to achieve artistic communication" was "a form of failure; and their repudiation of "the wealth of musical treasures to be discovered among American composers of the generation that produced Hanson, Cowell, Barber, Schuman, and others," a result of the narrowist thinking or intimidation by the ultramodernists. American art music, they realized, was in serious crisis.[2]

As we confront these new problems, are there any lessons to be learned from the experiences of the thirties, in particular? The answer is, yes. The "artist" image needs modification, and the mutual canonization of art composer by art composer must cease. It serves no purpose for a composer to declare listeners averse to his music to be philistines, "Macy's-basement types"—as has been said. The public is not duty-bound to make ceaseless efforts at fathoming the mysteries of a composition, however abstruse. On the other hand, the composer must make some effort at comprehensibility or stand up to criticism.[3] This does not mean that if a majority of listeners likes a composition, nothing else matters. Public taste does err. Nevertheless, the composer who can find no audience whatsoever to value and sustain his compositions has the obligation at least to reexamine the premises which guide his creativity, for he may be wrong. Was not reexamination of this sort behind the changes that took place in the styles of many composers during the thirties, among them Copland, Blitzstein, and Antheil? If the composer wishes to continue writing enigmatic music intelligible only to a limited audience, then he must scale down the performance forces needed to produce his music so that the expense of production approximates the modest gate his music will attract. Robert Schumann's admonition to musicians is worth quoting here: "Study your audience; yet never play [compose] anything of which in your heart you feel ashamed."[4]

We urgently need histories and other studies of American musical culture analyzing not the viewpoint of composer or performer, but the relation of the composer to the audience, the nature of musical communication, and the approaches to reconciliation of composer's and listener's needs. In this regard, one of the most valuable books in recent years on the relation of music to society is Alan P. Merriam's *The Anthropology of Music,* published by Northwestern University Press in 1964. Merriam observes that musical sound is produced by composers for a human audience, and that the two aspects are inseparable. Although nobody knows exactly what is communicated or how communication takes place, we must not forget that "the study of music as a means of communication" is, while complex, a necessary endeavor.[5] He points out that we tend to isolate the music heard and "analyze it as a thing in itself," as well as "an object divorced from context." This is a very limited approach to understanding.[6] He quotes David P. McAllester as saying:

> A peculiar trait in our own Western European culture [is] the bifurcation of the concept of culture. We can think of culture in the antropological sense of the total way of life of a people, but we also think of culture in the sense of "cultivated," with a particular emphasis on art forms and art for art's sake. The result of this cultural trait of ours has been a separation of art from culture-as-a-whole. . . . In music we are very prone to a consideration of music *qua* music outside of its cultural context . . . as an art form . . . outside of its principal cultural function.[7]

Aaron Copland has made a similar statement. Asked about the post-fifties music and the way it is explained, he replied: "One ought to be able to get some sort to charge out of it just by sitting there and listening to it in a dumb fashion. I think that basically we all listen to music in a rather dumb way, especially when we are presented with a new piece about which we know absolutely nothing. Too often you get the feeling, when you read an analysis, that there isn't much point to the music except the way the darn thing's put together."[8] These are among the matters requiring study—why we get a "charge out of" certain works and not others, and in what "dumb fashion" we all listen to music.

Historically speaking, we do know that every music has invariably been shaped by its culture. To some extent, getting a charge out of a composition means that it "is made of socially accepted patterns of sound." The general public does reach a consensus on "what it will and will not call music." Compositions falling outside the norm "are either unacceptable or are simply defined as something other than music."[9]

In the past, the composer has either faced oblivion or adapted his music to accommodate the norm. This was the choice of Monteverdi when the Italian public demanded melodic and visually splendid operas, which Cavalli, Cesti, and other composers were willing to supply. He put behind him his recitative-dominated style and wrote his superb *L'Incoronazione di Poppea* (1642). Did not Haydn compose symphonies according to the Viennese taste, the Parisian taste, and the London taste, and still preserve his integrity as a creative artist? When the European middle class of the nineteenth century desired music that was highly lyrical or dramatic, national or exotic, and capable of eliciting a variety of moods from the most intimate to the most flamboyant, any number of composers—among them, Berlioz, Dvorak, Mussorgsky, and Grieg—compiled and composed some of their finest works. Finally, in the American years of the Great Depression, when men and women said to the artists: "Tell us who we are, where we have come from," Thomson, Copland, Thompson, Siegmeister, and others wrote splendid works made up of "socially accepted patterns of sound," which responded to people's desires.

In the fifties, the fructifying union between composer and public ended. The composer wrote as if the approval of listeners did not matter; national characteristics disappeared from American compositions; internationalism took hold. And a wearying sameness dulled the ear, as composition after composition came out that might just as well have been done in Cologne, Vienna, or Paris. As a result, the strength of America's musical life has been vitiated, and we have to learn over again that a personal experience and its musical expression alone do not constitute any sort of culture. No matter how an artist may will it otherwise, culture still implies something whose meaning is shared.

A little before Koussevitzky died, he spoke of the democratic imperative to break down artificial barriers "between the initiated and the uninitiated," and to make "the language of music as accessible to the general understanding and emotion as is the spoken language." He said: "One of the greatest vices of European culture (of art, at any rate) has been that art was detached from the people."[10] In his estimate, all Americans, from the most sophisticated to the least educated, could appreciate beauty in artistic forms. The fact that people did go to concerts by the thousands established their need for such beauty and showed a true involvement with serious musical expression.

In contrast to the notion that popularity leads to the cheapening of an artistic work is the idea that rather, popularity attests to a broad-based agreement among listeners on the work's aesthetic value, and shows an understanding between public and composer. Only in this way can a community of art become established. The levelling effect of a musical culture that appeals to large numbers of people is a fear to be rejected in a democracy. Against it must be placed the question of how many potential music lovers, performers, and composers may be left without the opportunity to discover the finest in them because they were considered part of the masses and were denied exposure to the arts. The believer in democracy would rather give the opportunity to the majority to say: "No, I hate classical music," in order to encourage the minority that says: "I did not realize such beauty existed in the world." Such was the belief behind the WPA Federal Music Project; such is the equality of opportunity a democracy must foster. To believe otherwise, to act differently, is to compound the errors brought on by the accidents of birth.

Nevertheless, we must admit that the audience for art music will continue to resist any modern work that forgoes tonality, banishes melody, and abhors consonance. It will not give up what it finds pleasing and emotionally meaningful for what it finds to be ugly, cold, and overly abstract. After more than a half century of hearing post-tertian dissonant compositions, the general music public still refuses to absorb much of that music into its cultural tradition. Whether by Schoenberg and Webern or Ruggles and Sessions, inaccessible styles of music may never win wide acceptance by the public. The compositions that they wrote, if appreciated at all in the future, may have the allegiance of only a small group of partisans. Since the symphony orchestra, the opera company, and, increasingly, even chamber ensembles are "designed to reach audiences numbering in the thousands," music that fails to "communicate with such audiences" must expect to be bypassed.[11] Ruggles's *Sun-Treader* and Copland's *Short Sym-*

phony were bypassed for years, not only because of the performance difficulties of the score and the bias of foreign-born conductors, but also because, though written for symphony orchestra, they failed to communicate with the larger public that heard them.

What is meant by communication? For centuries, all art music contained direct and allusive significations about which composer, performer, and listener had at least implicitly come to an agreement. Merriam quotes Mantle Hood as saying: "Communication among people is a two-way street: speaking and listening, informing and being informed, constructively evaluating and welcoming constructive criticism. Communication is accurate to the extent that it is founded on a sure knowledge of the man with whom we would hold intercourse."[12]

Music is not a philosophy, nor a science, as Sessions implies. Music neither speculates about reality, nor imparts verifiable information about the physical world. Its chief province concerns feelings, the eliciting of sympathetic emotional responsiveness from the listener. The mechanistic explanation offered by some neo-classicists that music is "pure" and expresses nothing but itself is nonsense. For hundreds of years, people sensitive to the import of artistic sound have persisted in thinking that a composition is a composer's interpretation of what is happening within and around him and his listeners, enunciated through an imaginative and emotion-provoking diction.

Too many people through the ages have spoken of how much music has moved them; we dare not say their claim is absurd because they can prove nothing empirically. The insistence on proof falsely equates music with science. What happens within the psyche when music sounds can never be validated by evidence or verbal reasoning. Like René Descartes, who knew there was no external way to test his existence, we know there is no way to establish definitely just what music expresses to us. Twisting Descartes' words, we may say: "I feel its effects, therefore music has meaning for me."

Merriam describes music's function as emotional expression acting on a number of levels. Among these he mentions aesthetic enjoyment, entertainment, emotional communication to those who understand its idiom, symbolic representation, physical response, confirmation of social norms, the validation of socio-cultural institutions, the contributing to the continuity and validity of a culture, and societal integration.[13]

If American art music is to remain healthy, it must function on a majority of these levels. The question is, how can we bring composer, performer, and listener together, and foster understanding and interaction among the three? Another question involves America's past and present culture. How can we stop our endless inclination to repudiate our roots and depreciate our native talents? To decide that American musical culture has always occupied a wasteland, that American composers, conductors, and soloists are inferior to their European counterparts, and that American audiences are forever bent on stupidly vulgarizing every artistic expression is to judge that democracy and art must forever remain incompatible.

To answer these questions we must learn from what he have done right, not just from how we have erred. Here, the manifold activities of the second half of the thirties and the early forties can teach us a great deal. The promise of these years did not materialize, because the will and boldness of our politicians failed and the prejudice of influential reactionaires fearful of socialism prevailed. The threat of World War II was only the surface cause for ending the most noble cultural experiment the United States has ever undertaken—the Four Arts Project.

The time has come to resume what we started then and never finished. If we believe that the idea of America comprises more than a physical presence, an economic and political entity, and a military capability, then we must enhance our high culture by means of governmental aid. Art music must come to represent the best that is in us as a people. Nevertheless, governmental aid, federal and local, should not continue as now formulated but as a greatly increased assistance with conditions attached. A symphony orchestra should not receive a grant merely to repeat for the hundredth time Tchaikovsky's *Pathétique Symphony*, nor an opera company to mount still another version of Puccini's *La Boheme*, nor a ballet corps to execute once more Delibes's *Coppélia*. In exchange for governmental grants, at least twelve to fifteen percent of any group's total performance time should be devoted to American compositions, divided between music that is thirty or more years old and that which is more recent. These few minutes of performance time for an average concert are not an onerous burden for conductors. One would expect they would wish to do more than this; but regrettably, past experience has proved that they would much rather deny any time at all to American composers. Paine, Chadwick, MacDowell, Farwell, Gilbert, Carpenter, Griffes, Ives, Hadley, and composers of more recent vintage have all vanished into the limbo of disdainful neglect; yet they deserve far better than this.

Moreover, basic grants should regularly be sweetened following the employment of native conductors and soloists and the commissioning of native compositions. In addition, every board of directors should include one or more representatives from the subscription audience, the number of seats thus allotted to be in direct relation to the portion of income derived from the public. If special private groups want to retain total control of performance organizations, then they themselves should pay all expenses incurred and not look to the government or to the general public for funds to cover deficits in the expectation of public support without public representation.

Regularly conducted polls of the audience should take place in order to determine which pieces are enjoyed and which disliked; too often in the past unverified assumptions have been made concerning listeners' attitudes. In no way should the results of such polls absolutely decide what is to be included or excluded from programs. Rather, they should serve as recommendatory guides to conductors, managers, and boards to help in the scheduling of at least some of the program, and to determine what sorts of American works are really managing to communicate with the audience. As an added dividend, the contemporary composer can in this way have necessary evaluative, even corrective, information returned to him on what listeners hear as right or wrong in his compositions.

In the past, composers have heeded the wishes of the patrons who provided them with a living—Palestrina's Pope Julius III, Scarlatti's Queen Maria Barbera, Haydn's Prince Esterházy, Grieg's Norwegian people, and Stravinsky's Sergei Diaghilev. The twentieth-century patrons increasingly are the common citizens of a country; yet, in America, no liaison between composer and public exists. A dialogue must be encouraged.

We should be aware that artists cannot help but pay attention to the persons who are able to reward and punish them. Note the comment of Winthrop Sargeant, in 1957, that "given the economic conditions" composers "work under, they are likely to compose for the advisors of foundations and publishing houses (fellow-composers, usually) who have the power to award them fellowships, prizes, and contracts, instead of for the musical public—an extremely cultivated and knowledgeable one, by the way, and one that is unquestionably hungry for significant new compositions."[14]

Sargeant's faith in the musical public is refreshing. Quite disturbing, on the other hand, is his conclusion (corroborated in other accounts of the musical scene since World War II) that fellow-composers determine the recipients of fellowships, prizes, and contracts. Year after year the complaint is raised about the like-thinking advisors, who exact conformity to one or two currently accepted advanced styles in despite of how audiences react to those styles. One result has been that no announcement of a new prize winner causes anyone to rush to the concert hall or record counter. Of course, the advice of composers is both unavoidable and necessary; but at the same time, performing musicians also should serve as advisors.

To avoid the domination of any one viewpoint, I suggest that the names of competent musicians, representative of a variety of outlooks and having some degree of national recognition, be gathered. A blind drawing from these names would help eliminate the danger of sectarian monopoly on advisory committees. On the other hand, advisors should be empowered to select only the finalists, not the winners. At this point, the compositions, or portions of long compositions, of the finalists should be played or sung at a rehearsal, and replayed by way of a sound recording, for a volunteer audience chosen blindly from the subscribers to the group performing. It is this audience that votes on the winner. Thus, input into the selection process is insured to all concerned parties.

If it is a question of selecting composers for a grant, the process is the same. The candidates for grants are asked to submit tapes of typical compositions. Also, the candidate may additionally suggest for live hearing a work that best typifies his style. However cumbersome the system, it lessens the possibility of prejudicial decisions in favor of one aesthetic position and encourages diversity. It is also likely that the directors of foundations, seeing a democratic participation in the selection process and a good chance that their awards will not fall on barren ground, might increase their support of contemporary music.

There is no predicting what the results of such undertakings will be and, of course, experience must constantly modify their direction. Quite possibly a new generation may find less interest in any of the musics from before 1950 and more in a style not yet conceived. Yet, one hopes that these recommended actions might encourage a larger and more interested contemporary audience for twentieth-century American music.

In the private aid given to performing music groups, the same 12 to 15 percent rule already suggested for governmental aid should be encouraged. Non-profit, tax-exempt philanthropic organizations dispensing funds to the arts have an obligation to deepen our acquaintance with our own native culture.

Another way government can set an example is by guaranteeing financial support to performance groups desiring to reach out to a wider audience in their community through free or cheaply priced concerts, who tour outlying areas of their state where live concerts are unusual, who make room for gifted young musicians to play beside experienced performers or even to solo, and who put on the works of local composers at rehearsals and, if these have special merit, at scheduled concerts. Some of these suggestions have been advanced by Edward Arian. He also advocates the establishment of a new position, that of arts administrator, to plan and direct programs like the ones just described.[15]

To give maximum exposure to American music, public money should help underwrite television and radio broadcasts, sound recordings, and publications of American works. Today, it is possible for us to have every kind of American music, past and present, readily available by way of film, tape, and disc recording. An American work performed in one locality should be preserved so that interested music lovers living elsewhere can also hear it. If an ensemble specializes in the presentation of some segment of American music, its performances, made available in film or sound recording, would prove invaluable.

Several performances and at least one publicly available recording of an American composition are vital for allowing listeners to familiarize themselves with its sound and for setting up the possibility of its acceptance. Let a new work reach its special audience, if one can be found, without the fatal handicap of one performance and nothing else. Some years ago, Howard Hanson remarked: "The music public may know what it likes, but it can like only what it knows—and knows well."[16] This will always be true.

A further recommendation is that an American Symphony Orchestra, with its ancillary chamber-music groups, and an American Opera Company, with its ancillary chamber-opera, choral, and art-song groups be established to perform only American works. The music played should represent all styles that native composers have worked in and are working in—not merely those styles in favor with a particular group of intellectuals, from the most conservative to the most daring. Care must be taken that no one viewpoint predominate in the selection committees. To make certain no work is overlooked, an advisory staff of musicologists knowledgeable about music in the United States is required, which will gather the music of our past and present, prepare study and performing editions of it, record it, and preserve it in score and sound. Publication on demand and taped music on demand must be a service offered all interested music lovers. In many areas, the staff need not operate solely on its own but may work in cooperation with already extant organizations. Certainly, several institutions now exist whose activities on behalf of American music can receive encouragment and backing: the Library of Congress's Music Division, the Smithsonian Institute, the American Music Center, New World Records, and the Sonneck Society, to name five.

To insure the idiomatic performance of American works and to provide a showcase for native talent, the American Orchestra and the American Opera Company must consist entirely of American instrumentalists and singers. Keep in mind how the WPA ensembles first brought American players to the fore and sent them on to employment in established musical organizations. We must do no less.

Finally, regional composers' workshops and forums must again come into existence. Composers need to be able to try out their new works and engage in open discussion with colleagues and audience over the meaning of what they are attempting to accomplish. We would expect that works from innocuous to outrageous can be aired. Composers would keep in touch with the latest thinking of their colleagues. Advisors to foundations would get some inkling of who are the rising talents to be encouraged. Performers would discover new, potentially attractive works to add to their repertoire. And the ferment necessary for sustained creativity and for feeling that American musical culture is on the move will affect all participants.

What is proposed is not an illusory plan. European governments already do a great deal more than we do to support municipal orchestras and opera companies, radio and television ensembles of every description, and publication of the scores and recordings of what are regarded as national musical monuments. They have given this support over many decades, in times of prosperity and of economic malaise.

In the United States, it is true that a great deal of private and public money does go into support of the arts. But the spending is aimless. No abiding results ensue. These pages have suggested a structure that can provide overall guidance and convey a sense of cultural direction. Most important, for those of us who love music, believe that democracy can demonstrate its own cultural excellences, and watch in despair as American flounders on from cultural crisis to cultural crisis, it offers us something to believe in and work for. To quote Franklin Delano Roosevelt: "The only limit to our realization of tomorrow will be our doubts of today. Let us move forward with strong and active faith."

Notes

1 The Composer Speaks (pp. 1-53)

1. Louis Moreau Gottschalk, *Notes of a Pianist*, ed. Jeanne Behrend (New York: Knopf, 1964), pp. 51-52.
2. Edward T. Cone, "Conversations with Aaron Copland," *Perspectives of New Music* (Spring–Summer 1968), p. 59.
3. These statements were still coming out in the late thirties; see F. Bonavia, "Reformers Convened," *New York Times*, 26 June 1938, sec. IX, 5.
4. David Ewen, *Composers Since 1900* (New York: Wilson, 1969), pp. 9, 89.
5. Cone, "Conversations," p. 64.
6. See Charles Seeger, "Carl Ruggles," *The Musical Quarterly* 18 (1932), 578-92; Joseph Machlis, *American Composers of Our Time* (New York: Crowell, 1963), p. 59; Marc Blitzstein, "Forecast and Review," *Modern Music* 9 (1931-32), 82; Roger Sessions, "On the American Future," *Modern Music* 17 (1939-40), 73-74.
7. Aaron Copland, in *Modern Music* 9 (1931-32), 22.
8. Arthur Berger, *Aaron Copland* (New York: Oxford, 1953), p. 22.
9. For a full exposure of this viewpoint, see Carlos Chavez, *Musical Thought* (Cambridge: Harvard Univ. Press, 1961), pp. 89, 99; John H. Mueller, in *The American Symphony Orchestra* (Bloomington: Indiana Univ. Press, 1951), p. 388, terms this attitude an "elliptical fallacy."
10. Claire R. Reis, *Composers, Conductors, and Critics* (New York: Oxford Univ. Press, 1951), p. 53.
11. Aaron Copland, in *Modern Music* 9 (1931-32), 21; Copland, *Music and Imagination* (New York: New American Library, 1959), pp. 20-21.

12. See Roger Sessions, "New Vistas in Musical Education," *Modern Music* 11 (1933-34), 115; Sessions, "American Music and the Crisis," *Modern Music* 18 (1940-41), 211-17; Mark A. Schubart, "Roger Sessions," *The Musical Quarterly* 32 (1946), 197; *The American Composer Speaks*, ed. Gilbert Chase (Baton Rouge: Louisiana State Univ. Press, 1966), pp. 272-73; Sessions, *Questions About Music* (Cambridge: Harvard Univ. Press, 1970), pp. 11-12, 20, 132.

13. ROGER SESSIONS, *The Musical Experience* (New York: Atheneum, 1965), p. 100.

14. NED ROREM, *The Paris Diary* (New York: Braziller, 1960), p. 14. Though the reference is to American compositions of the 1950s, similar comments were made on earlier works; see Mueller, *American Symphony Orchestra*, p. 291; Olin Downes, "Slashing Attack," *New York Times*, 20 March 1955, sec. II, 7; Arthur Lourie, "Neogothic and Neoclassic," *Modern Music* 5, no. 3 (1927-28), 6.

15. CHARLES SEEGER, "Carl Ruggles," *The Musical Quarterly* 18 (1932), 579-80, 590; Seeger, "Carl Ruggles," in *American Composers on American Music*, ed. Henry Cowell (New York: Ungar, 1962), pp. 15, 32. The Cowell book was first published in 1933.

16. LOU HARRISON, *About Carl Ruggles* (Yonkers, N.Y.: Bavadinsky, 1946), p. 2.

17. PAUL BOWLES, *Without Stopping* (New York: Putnam's, 1972), p. 103.

18. MARC BLITZSTEIN, reviewing Thompson's Second Symphony, in *Modern Music* 11 (1933-34), 37; Theodore Chanler, in *Modern Music* 11 (1933-34), 146.

19. OLIN DOWNES, "What Makes Music Modern?" *New York Times*, 26 May 1940, sec. IX, 5.

20. JOHN BRIGGS, "Crusty Composer," *New York Times*, 12 October 1958, sec. II, 11.

21. PAUL ROSENFELD, *Discoveries of a Music Critic* (1936; reprint, New York: Vienna House, 1972), p. 271; Reis, *Composers*, p. 47. See also Paul Rosenfeld, *An Hour with American Music* (Philadelphia: Lippincott, 1929).

22. VERNON DUKE, *Passport to Paris* (Boston: Little, Brown, 1955), pp. 3-4, 88-89.

23. ALEXANDER FRIED, "For the People," *The Musical Quarterly* 4 (1927), 33; David Epstein, "Sessions at 60," *Musical America*, September 1957, p. 28.

24. NOEL STRAUS, "Nadia Boulanger Discusses the Moderns," *New York Times*, 2 April 1939, sec. X, 7.

25. SESSIONS, *Musical Experience*, p. 87.

26. OTTO LUENING, *The Odyssey of an American Composer* (New York: Scribner's, 1980), p. 320.

27. DUKE, *Passport*, p. 251.

28. See Harrison Kerr, "The Composer's Lot Is Not a Happy One," *Musical America*, 10 February 1934, p. 8; Emerson Whithorne, "Where Do We Go from Here?" *The Musical Quarterly* 4 (1927), 9–14, respectively, for the first quotation. For the lengthy second quotation, see Edward Robinson, "The Life and Death of an American Composer," *The American Mercury* 30 (1933), 347–48.

29. See, for example, Paul Bowles's comment, in *Without Stopping*, pp. 98–99, that when he found Copland's music ridiculed, he "assumed automatically that he was the most important composer in the United States."

30. ALEXANDER FRIED, "The Prestige of Good Music," *The Musical Quarterly* 5 (1928), 129–132. For an opposite view of the eighteenth century, see Jacques Barzun, "Artist Against Society," *The Partisan Review* 19 (1952), 63.

31. JOHN TASKER HOWARD, with the assistance of Arthur Mendel, *Our Contemporary Composers* (New York: Crowell, 1941), p. 10; Charles Wakefield Cadman, letter to the *New York Times*, 6 March 1932, sec. VIII, 8.

32. EDWARD JABLONSKI and LAWRENCE D. STEWART, *The Gershwin Years* (Garden City, N.Y.: Doubleday, 1973), p. 108.

33. GILBERT CHASE, *America's Music*, 2nd ed. (New York: McGraw-Hill, 1966), p. 550; *Olin Downes on Music*, ed. Irene Downes (New York: Simon & Schuster, 1957), p. 181; Machlis, *American Composers*, pp. 72–73; news item in the *New York Times*, 19 September 1937, sec. XI, 7.

34. RICHARD JACKSON, in *New Grove Dictionary*, s.v. "Barber, Samuel."

35. HENRY COWELL, "Paul Creston," *The Musical Quarterly* 34 (1948), 534–35, 538; Madeleine Goss, *Modern Music-Makers* (New York: Dutton, 1952), p. 377; David Ewen, *The World of Twentieth-Century Music* (Englewood Cliffs, N.J.: Prentice-Hall, 1968), p. 183; Ewen, *Composers Since 1900*, p. 148.

36. BOWLES, *Without Stopping*, pp., 168–169.

37. JOSHUA C. TAYLOR, *The Fine Arts in America* (Chicago: Univ. of Chicago Press, 1979), p. 192. For more on the subject of the change in artists' attitudes, see Frederick Lewis Allen, *Since Yesterday* (New York: Harper, 1940), pp. 41–42; Sheldon Cheney, in *America Now*, ed. Harold E. Stearns (New York: Literary Guild, 1938), p. 97; for a discussion of rights versus obligations, see Simone Weil, *The Need for Roots*, trans. Arthur Wills (New York: Harper & Row, 1971), p. 3.

38. ROGER SESSIONS, "Music in Crisis," *Modern Music* 10 (1932-33), 76; Marion Bauer, *Twentieth-Century Music* (New York: Putnam's, 1933), p. 294; Virgil Thomson, *Virgil Thomson* (New York: Knopf, 1966), p. 156.

39. ARTHUR FARWELL, "Roy Harris," *The Musical Quarterly* 18 (1932), 23-24; Randall Thompson, "The Contemporary Scene in American Music," *The Musical Quarterly* 18 (1932), 12.

40. OLIN DOWNES, "A Nation's Musical Frontiers," *New York Times*, 3 June 1934, sec. IX, 5; Downes, "America's Awakening," *New York Times*, 1 November 1932, p. 23; Charles Seeger, "Ruggles," p. 34.

41. THOMAS HART BENTON, *An Artist in America*, 3rd ed. revised (Columbia: Univ. of Missouri Press, 1968), p. 262.

42. NELSON PRICE, in the *New York Times*, 2 July 1933, sec. IX, 5.

43. See, respectively, Dixon Wecter, *The Age of Depression, 1929-1941* (New York: Macmillan, 1948), p. 251; Bowles, *Without Stopping*, p. 193; George Antheil, *Bad Boy of Music* (Garden City, N.Y.: Doubleday, Doran, 1945), p. 277.

44. AARON COPLAND, *The New Music*, rev. ed. (New York: Norton, 1968), p. 160.

45. ARTHUR BERGER, "The Music of Aaron Copland," *The Musical Quarterly* 31 (1945), 424-25. For a more general discussion of the "desertion from the ranks," see Louise Bogan, in *America Now*, p. 57.

46. ANTHEIL, *Bad Boy*, pp. 762-63.

47. SIDNEY ROBERTSON COWELL, "Charles Seeger," *The Musical Quarterly* 65 (1979), 306; Henry Cowell, *American Composers*, p. viii.

48. CHARLES R. HEARN, *The American Dream in the Great Depression* (Westport: Greenwood, 1977), p. 197. See also Leo Gurko, *The Angry Decade* (New York: Dodd, Mead, 1947), pp. 57-66; Louise Bogan, in *America Now*, p. 59; Wecter, *Age of Depression*, pp. 195, 254.

49. SAMUEL LIPMAN, *Music After Modernism* (New York: Basic Books, 1979), p. 73; Bowles, *Without Stopping*, pp. 102, 186, 215; Ewen, *Composers*, p. 82.

50. ELIE SIEGMEISTER, "Three Points of View," *The Musical Quarterly* 65 (1979), 282; Siegmeister, in *The Music Lover's Handbook*, ed. Elie Siegmeister (New York: Morrow, 1943), p. 771.

51. SIEGMEISTER, *Music Lover's Handbook*, p. 772.

52. CHARLES SEEGER, "On Proletarian Music," *Modern Music* 11 (1933-34), 126-27.

53. See, for example, the *New York Times*, 2 October 1933, p. 23; *Modern Music* 11 (1933-34), pp. 41, 93. Volume 11 began with the Nov.-Dec. 1933 issue.

54. OSCAR LEVANT, *The Memoirs of an Amnesiac* (New York: Putnam's, 1965), p. 107; Aaron Copland, "The Composer and His Critic," *Modern Music* 9 (1931-32), 144; Copland, "The Composer in America," *Modern Music* 10 (1932-33), 91; Berger, "The Music of Aaron Copland," p. 423; Berger, *Copland*, p. 14.

55. CHARLES SCHWARTZ, *Gershwin, His Life and Music* (Indianapolis: Bobbs-Merrill, 1973), pp. 266-67; Allen, *Since Yesterday*, p. 44.

56. Moore is quoted in the New York *Herald Tribune*, 17 May 1931, p. 85.

57. VIRGIL THOMSON, *American Music Since 1910* (New York: Holt, Rinehart & Winston, 1971), p. 55; see also Berger, *Copland*, pp. 26-27.

58. ELLIOT FORBES, "The Music of Randall Thompson," *The Musical Quarterly* 35 (1949), 1. Though the quotations come from a talk at Princeton University that he gave in 1946, Thomspon assured the author, who spoke with him a year later, that what he said in 1946 he had also believed in 1932.

59. Thomson, *American Music,* p. 66.

60. PAUL BRODER, *One Hundred Years of Music in America,* ed. Paul Henry Lang (New York: Schirmer, 1961), p. 31.

61. COPLAND, *Music and Imagination,* p. 86.

62. RICHARD SCHICKEL, *The World of Carnegie Hall* (New York: Messner, 1960), p. 319-20.

63. *William Grant Still,* ed. Robert Bartlett Haas (Los Angeles: Black Sparrow, 1972), p. 134.

64. EWEN, *Composers,* p. 538.

65. MARC BLITZSTEIN, "Weill Scores for Johnny Johnson," *Modern Music* 14 (1936-37), 44-45.

66. BERGER, *Copland*, pp. 28-29; see also Julia Smith, *Aaron Copland* (New York: Dutton, 1955), p. 120.

67. ASHLEY PETTIS, "The WPA and the American Composer," *The Musical Quarterly* 26 (1940), 109.

68. BENTON, *Artist*, pp. 314-15.

69. ANTHEIL, *Bad Boy,* p. 295; Ewen, *Composers Since 1900,* pp. 10-11.

70. ROY HARRIS, "Sources of a Musical Culture," *New York Times,* 1 January 1939, sec. IX, 7.

71. Almost a year and a half before, on 29 August 1937, a Harris letter which said the same thing had appeared in the *Times.*

72. See, respectively, *William Grant Still,* ed. Haas, pp. 11, 120; Marc

Blitzstein, "On Writing for the Theatre," *Modern Music* 15 (1937–38), 83; *Music Lover's Handbook*, ed. Siegmeister, pp. 735, 773; Smith, *Copland*, p. 185.

73. COPLAND, *Music and Imagination*, p. 115; Copland, *The New Music*, pp. 136–37.

74. OLIN DOWNES, "Composing to Please the Public," *New York Times*, 27 March 1938, sec. X, 7.

75. HOWARD, *Our Contemporary Composers*, pp. 152–53.

76. *Film Scores*, ed. Tony Thomas (South Brunswick, N.J.: Barnes, 1979), pp. 19–20; Copland, *The New Music*, pp. 161–62; Berger, *Copland*, p. 27.

77. *Music Lover's Handbook*, p. 773.

78. MACHLIS, *American Composers*, p. 94.

79. HARRIS, "Sources," p. 7.

80. VIRGIL THOMSON, review of 21 November 1940, in *Music Reviewed, 1940–1954* (New York: Vintage, 1967), p. 15.

81. BERGER, *Copland*, p. 32.

82. COPLAND, *Music and Imagination*, pp. 20–21, 26.

83. THOMSON, *American Music*, p. 54.

84. ANTHEIL, *Bad Boy*, p. 324.

85. The Carter quotations appeared in *Modern Music* 15 (1937–38); 16 (1938–39); and 17 (1939–40).

86. ALLEN EDWARDS, *Flawed Words and Stubborn Sounds: A Conversation with Elliott Carter* (New York: Norton, 1971), p. 57.

87. RICHARD F. GOLDMAN, "Current Chronicle," *The Musical Quarterly* 36 (1950), 446–47.

88. EWEN, *Composers Since 1900*, p. 21.

89. BARRY ULANOV, *The Two Worlds of American Art* (New York: Macmillan, 1965), pp. 26–28. Ulanov was professor of English at Barnard College and author of books whose subjects range from jazz to Judeo-Christian studies.

90. NED ROREM, in the *New York Times*, Book Review section, 23 May 1982, p. 29.

91. NED ROREM, *Pure Contraption* (New York: Holt, Rinehart & Winston, 1974), pp. 92–93.

2 The Intermediaries Between Composer and Listener (pp. 55-119)

1. MUELLER, *American Symphony Orchestra*, p. 11; Helen Thompson, in *One Hundred Years*, p. 41.

2. HERBERT KUPFERBERG, *Those Fabulous Philadelphians* (New

York: Scribner's, 1969), p. 196; *New York Times*, 21 November 1931, sec. VIII, 8.

3. *Musical America*, 10 January 1939, p. 16; Howard Shanet, *Philharmonic: A History of New York's Orchestra* (Garden City, N.Y.: Doubleday, 1975), pp. 272-73; Moses Smith, *Koussevitzky* (New York: Allen, Towne & Heath, 1947), p. 232.

4. COPLAND, *Music and Imagination*, pp. 65-66.

5. VIRGIL THOMSON, *The Musical Scene* (New York: Greenwood, 1968), p. 31.

6. DUKE, *Passport*, pp. 270-71, 278-79.

7. "Mephisto's Musings," *Musical America*, 25 May 1937, p. 9.

8. HOWARD TAUBMAN, *The Maestro: The Life of Arturo Toscanini* (New York: Simon & Schuster, 1951), pp. 203, 205; Shanet, *Philharmonic*, p. 268.

9. KUPFERBERG, *Those Fabulous Philadelphians*, p. 90; Edward Arian, *Bach, Beethoven, and Bureaucracy: The Case of the Philadelphia Orchestra* (University, Ala.: Univ. of Alabama Press, 1971), p. 14; "Mephisto's Musings," *Musical America*, 25 December 1934, p. 9.

10. *Musical America*, 25 May 1940, p. 29; Smith, *Koussevitzky*, pp. 245-46; Mueller, *American Symphony Orchestra*, p. 362.

11. HALINA RODZINSKI, *Our Two Lives* (New York: Scribner's, 1976), p. 164; Smith, *Koussevitzky*, pp. 251-52.

12. SMITH, *Koussevitzky*, pp. 238-39.

13. LEVANT, *Memoirs*, p. 206; Kupferberg, *Those Fabulous Philadelphians*, pp. 88-89, 93.

14. GEORGE R. MAREK, *Toscanini* (New York: Atheneum, 1975), p. 151.

15. TAUBMAN, *Maestro*, pp. 198-99; Paul Henry Lang, *Music in Western Civilization* (New York: Norton, 1941), p. 1026.

16. SAMUEL CHATZINOFF, *Toscanini* (New York: Knopf, 1956), p. 26.

17. *Musical America*, 25 February 1938, p. 9.

18. *Musical Courier*, 2 November 1929, p. 7.

19. *New York Times*, 1 February 1930, p. 14.

20. *New York Times*, 9 March 1930, sec. X, 9.

21. *New York Times*, 20 April 1930, sec. VIII, 7.

22. OLIN DOWNES, "Barring Applause," the *New York Times*, 21 August 1938, sec. IX, 5.

23. ROY HARRIS, in *The American Composer Speaks*, p. 160; see also Nathan Broder, "American Music and American Orchestras," *The Musical Quarterly* 28 (1942), 490, 493.

24. EDWARD C. POTTER, in the *New York Times*, 14 January 1940, sec. IX, 8; see also Arthur Berger, in *Culture and Commitment, 1929-1945*, ed. Warren Susman (New York: Braziller, 1973), p. 112.

25. Duke, *Passport*, p. 237.

26. Deems Taylor, *Music to My Ears* (New York: Simon & Schuster, 1949), p. 56; Copland, *Music and Imagination*, p. 27; Peter Jona Korn, "The Symphony in America," in *The Symphony* II, ed. Robert Simpson (Baltimore: Penguin, 1967), 243.

27. *New York Times*, 31 January 1932, sec. VIII, 9; 20 October 1932, p. 24.

28. Robert Gelatt, *Music Makers* (1953; reprint, New York: Da Capo, 1972), p. 56.

29. Shanet, *Philharmonic*, pp. 275-76; Taubman, *Maestro*, p. 290; Mueller, *American Symphony Orchestra*, pp. 67-68; Schwartz, *Gershwin*, p. 204.

30. *Musical America*, 10 May 1936, p. 9; Michael Kennedy, *Barbirolli* (London: MacGibbon & Kee, 1971), pp. 111-18, 153-58.

31. Robin Moore, *Fiedler* (Boston: Little, Brown, 1968), p. 114.

32. Mueller, *American Symphony Orchestra*, p. 136. The Stokowski quotation, and several others like it, are found in Leopold Stokowski, *Music for All of Us* (New York: Simon & Schuster, 1943).

33. Rodzinski, *Our Two Lives*, pp. 245-46.

34. Elliott Carter, in *Modern Music* (Jan.-Feb. 1938); *New York Times*, 23 May 1933, p. 22; *Musical America*, 25 January 1935, p. 9; Antheil, *Bad Boy*, p. 276; Thomson, *Virgil Thomson*, p. 276.

35. Edwards, *Flawed Words*, p. 59.

36. Smith, *Copland*, pp. 183-85.

37. Mueller, *American Symphony Orchestra*, pp. 95-96, 122; Aaron Copland, *Copland on Music* (Garden City: Doubleday, 1960), p. 82; Smith, *Koussevitzky*, pp. 269-70, 330-31.

38. Smith, *Koussevitzky*, p. 206.

39. Smith, *Koussevitzky*, pp. 225-26.

40. Thomson, *Music Reviewed*, p. 104.

41. Shanet, *Philharmonic*, p. 273.

42. Thomson, *Music Reviewed*, p. 169.

43. Mueller, *American Symphony Orchestra*, pp. 276-79, 283.

44. Thomson, *Musical Scene*, pp. 15-17.

45. *Musical America*, 25 February 1935, p. 11.

46. Herbert Graf, *Opera for the People* (Minneapolis: Univ. of Minnesota Press, 1951), pp. 68-69, 152-57.

47. Graf, *Opera for the People*, p. 66.

48. Moore, *Fiedler*, p. 118.

49. *Musical America*, 10 February 1934, p. 3.

50. *Musical America*, 10 February 1934, p. 15.

51. Schickel, *Carnegie Hall,* p. 287; Graf, *Opera for the People,* pp. 75–76; *Musical America,* 25 February 1935, p. 17.

52. Mueller, *American Symphony Orchestra,* p. 156.

53. Arian, *Bach,* pp. 51–52, 66–67.

54. *Musical America,* 24 January 1929, p. 38.

55. Kennedy, *Barbirolli,* p. 159.

56. Schickel, *Carnegie,* pp. 325–326.

57. See, for example, Arian, *Bach, Beethoven, and Bureaucracy,* pp. 66–70.

58. Machlis, *American Composers,* pp. 69–70.

59. Sessions, *Musical Experience,* pp. 85–86.

60. Milton Goldin, *The Musical Merchants* (Toronto: Macmillan, 1969), pp. 164–65.

61. Goldin, *Music Merchants,* p. 166.

62. *Musical America,* 10 January 1935, p. 18; 10 January 1940, p. 18.

63. Cecil Smith, *Worlds of Music* (1952; reprint, Westport: Greenwood, 1973), p. 13.

64. *New York Times,* 28 March 1931, p. 7; Smith, *Worlds of Music,* p. 28.

65. Duke, *Passport to Paris,* p. 102.

66. See Smith, *Worlds of Music,* p. 79.

67. Olin Downes, "Toscanini Returns," *New York Times,* 22 November 1931, sec. VIII, 8; Philip Hart, *Orpheus in the New World* (New York: Norton, 1973), pp. 71, 78, 81–82; Goldin, *Music Merchants,* pp. 166, 168–69.

68. Kerr, in *Musical America,* 10 February 1934, p. 8. Also see Dennison Nash, "The Alienated Composer," in *The Arts in Society,* ed. Robert N. Wilson (Englewood Cliffs, N.J.: Prentice-Hall, 1964), pp. 42–44.

69. Bowles, *Without Stopping,* pp. 189–90.

70. Olin Downes, "The Composer's Lot," *New York Times,* 14 March 1937, sec. XI, 5; Arian, *Bach, Beethoven, and Bureaucracy,* p. 109; David Ewen, *Music Comes to America* (New York: Allen, Towne & Heath, 1947), pp. 255–56.

71. Schwartz, *Gershwin,* p. 89.

72. Smith, *Copland,* p. 172; Aaron Copland, "Scores and Records," *Modern Music* 14 (1936–37), 100.

73. Lehman, Engel, *This Bright Day: An Autobiography* (New York: Macmillan, 1974), p. 89.

74. Ewen, *Composers,* pp. 42–43.

75. Marion Bower and Claire R. Reis, "Twenty-Five Years with the League of Composers," *The Musical Quarterly* 34 (1948), 1–3.

76. *Musical America,* September 1933, p. 12; 25 March 1934, p. 4.
77. SMITH, *Copland,* p. 173.
78. *Modern Music* 15 (1938), 92; Thomson, *Virgil Thomson,* p. 278.
79. EMANUEL BALABAN, "Progress at Rochester," *Modern Music* 9 (1931-32), 182; see also Martha Alter, "Howard Hanson," *Modern Music* 18 (1940-41), 84-86; Machlis, *American Composers,* pp. 68-71.
80. KERR, in *Musical America,* 10 February 1934, p. 182.
81. NATHAN BRODER, *Samuel Barber* (New York: Schirmer, 1954), p. 29; see also Ned Rorem, *An Absolute Gift* (New York: Simon & Schuster, 1978, p. 116.
82. SHANET, *Philharmonic,* p. 286.
83. *Musical America,* 25 March 1939, pp. 3-4; 25 April 1939, p. 6; 25 May 1939, p. 3.
84. GELATT, *The Fabulous Phonograph,* 2nd ed. (New York: Macmillan, 1977), p. 189; Colin McPhee, in *Modern Music* 20 (1942-43), 126-27.
85. HUGO FRIEDHOFER, in *Film Score,* p. 66.
86. IRWIN BAZELON, *Knowing the Score* (New York: Van Nostrand Reinhold, 1975), pp. 25, 184.
87. TONY THOMAS, in *Film Score,* p. 127; *Baker's Biographical Dictionary,* 6th ed., rev. Nicolas Slonimsky (New York: Schirmer, 1978), s.v. "Newman, Alfred."
88. TONY THOMAS, in *Film Score,* pp. 15-16.
89. WARREN SLOAT, *1929* (New York: Macmillan, 1979), pp. 103-4.
90. LOUIS R. REID, in *America Now,* p. 6.
91. Ibid., pp. 6, 8.
92. The first quotation is from Allen, *Since Yesterday;* the second, from *Musical America,* 10 January 1938, p. 16.
93. *Musical America,* 10 February 1937, p. 29; *Modern Music* 14 (1936-37), 113-14, 177-78.
94. DAVIDSON TAYLOR, "To Order, for Radio," *Modern Music* 14 (1936-37), 13; Goddard Lieberson, "Over the Air," *Modern Music* 15 (1937-38), 88-89.
95. ROY HARRIS, in *The American Composer Speaks,* p. 154; Carter, *Writings,* pp. 34-35.
96. OLIN DOWNES, in the *New York Times,* 26 February 1939, sec. IX, 7.
97. IRVING KOLODIN, *The Musical Life* (New York: Knopf, 1958), p. 69; Lang, *Music in Western Civilization,* p. 1027.
98. *Musical Courier,* 3 January 1929, p. 10; Aaron Copland, in *Modern Music* 9 (1931-32), 145; Roy Harris, in *The American Composer Speaks,* p. 157.

99. The several reviews are excerpted in *Musical America*, 25 January 1933, p. 21.

100. *Musical America*, 25 October 1933, p. 24.

101. The comments, appearing in *The American Mercury*, were reprinted in the *New York Times*, 23 March 1930, sec. IX, 10. The Nathan statement underlines John A. Kouwenhoven's observation: "Those who might have been expected to help in the exploration of new values too often spent their time ridiculing or denouncing or lamenting what they called America's bourgeois taste;" see *The Arts in Modern American Civilization* (New York: Norton, 1967), p. 201.

102. "Mephisto's Musings," *Musical America*, 25 November 1933, p. 9; Carter, *Writings*, pp. 45-46.

103. COPLAND, *The New Music*, p. 119.

104. *Musical America*, 25 March 1939, pp. 3-4; 25 May 1939, p. 3; Sigmund Spaeth, *At Home with Music* (Garden City, N.Y.: Doubleday, Doran, 1945), pp. 6-8, 265-67.

105. *Musical America*, 10 January 1931, p. 48; 10 November 1933, p. 16.

106. THOMPSON, "Contemporary Scene," p. 16.

107. See, respectively, *Musical America*, 10 October 1935, p. 12; Schwartz, *Gershwin*, pp. 265-66; Nicolas Slonimsky, *A Thing or Two About Music* (1948; reprint, New York: Greenwood, 1972), pp. 213-14; Schickel, *Carnegie Hall*, p. 328.

108. FRANK R. ROSSITER, *Charles Ives and His America* (New York: Liveright, 1975), p. 279.

109. OLIN DOWNES, in the *New York Times*, 8 May 1932, sec. VIII, 6; 20 January 1935, sec. X, 7.

110. THOMSON, *The Musical Scene*, p. xiv.

111. GRACE OVERMYER, *Government and the Arts* (New York: Norton, 1939), pp. 133-34, 185-87.

112. *Musical America*, 10 November 1933, p. 15.

113. *New York Times*, 21 April 1938, p. 17.

114. ENGEL, *This Bright Day*, p. 79.

115. *Musical America*, August 1935, p. 3; Ewen, *Music Comes*, pp. 204-5. The quotations are from Overmyer, *Government and the Arts*, pp. 109, 111.

116. WECTER, *Age of Depression*, p. 266.

117. NIKOLAI SOKOLOFF, in *Musical America*, 10 February 1936, p. 8. See also Moore, *Fiedler*, p. 155; Wecter, *Age of Depression*, p. 224. The Vermont project is described in Luening, *Odyssey*, pp. 380-81.

118. *New York Times*, 25 August 1935, sec. II, 6.

119. Overmyer, *Government and the Arts*, p. 132.
120. Overmyer, *Government and the Arts*, pp. 130-31; Wecter, *Age of Depression*, p. 97; Graf, *Opera for the People*, pp. 64, 67-68.
121. Gurko, *Angry Decade*, pp. 94-96; Overmyer, *Government and the Arts*, p. 112.
122. *New York Times*, 24 April 1938, p. 14.
123. Overmeyer, *Government and the Arts*, pp. 120, 180.
124. Hope Stoddard, *Symphony Conductors of the U.S.A.* (New York: Crowell, 1957), p. 195; *Modern Music* 14 (1936-37), 97.
125. *Musical America*, 10 February 1937, p. 163; see also 25 January 1936, p. 20.
126. Thomson, *Musical Scene*, p. 267.
127. Overmyer, *Government and the Arts*, pp. 112-13, 117-18; Wecter, *Age of Depression*, pp. 266-67.
128. Overmyer, *Government and the Arts*, p. 119.
129. Isadore Fried, "Forum Portraits," *Modern Music* 14 (1936-37), 34.
130. Virgil Thomson, "In the Theater," *Modern Music* 15 (1937-38), 183.
131. Bowles, *Without Stopping*, pp. 192-93; Carter, *Writings*, p. 42.
132. Arthur Cohn, "How News Comes to Philadelphia," *Modern Music* 15 (1937-38), p. 237.
133. Copland, *The New Music*, p. 162.
134. Thomson, *Virgil Thomson*, pp. 259-60, 262, 279-80.
135. Gurko, *Angry Decade*, pp. 96-97.
136. Engel, *This Bright Day*, p. 76.
137. *New York Times*, 23 November 1935, p. 23.
138. *New York Times*, 25 November 1935, p. 23.
139. *New York Times*, 25 October 1936, sec. I, 29.
140. *Musical America*, 10 February 1939, p. 183; 10 February 1940, p. 195; *Modern Music* 17 (1939-40), 67; Ewen, *Music Comes*, pp. 205-8.
141. Engel, *This Bright Day*, p. 76.
142. Moore, *Fiedler*, pp. 154-55.
143. Stoddard, *Symphony Conductors*, pp. 22, 212.

3   The General Audience for Art Music (pp. 121-156)

1. Sessions, *Musical Experience*, pp. 100-101.
2. Ibid., pp. 88-89, 92-93.
3. Copland, *Music and Imagination*, p. 19.
4. Ibid., p. 21.

5. Ibid., p. 26.
6. ROREM, *Absolute Gift,* p. 21.
7. AARON COPLAND, "Modern Music: Fresh and Different," *New York Times,* 13 March 1955, sec. VI, 15.
8. ROREM, *Pure Contraption,* p. 17.
9. A. W. ZELOMEK, *A Changing America* (New York: Wiley, 1959), p. 91.
10. HERBERT GANS, in *The Arts in a Democratic Society,* ed. Dennis Alan Mann (Bowling Green, Ohio: Bowling Green Univ. Popular Press, 1977), p. 149; Sigmund Spaeth, *The Importance of Music* (New York: Fleet, 1963), pp. 15-16.
11. MUELLER, *American Symphony Orchestra,* p. 393; Henry Pleasants, *The Agony of Modern Music* (New York: Simon & Schuster, 1955), p. 10. Richard Dyer, "Berger's Composing Career," *The Boston Globe,* 18 April 1982, sec. B, 5, quotes Arthur Berger as saying of the thirties: "In the early days when I was starting, new music had the intellectual audience. There was a certain cachet to knowing the newest music. A certain snobbism went with it, but it was a small price to pay for the results. . . . New music has always been for a small audience."
12. MADELEINE GOSS, *Modern Music-Makers* (New York: Dutton, 1952), pp. 52-53.
13. BENTON, *Artist in America,* pp. 234-35.
14. Beginning in 1965, the author asked all students taking his course in American music to write a cultural history of their family. Whenever possible, the author interviewed the parent and grandparent generation. The agreement was that he could use the information gained in this way, so long as he did not divulge the names of the contributors. Altogether some 800 reports and recorded interviews were a consequence of this activity. The student's report quoted here and the interview with the father took place in April 1972.
15. Quoted from a report submitted to the author in April 1971.
16. JANE FEUER, "The Theme of Popular vs. Elite Art in the Hollywood Musical," *Journal of Popular Culture* 13 (1978), 194.
17. *Musical America,* 10 May 1935, p. 16; Lawrence Tibbett, in *Musical America,* 10 October 1934, p. 12; Graf, *Opera for the People,* p. 19; Deems Taylor, *Of Men and Music* (New York: Simon & Schuster, 1945), pp. 207-8.
18. MUELLER, *American Symphony Orchestra,* pp. 339-41; see also Pleasants, *Agony of Modern Music,* p. 5.
19. EUGENE GOOSSENS, "The Public—Has It Changed?" *Modern Music* 20 (1942-43), 71-77.

20. Thomson, *Musical Scene*, p. xiii.

21. These arguments for and against the general public and its musicality were aired continually in *Modern Music* and in the Sunday edition of the *New York Times* all through the thirties.

22. Engel, *This Bright Day*, p. 44; Antheil, *Bad Boy*, p. 277; Olin Downes, in the *New York Times*, 7 August 1938, sec. IX, 5.

23. Levant, *Memoirs*, p. 221.

24. *William Grant Still*, ed. Haas, pp. 118–19.

25. Carol J. Oja, "The Copland-Sessions Concerts and Their Reception in the Contemporary Press," *The Musical Quarterly* 65 (1979), 224; Berger, *Copland*, p. 44.

26. Duke, *Passport*, p. 89.

27. Benton, *Artist*, p. 242.

28. Kolodin, *Musical*, p. 87; Virgil Thomson, "In the Theatre," *Modern Music* 15 (1937–38), 113.

29. Studs Terkel, *Hard Times* (New York: Pantheon, 1970), pp. 366–67.

30. Reis, *Composers, Conductors and Critics*, p. 3; Olin Downes, in the *New York Times*, 21 February 1934.

31. Olin Downes, in the *New York Times*, 25 February 1939, p. 270.

32. Howard, *Our Contemporary Composers*, p. 133.

33. The incident is described in Paul Bowles, *Without Stopping: An Autobiography*, published by Putnam, in 1972.

34. Mueller, *American Symphony Orchestra*, pp. 289–90.

35. *Musical Courier*, 3 January 1929, p. 10.

36. *New York Times*, 6 January 1929, sec. III, 1.

37. *New York Times*, 15 February 1929, p. 27.

38. Allen, *Since Yesterday*, pp. 268–70.

39. *New York Times*, 5 February 1933, sec. IX, 8; 8 November 1931, sec. VIII, 10, respectively.

40. Warren Susman, in *Culture and Commitment*, pp. 20–21.

41. Dennis Alan Mann, "Why Be Original when You Can Be Good?" *Journal of American Culture* 1 (1978), 219; Fred E. H. Schroeder, "The Discovery of Popular Culture Before Printing," *Journal of Popular Culture* 11 (1977), 632–33; Kouwenhoven, *Arts*, p. 197.

42. Carter, *Writings*, p. 28.

43. C. W. Valentine, *The Experimental Psychology of Beauty* (London: Methuen, 1962), pp. 201, 229–32.

44. Mueller, *American Symphony Orchestra*, pp. 388–89.

45. Valentine, *Experimental Psychology of Beauty*, p. 213.

46. The author was the second violinist.

47. "The Lewisohn Stadium Concerts," *New York Times*, 21 August 1932, sec. IX, 4.

48. KUPFERBERG, *Philadelphia,* p. 191.
49. GOOSSENS, "The Public," p. 76.
50. Concerning this point, see Valentine, *Experimental Psychology of Beauty,* p. 252.
51. This statement is not meant to indicate that such modern works might be found lacking in excellence by a small, sophisticated group; simply that they failed to please the much larger public.
52. GRAF, *Opera for the People,* p. 13.
53. CHARLES REPPER, "Only a Composer," *Musical America,* 10 February 1936, p. 6; Ulanov, *Two,* pp. 16-17.
54. THOMSON, *Musical Scene,* p. xiii.
55. ALEXANDER SMALLENS, in *Modern Music* 8, No. 1 (1930-1931), 40; Ulanov, *Two Worlds,* pp. 18-19; Reis, *Composers, Conductors and Critics,* pp. 50-51; Taylor, *Of Men,* p. 134; Olin Downes, in the *New York Times,* 6 October 1935, sec. X, 7.
56. See Oscar Handlin, *The American People* (Boston: Beacon, 1963), pp. 146-47; Schickel, *Carnegie Hall,* pp. 282-83.
57. TAYLOR, *Music,* pp. 264, 269.
58. *New York Times,* 28 April 1935, sec. X, 6.
59. *New York Times,* 4 February 1940, sec. IX, 8.
60. THOMSON, *Music Reviewed,* pp. 320-21.
61. ALFRED FRANKENSTEIN, "How to Make Friends by Radio," *Modern Music* 21 (1943-44), 6-9.
62. *Musical America,* 10 March 1935, p. 12; see also Hugo Leichtentritt, *Serge Koussevitzky* (Cambridge: Harvard Univ. Press, 1946), p. 19. Margie McLeod reports on a reaction similar to that in Boston, when Stock conducted the work in Chicago—see *Musical America,* 10 February 1934, p. 117.
63. *New York Times,* 11 August 1935, sec. IX, 4.

4   Music of Two Decades (pp. 157-211)

1. See Virgil Thomson, *Music Right and Left* (1951; reprint, New York: Greenwood, 1969), p. 188.
2. LIPMAN, *Music After Modernism,* p. viii; Nicolas Nabokov, Introduction to *American Music,* by Virgil Thomson, pp. xi, xiv-xv.
3. ELIE SIEGMEISTER, "Three Points of View," *The Musical Quarterly* 65 (1979), 282.
4. CHARLES SEEGER, in *American Composers,* ed. Cowell, pp. 23-24, 27-28; Seeger, "Ruggles," pp. 584-85, 587.
5. NICOLAS SLONIMSKY, in *Modern Music* 7, No. 2 (1929-30), p. 26; Lazare Saminsky, in *Modern Music* 9 (1931-32), 39.

6. *Musical America*, 10 April 1936, p. 14.
7. SEEGER, "Ruggles," p. 584.
8. EDWARDS, *Flawed Words*, pp. 32–33.
9. PAUL ROSENFELD, *By Way of Art* (1928; reprint, Freeport: Books for Libraries, 1967), pp. 74, 76.
10. OSCAR THOMPSON, in *Modern Music* 6, no. 4 (1928–29), p. 23; Richard Franko Goldman, "The Music of Wallingford Riegger," *The Musical Quarterly* 36 (1950), 43–44; Richard Franko Goldman, "Wallingford Riegger," *HiFi/Stereo Review* (April 1968), pp. 60–61; Ewen, *Twentieth-Century Music*, pp. 656–57.
11. GOLDMAN, "Music of Wallingford Riegger," p. 47; Goldman, "Wallingford Riegger," p. 61.
12. See *Modern Music* 10 (1932–33), 112.
13. See *Modern Music* 17 (1939–40), 192.
14. RAY BROWN, in *Modern Music* 21 (1943–44), 257.
15. *Musical America*, 25 January 1936, pp. 26, 28.
16. ROY D. WELCH, "A Symphony Introduces Roger Sessions," *Modern Music* 4, No. 4 (1926–27), 27–29.
17. LAZARE SAMINSKY, "The Work of Roger Sessions," *Modern Music* 13, no. 2 (1935–36), 40.
18. ROSENFELD, *Discoveries*, p. 357; Carter, *Writings*, pp. 70–71.
19. RANDALL THOMPSON, "Jacobi's Quartet and Sessions' Sonata," *Modern Music* 12 (1934–35), 137–38.
20. EDWARD T. CONE, "Roger Sessions' String Quartet," *Modern Music* 18 (1940–41), 59, 61, 63.
21. AARON COPLAND, "Scores and Records," *Modern Music* 15 (1937–38), 244–45.
22. THOMSON, *Music Reviewed*, p. 211.
23. HOWARD, *Our Contemporary Composers*, p. 159.
24. Concerning these points, see Copland, *The New Music*, pp. 131–33; Elliott Carter, "Walter Piston," *The Musical Quarterly* 32 (1946), 356, 361–62.
25. SMITH, *Copland*, pp. 119, 160.
26. *Modern Music* 16 (1938–39), 262.
27. *Modern Music* 9 (1931–32), 92–93.
28. *Modern Music* 8, no. 2 (1930–31), 41–42.
29. HUGO WEISGALL, "The Music of Henry Cowell," *The Musical Quarterly* 45 (1959), 492.
30. ABRAM CHASINS, *Music at the Crossroads* (New York: Macmillan, 1972), pp. 185–86.
31. WILFRED MELLERS, *Music in a New Found Land* (New York: Knopf, 1965), p. 66.

32. ROBERT SABIN, "Twentieth-Century Americans," *Choral Music*, ed. Arthur Jacobs (Baltimore: Penguin, 1963), pp. 373–74.
33. LEICHTENTRITT, *Koussevitzky*, p. 40; Machlis, *American Composers*, p. 72.
34. COLIN MCPHEE, in *Modern Music* 17 (1939–40), 260; Virgil Thomson, *The Art of Judging Music* (1948; reprint, New York: Greenwood, 1969), p. 151.
35. EWEN, *Composers Since 1900*, p. 259.
36. The 25 February 1934 issue of *Musical America* examines the several criticisms of the opera.
37. DONALD JAY GROUT, *A Short History of Opera* (New York: Columbia Univ. Press, 1947), p. 504.
38. THOMSON, *American Music*, p. 121.
39. BRODER, *Samuel Barber*, p. 58.
40. See Walter Simmons's review of a recording of Barber's Essay No. 3, in *Fanfare* (May–June 1981), p. 49.
41. BRODER, *Samuel Barber*, p. 44.
42. JOHN GRUEN, *Menotti* (New York: Macmillan, 1978), pp. 38–39.
43. See *Fanfare* (May–June 1981), pp. 49–50.
44. COWELL, "Paul Creston," pp. 533, 539–40.
45. *Musical Courier*, 15 November 1956, pp. 9–10.
46. *Modern Music*, 3, no. 4 (1925–26), 7.
47. *Modern Music* 4, no. 4, 35–37; and *Modern Music* 10 (1932–33), 101.
48. *Modern Music* 9 (1931–32), 67.
49. *Modern Music* 9 (1931–32), 5.
50. See the review of Olin Downes, in the *New York Times*, 8 January 1933; also see *Musical America*, 25 January 1933, pp. 16, 29; and *Modern Music* 10 (1932–33), 7.
51. VIRGIL THOMSON'S *American Music Since 1910* (New York, 1971) says not one word about Gruenberg and his considerable contributions to American musical culture.
52. SCHWARTZ, *Gershwin*, pp. 132–33; Rosenfeld, *Discoveries*, p. 264.
53. THOMSON, *American Music*, p. 146.
54. SCHWARTZ, *Gershwin*, p. 164.
55. SYDNEY FINKELSTEIN, *Composer and Nation* (New York: International, 1960), p. 312.
56. OCTAVIA HENSEL, *Life and Letters of Louis Moreau Gottschalk* (Boston: Ditson, 1970), p. 209.
57. NICOLAS NABOKOV, Introduction to *American Music*, by Virgil Thomson, p. xii.
58. COPLAND, *Music and Imagination*, p. 110.

59. Thomson, *American Music*, p. 55.
60. Paul Rosenfeld, "'Americanism' in American Music," *Modern Music* 17 (1939-40), 231-32.
61. Copland, *Music and Imagination*, pp. 100-101.
62. Both quotations are from the jacket notes, written by Otto Luening for a recording of the opera (Desto DST 6450).
63. *William Grant Still*, ed. Haas, p. 713; Albert Goldberg, in *Musical America*, 10 February 1937, p. 201; Finkelstein, *Composer*, p. 317.
64. See Eileen Southern, *The Music of Black Americans* (New York: Norton, 1971), pp. 454-62.
65. Howard, *Our Contemporary Composers*, pp. 109-110; Copland, *Copland on Music*, pp. 155-56.
66. See also reports on later performances, in *Musical America*, 25 October 1939, p. 7; 25 January 1940, p. 21.
67. Thomson, *Judging Music*, p. 77.
68. See Forbes, "The Music of Randall Thompson," *The Musical Quarterly* 35 (1949), 1-25, for a fuller discussion of these works.
69. Peggy Glanville-Hicks, "Virgil Thomson," *The Musical Quarterly* 35 (1949), 214-15.
70. Jane Hobhouse, *Everybody Who Was Anybody: A Biography of Gertrude Stein* (New York: Putnam's, 1975), pp. 142-43.
71. For a discussion of Thomson's operas, see Victor Fell Yellin, "The Operas of Virgil Thomson," in Thomson, *American Music*, pp. 91-109.
72. Carter, *Writings*, p. 26; see also Thomson *Virgil Thomson*, p. 275.
73. *Musical America*, 10 February 1934, p. 102; Theodore Chanler, in *Modern Music* 11 (1933-34), 142-43.
74. *Musical America*, 10 November 1935, p. 9.
75. Charles Seeger, in *Modern Music* 17 (1939-40), 252.
76. Thomson, *Music Reviewed*, pp. 15-16.
77. Copland, *The New Music*, pp. 122-23.
78. *Musical America*, 25 February 1937, p. 26; Goddard Lieberson, in *Modern Music* 14 (1936-37), 155; Howard, *Our Contemporary Composers*, p. 143.
79. *Olin Downes on Music*, pp. 282-83; Leichtentritt, *Koussevitzky*, p. 232; Copland, *The New Music*, p. 124; Thomson, *Musical Scene*, pp. 123-24; Carter, *Writings*, p. 69; Colin McPhee, in *Modern Music* 17 (1939-40), 260.
80. Thomson, *American Music*, p. 53.
81. Elie Siegmeister, "Three Points of View," pp. 282-83.
82. Thomson, *American Music*, pp. 55-56; Berger, *Copland*, pp. 57, 65, 70; Lipman, *Music After Modernism*, pp. 70-71.
83. Lipman, *Music After Modernism*, p. 71.

84. SMITH, *Copland*, pp. 165-66, 169.
85. SMITH, *Copland*, pp. 174-75; Berger, *Copland*, p. 30; Carter, *Writings*, p. 46.
86. See Colin McPhee, in *Modern Music* 19 (1941-42), 48; Smith, *Copland*, pp. 88-90.
87. EDWARD DENBY, in *Modern Music* 19 (1941-42), 53-54; Smith, *Copland*, pp. 191-93.
88. *Culture and Commitment*, ed. Susman, p. 22. Also see Thomson, *Music Reviewed*, p. 152; S. L. M. Barlow, in *Modern Music* 21 (1943-44), 42.
89. THOMAS, in *Film Score*, pp. 16-17, 21-22.
90. THOMSON, *Music Right and Left*, pp. 74-75.

5 Lessons from Experience (pp. 213-225)

1. JOSEPH WOOD KRUTCH, *The Measure of Man* (New York: Grosset & Dunlap, 1954), p. 237.
2. WALTER SIMMONS, "Contemporary Music," *Fanfare* (May/June 1981), pp. 22-23.
3. For more on the obligations of the artist, see Trevor Wishart, in John Shepherd et al., *Whose Music?* (London: Latimer, 1977), p. 238; Nabakov, Introduction to *American Music*, by Virgil Thomson, p. xv.
4. ROBERT SCHUMANN, *On Music and Musicians*, ed. Konrad Wolff, trans. Paul Resenfeld (New York: McGraw-Hill, 1964), p. 33.
5. ALAN P. MERRIAM, *The Anthropology of Music* (Evanston: Northwestern Univ. Press, 1964), pp. 6, 13, 15.
6. Ibid., pp. 261-62.
7. Ibid., p. 30.
8. EDWARD T. CONE, "Conversations with Aaron Copland," *Perspectives on American Composers*, ed. Benjamin Boretz and Edward T. Cone (New York: Norton, 1971), p. 144.
9. MERRIAM, *Anthropology of Music*, p. 27.
10. *The Music Journal* (March-April 1948), p. 11.
11. HART, *Orpheus*, p. 422.
12. MERRIAM, *Anthropology of Music*, p. 10.
13. Ibid., pp. 219, 223-26.
14. WINTHROP SARGEANT, in *The New Yorker* (23 February 1957), p. 108.
15. ARIAN, *Bach*, pp. 123-27.
16. HOWARD HANSON, in *The Music Journal* (May-June 1948), p. 40.

A Selective
Bibliography Of
Works Consulted

ALLEN, FREDERICK LEWIS. *Since Yesterday.* New York: Harper, 1940.
ALLEN, WARREN DWIGHT. *Philosophies of Music History.* 1939. Reprint. New York: Dover, 1962.
America Now, ed. Harold E. Stearns. New York: Literary Guild, 1938.
American Composers on American Music, ed. Henry Cowell. New York: Ungar, 1962. The book was first published in 1933.
The American Composer Speaks, ed. Gilbert Chase. Baton Rouge: Louisiana State Univ. Press, 1966.
The American Imagination, from the *Times Literary Supplement,* intro. Alan Pryce-Jones. New York: Atheneum, 1960.
ANTHEIL, GEORGE. *Bad Boy of Music.* Garden City N.Y.: Doubleday, Doran, 1945.
An Anthology of Music Criticism. History of Music in San Francisco 7. No. Cal. Writer's Project, WPA. 1942. Reprint. New York: AMS, 1972.
ARDION, JOHN. "Samuel Barber at Capricorn." *Musical America,* March 1960, pp. 4-5, 46.
ARIAN, EDWARD. *Bach, Beethoven, and Bureaucracy: The Case of the Philadelphia Orchestra.* University: Univ. of Alabama Press, 1971.
The Arts in a Democratic Society, ed. Demus Alan Mann. Bowling Green, Ohio: Bowling Green State Univ. Popular Press, 1977.
The Arts in Society, ed. Robert N. Wilson. Englewood Cliffs, N.J.: Prentice-Hall, 1964.
AUSTEN, WILLIAM W. *Music in the 20th Century.* New York: Norton, 1966.
Baker's Biographical Dictionary of Musicians, 6th ed., rev. Nicolas Slonimsky. New York: Schirmer, 1978.

BARZUN, JACQUES, "Artist Against Society." *Partisan Review* 19 (1952), 60–77.

BARZUN, JACQUES. *Classic, Romantic, and Modern.* Boston: Little, Brown, 1961.

BARZUN, JACQUES. *Music in American Life.* Garden City, N.Y.: Doubleday, 1956.

BAUER, MARION. "Have We an American Music?" *Musical America,* 10 February 1940, pp. 22, 271–72.

BAUER, MARION. *Twentieth-Century Music.* New York: Putnam's Sons, 1933.

BAUER, MARION, and CLAIRE R. REIS. "Twenty-Five Years with the League of Composers." *Musical Quarterly* 34 (1948), 1–14.

BAZELON, IRWIN. *Knowing the Score.* New York: Van Nostrand Reinhold, 1975.

BENTON, THOMAS HART. *An Artist in America,* 3rd rev. ed. Columbia: Univ. of Missouri Press, 1968.

BERGER, ARTHUR. *Aaron Copland.* New York: Oxford Univ. Press, 1953.

BERGER, ARTHUR. "The Music of Aaron Copland." *Musical Quarterly* 31 (1945), 420–47.

BORETZ, BENJAMIN. "Current Chronicle; United States, Evanston, Ill." *Musical Quarterly* 47 (1961), 386–96.

BOWLES, PAUL. *Without Stopping: An Autobiography.* New York: Putnam's Sons, 1972.

BRODER, NATHAN. "American Music and American Orchestras." *Musical Quarterly* 28 (1942), 488–93.

BRODER, NATHAN. *Samuel Barber.* New York: Schirmer, 1954.

CARTER, ELLIOTT. "Walter Piston." *Musical Quarterly* 32 (1946), 354–73.

[Carter, Elliott]. *The Writings of Elliott Carter.* Bloomington: Indiana Univ. Press, 1977.

CHASE, GILBERT. *America's Music,* 2nd ed. New York: McGraw-Hill, 1966.

CHASINS, ABRAM. *Leopold Stokowski.* New York: Hawthorn, 1979.

CHASINS, ABRAM. *Music at the Crossroads.* New York: Macmillan, 1972.

CHAVEZ, CARLOS. *Musical Thought.* Cambridge: Harvard Univ. Press, 1961.

CHESLOCK, LOUIS. *H. L. Mencken on Music.* New York: Knopf, 1961.

CHOTZINOFF, SAMUEL. *Toscanini.* New York: Knopf, 1956.

CLURMAN, HAROLD. *The Fervent Years.* New York: Knopf, 1945.

COEUROY, ANDRE. "The Cure of Literature." *Musical Quarterly* 2 (1925), 3–6.

CONE, EDWARD T. "Conversations with Aaron Copland." *Perspectives of New Music,* Spring–Summer 1968, pp. 57-72.

COPLAND, AARON. *Copland on Music.* Garden City, N.Y.: Doubleday, 1960.

COPLAND, AARON. "Modern Music: 'Fresh and Different'." *New York Times,* 13 March 1955, sec. VI, 60, 62.

COPLAND, AARON. *Music and Imagination.* New York: New American Library, 1959.

COPLAND, AARON. *The New Music,* rev. ed. New York: Norton, 1968.

COWELL, HENRY. "Paul Creston." *Musical Quarterly* 34 (1948), 533–43.

Culture and Commitment, 1929–1945, ed. Warren Susman. New York: Braziller, 1973.

Culture for the Millions, ed. Norman Jacobs. Boston: Beacon, 1964.

DORIAN, FREDERICK. *Commitment to Culture.* Pittsburgh: Univ. of Pittsburgh Press, 1964.

DOWNES, OLIN. "The American Talent." *New York Times,* 24 February 1929, sec. IX, 9.

[Downes, Olin]. *Olin Downes on Music,* ed. Irene Downes. New York: Simon & Schuster, 1957.

DOWNES, OLIN. "Slashing Attack." *New York Times,* 20 March 1955, sec. II, 7.

DUKE, VERNON. *Listen Here!* New York: Obolensky, 1963.

DUKE, VERNON. *Passport to Paris.* Boston: Little, Brown, 1955.

EATON, FRANCES QUAINTANCE. "Paul Creston." *Musical America,* October 1944, pp. 7, 25.

EDWARDS, ALLEN. *Flawed Words and Stubborn Sounds: A Conversation with Elliott Carter.* New York: Norton, 1971.

ENGEL, LEHMAN. *This Bright Day: An Autobiography.* New York: Macmillan, 1974.

EVANS, MARK. *Soundtrack: The Music of the Movies.* New York: Hopkinson & Blake, 1975.

EWEN, DAVID. *Composers Since 1900.* New York: Wilson, 1969.

EWEN, DAVID. *Music Comes to America.* New York: Allen, Towne & Heath, 1947.

EWEN, DAVID. *The World of Twentieth-Century Music.* Englewood Cliffs, N.J.: Prentice-Hall, 1968.

FARWELL, ARTHUR. "Roy Harris." *Musical Quarterly* 18 (1932), 18–32.

Film Score, ed. Tony Thomas. South Brunswick N.J.: Barnes, 1979.

FINKELSTEIN, SYDNEY. *Composer and Nation.* New York: International, 1960.

FORBES, ELLIOT. "The Music of Randall Thompson." *Musical Quarterly* 35 (1949), 1–25.

FRIED, ALEXANDER. "For the People." *Musical Quarterly* 4 (1927), 33–37.

FRIED, ALEXANDER. "The Prestige of Good Music." *Musical Quarterly* 5 (1928), 29–32.

GARDNER, JOHN W. *Excellence.* New York: Harper & Row, 1971.

GELATT, ROLAND. *The Fabulous Phonograph,* 2nd rev. ed. New York: Macmillan, 1977.

GELATT, ROLAND. *Music Makers.* 1953. Reprint. New York: Da Capo, 1972.

GLANVILLE-HICKS, PEGGY. "Virgil Thomson." *Musical Quarterly* 35 (1949), 209–25.

GOLDIN, MILTON. *The Music Merchants.* Toronto: Macmillan, 1969.

GOLDMAN, RICHARD FRANKO. "Aaron Copland." *Musical Quarterly* 47 (1961), 1–3.

GOLDMAN, RICHARD FRANKO. "The Music of Wallingford Riegger." *Musical Quarterly* 36 (1950), 39–61.

GOLDMAN, RICHARD FRANKO. "Wallingford Riegger." *HiFi/Stereo Review,* April 1968, pp. 57–67.

GOOSSENS, EUGENE. "The Public—Has It Changed?" *Modern Music* 20 (1942–43), 71–77.

GOSS, MADELEINE. *Modern Music-Makers: Contemporary American Composers.* New York: Dutton, 1952.

GOTTSCHALK, LOUIS MOREAU. *Notes of a Pianist,* ed. Jeanne Behrend. New York: Knopf, 1964.

GRAF, HERBERT. *Opera for the People.* Minneapolis: Univ. of Minnesota Press, 1951.

GROUT, DONALD JAY. *A Short History of Opera.* New York: Columbia Univ. Press, 1947.

GRUEN, JOHN. *Menotti.* New York: Macmillan, 1978.

GURKO, LEO. *The Angry Decade.* New York: Dodd, Mead, 1947.

HAAS, ROBERT BARTLETT, ed. *William Grant Still.* Los Angeles: Black Sparrow, 1972.

HANDLIN, OSCAR. *The American People.* Boston: Beacon, 1963.

HARRIS, ROY. "Sources of a Musical Culture." *New York Times,* 1 January 1939, sec. IX, 7–8.

HARRISON, LOU. *About Carl Ruggles.* Yonkers, N.Y.: Bardiansky, 1946.

HART, PHILIP. *Orpheus in the New World.* New York: Norton, 1973.

HEARN, CHARLES R. *The American Dream in the Great Depression.* Westport, Conn.: Greenwood, 1977.

HENDERSON, W. J. "Is Romantic Music Dead?" *Musical America,* 10 February 1936, pp. 5, 196.

HENDERSON, WILLIAM. "Modern Homage to Doctrine." *Musical Quarterly* 1 (1925), 8–11.

HITCHCOCK, H. WILEY. *Music in the United States,* 2nd ed. Englewood Cliffs, N.J.: Prentice-Hall, 1974.

HOBHOUSE, JANE. *Everybody Who Was Anybody: A Biography of Gertrude Stein*. New York: Putnam's Sons, 1975.

[Honigsheim, Paul]. *Music and Society: The Late Writings of Paul Honigsheim*, ed. K. Peter Etzkorn. New York: Wiley, 1973.

HOOVER, KATHLEEN, and JOHN CAGE. *Virgil Thomson*. New York: Yoseloff, 1959.

HORAN, ROBERT. "Samuel Barber." *Modern Music* 20 (1942-43), 161-69.

HOWARD, JOHN TASKER. *Deems Taylor*. New York: J. Fischer, 1940.

HOWARD, JOHN TASKER, with the assistance of Arthur Mendel. *Our Contemporary Composers*. New York: Crowell, 1941.

HUGHES, CHARLES W. *The Human Side of Music*. New York: Philosophical Library, 1948.

JABLONSKI, EDWARD, and LAWRENCE D. STEWART. *The Gershwin Years*. Garden City, N.Y.: Doubleday, 1973.

JACOBS, ARTHUR. *A Short History of Western Music*. Baltimore: Penguin, 1972.

KAVOLIS, VYTAUTAS. *Artistic Expression—A Sociological Analysis*. Ithaca, N.Y.: Cornell Univ. Press, 1968.

KAVOLIS, VYTAUTAS. *History on Art's Side*. Ithaca, N.Y.: Cornell Univ. Press, 1972.

KAZIN, ALFRED. *On Native Grounds*. New York: Harcourt, Brace & World, 1942.

KENNEDY, MICHAEL. *Barbirolli*. London: MacGibbon & Kee, 1971.

KERR, HARRISON. "The Composer's Lot Is Not a Happy One." *Musical America*, 10 February 1934, pp. 8, 182.

KIRKPATRICK, JOHN. "Aaron Copland's Piano Sonata." *Modern Music* 19 (1941-42), 246-50.

KOLODIN, IRVING. *The Musical Life*. New York: Knopf, 1958.

KORN, PETER JONA. "The Symphony in America." *The Symphony*, vol. 2, ed. Robert Simpson. Baltimore: Penguin, 1967, pp. 243-67.

KOUWENHOVEN, JOHN A. *The Arts in Modern American Civilization*. New York: Norton, 1967.

KRENEK, ERNST. *Exploring Music*. New York: October House, 1966.

KRONENBERGER, LOUIS. *Company Manners: A Cultural Inquiry into American Life*. Indianapolis: Bobbs-Merrill, 1954.

KUPFERBERG, HERBERT. *Those Fabulous Philadelphians*. New York: Scribner's Sons, 1969.

LAMBERT, CONSTANT. *Music Ho!* New York: October House, 1967.

LANG, PAUL HENRY. *Music in Western Civilization*. New York: Norton, 1941.

LEICHTENTRITT, HUGO. *Serge Koussevitzky*. Cambridge: Harvard Univ. Press, 1946.

LEVANT, OSCAR. *The Memoirs of an Amnesiac*. New York: Putnam's Sons, 1965.

LEVANT, OSCAR. *The Unimportance of Being Oscar*. New York: Putnam's Sons, 1968.

LEWIS, GEORGE H. "Between Consciousness and Existence." *Journal of Popular Culture* 15 (1982), 81-92.

LIPMAN, SAMUEL. *Music After Modernism*. New York: Basic Books, 1979.

LOURIE, ARTHUR. "Neogothic and Neoclassic." *Modern Music* 5, no. 3. (1927-28), 3-8.

LUENING, OTTO. *The Odyssey of an American Composer*. New York: Scribner's Sons, 1980.

LUKACS, JOHN. *The Passing of the Modern Age*. New York: Harper & Row, 1970.

MACHLIS, JOSEPH. *American Composers of Our Time*. New York: Crowell, 1963.

MCMULLEN, ROY. *Art, Affluence, and Alienation*. New York: Praeger, 1968.

MAREK, GEORGE R. *Toscanini*. New York: Atheneum, 1975.

MASON, DANIEL GREGORY. *Tune In, America*. 1931. Reprint. Freeport, N.Y.: Books for Libraries, 1969.

MELLERS, WILFRID. *Music in a New Found Land*. New York: Knopf, 1965.

MERRIAM, ALAN P. *The Anthropology of Music*. Evanston, Ill.: Northwestern Univ. Press, 1964.

MOORE, ROBIN. *Fiedler*. Boston: Little, Brown, 1968.

MUELLER, JOHN H. *The American Symphony Orchestra*. Bloomington: Indiana Univ. Press, 1951.

The Music Lover's Handbook, ed. Elie Siegmeister. New York: Morrow, 1943.

The New Book of Modern Composers, 3rd ed., ed. David Ewen. New York: Knopf, 1961.

OJA, CAROL J. "The Copland-Sessions Concerts and Their Reception in the Contemporary Press." *Musical Quarterly* 65 (1979), 212-29.

One Hundred Years of Music in America, ed. Paul Henry Lang. New York: Schirmer, 1961.

The Orchestral Composer's Point of View, ed. Robert Stephen Hines. Norman: Univ. of Oklahoma Press, 1970.

OVERMYER, GRACE. *Government and the Arts*. New York: Norton, 1939.

Perspectives on American Composers, ed. Benjamin Boretz, and Edward T. Cone. New York: Norton, 1971.

PETTIS, ASHLEY. "The WPA and the American Composer." *Musical Quarterly* 26 (1940), 101-12.

PEYSER, JOAN. *The New Music*. New York: Delacorte, 1970.

PLEASANTS, HENRY. *The Agony of Modern Music*. New York: Simon & Schuster, 1955.

PLEASANTS, HENRY. "Modern Music: 'A Dead Art'." *New York Times,* 13 March 1955, sec. VI, 14, 57, 62.

PLEASANTS, HENRY. *Serious Music—and All That Jazz!* New York: Simon & Schuster, 1969.

POLLACK, HOWARD. *Walter Piston.* Ann Arbor, Mich.: UMI Research Press, 1981.

Problems of Modern Music, ed. Paul Henry Lang. New York: Norton, 1962.

RAYNOR, HENRY. *Music and Society Since 1815.* New York: Schocken, 1976.

REIS, CLAIRE R. *Composers, Conductors, and Critics.* New York: Oxford Univ. Press, 1955.

REIS, CLAIRE R. *Composers in America.* New York: Macmillan, 1947.

REPPER, CHARLES. "Only a Composer." *Musical America,* 10 February 1936, pp. 6, 197.

RODZINSKI, HALINA. *Our Two Lives.* New York: Scribner's Sons, 1976.

ROREM, NED. *An Absolute Gift.* New York: Simon & Schuster, 1978.

ROREM, NED. *Critical Affairs, A Composer's Journal.* New York: Braziller, 1970.

ROREM, NED. *The Paris Diary.* New York: Braziller, 1960.

ROREM, NED. *Pure Contraption.* New York: Holt, Rinehart & Winston, 1974.

ROSENFELD, PAUL. *By Way of Art.* 1928. reprint. Freeport, N.Y.: Books for Libraries, 1967.

ROSENFELD, PAUL. *Discoveries of a Music Critic.* 1936. Reprint. New York: Vienna House, 1972.

[Rosenfeld, Paul]. *Musical Impressions: Selections from Paul Rosenfeld's Criticisms,* ed. Herbert A. Leibowitz. New York: Hill & Wang, 1969.

ROSSITER, FRANK R. *Charles Ives and His America.* New York: Liveright, 1975.

ROTHSTEIN, EDWARD. "Why We Live in the Musical Past." *New York Times,* 11 April 1982, sec. II, 1, 26.

ROUSSEL, HERBERT. *The Houston Symphony Orchestra, 1913-71.* Austin: Univ. of Texas Press, 1972.

SABIN, ROBERT. "Twentieth Century Americans," in *Choral Music,* ed. Arthur Jacobs. Baltimore: Penguin, 1963, pp. 370-86.

SABLOSKY, IRVING. *American Music.* Chicago: Univ. of Chicago Press, 1969.

SACHS, CURT. *The Wellsprings of Music,* ed. Jaap Kunst. New York: McGraw-Hill, 1965.

SANDERS, RONALD. *The Days Grow Short: The Life and Music of Kurt Weill.* New York: Holt, Rinehart & Winston, 1980.

SARGEANT, WINTHROP. *Geniuses, Goddesses, and People.* New York: Dutton, 1949.

SCHICKEL, RICHARD. *The World of Carnegie Hall.* New York: Messner, 1960.

SCHUBART, MARK A. "Roger Sessions: Portrait of an American Composer." *Musical Quarterly* 32 (1946), 196-214.

SCHWARTZ, CHARLES. *Gershwin, His Life and Music.* Indianapolis: Bobbs-Merrill, 1973.

SEEGER, CHARLES. "Carl Ruggles." *Musical Quarterly* 18 (1932), 578-92.

SESSIONS, ROGER. "Music in Crisis." *Modern Music* 10 (1932-33), 63-78.

SESSIONS, ROGER. *The Musical Experience.* 1950. Reprint. New York: Atheneum, 1965.

SESSIONS, ROGER. *Questions About Music.* Cambridge: Harvard Univ. Press, 1970.

SHANET, HOWARD. *Philharmonic: A History of New York's Orchestra.* Garden City, N.Y.: Doubleday, 1975.

SHEPHERD, JOHN, and PHIL VIRDEN, GRAHAM VULLIAMY, and TREVOR WISHART. *Whose Music?* London: Latimer, 1977.

SHERMAN, JOHN K. *Music and Maestros: The Story of the Minneapolis Symphony Orchestra.* Minneapolis: Univ. of Minnesota Press, 1952.

SIEGMEISTER, ELIE. "Three Points of View," *Musical Quarterly* 65 (1979), 281-86.

SLOAT, WARREN. *1929.* New York: Macmillan, 1979.

SLONIMSKY, NICOLAS. "Roy Harris." *Musical Quarterly* 33 (1947), 17-37.

SLONIMSKY, NICOLAS. *A Thing or Two About Music.* 1948. Reprint. Westport, Conn.: Greenwood, 1972.

SMITH, CECIL. *Worlds of Music.* 1952. Reprint. Westport, Conn.: Greenwood, 1973.

SMITH, JULIA. *Aaron Copland.* New York: Dutton, 1955.

SMITH, MOSES. *Koussevitzky.* New York: Allen, Towne & Heath, 1947.

SOUTHERN, EILEEN. *The Music of Black Americans.* New York: Norton, 1971.

SOROKIN, PITRIM A. *The Crisis of Our Age.* New York: Dutton, 1942.

SOROKIN, PITRIM A. *Society, Culture, and Personality.* New York: Cooper Square Publishers, 1969.

SPAETH, SIGMUND. *At Home with Music.* Garden City, N.Y.: Doubleday, Doran, 1945.

SPAETH, SIGMUND. *The Importance of Music.* New York: Fleet, 1963.

STODDARD, HOPE. *Symphony Conductors of the U.S.A.* New York: Crowell, 1957.

STOKOWSKI, LEOPOLD. *Music for All of Us.* New York: Simon & Schuster, 1943.

STRAUS, NOEL. "Nadia Boulanger Discusses the Moderns." *New York Times,* 2 April 1939, sec. X, 7.

TAUBMAN, HOWARD. *The Maestro: The Life of Arturo Toscanini.* New York: Simon & Schuster, 1951.

TAYLOR, DEEMS. *Music to My Ears.* New York: Simon & Schuster, 1949.

TAYLOR, DEEMS. *Of Men and Music.* New York: Simon & Schuster, 1945.

TAYLOR, JOSHUA C. *The Fine Arts in America.* Chicago: Univ. of Chicago Press, 1979.

TERKEL, STUDS. *Hard Times.* New York: Pantheon, 1970.

TERRY, WALTER. *The Dance in America,* rev. ed. New York: Harper & Row, 1971.

THOMPSON, RANDALL. "The Contemporary Scene in American Music." *Musical Quarterly* 18 (1932), 9-17.

THOMSON, VIRGIL. *American Music Since 1910.* New York: Holt, Rinehart & Winston, 1971.

THOMSON, VIRGIL. *The Art of Judging Music.* 1948. Reprint. Westport, Conn.: Greenwood, 1969.

THOMSON, VIRGIL. *Music Reviewed, 1940-1954.* New York: Vintage, 1967.

THOMSON, VIRGIL. *Music Right and Left.* 1951. Reprint. Westport, Conn.: Greenwood, 1969.

THOMSON, VIRGIL. *The Musical Scene.* 1945. Reprint. Westport, Conn.: Greenwood, 1968.

THOMSON, VIRGIL. *Virgil Thomson.* New York: Knopf, 1966.

ULANOV, BARRY. *The Two Worlds of American Art.* New York: Macmillan, 1965.

VALENTINE, C. W. *The Experimental Psychology of Beauty.* London: Methuen, 1962.

WECTER, DIXON. *The Age of Depression, 1929-1941.* New York: Macmillan, 1948.

WEIL, IRVING. "The American Scene Changes." *Modern Music* 6, no. 4 (1928-29), 3-9.

WEIL, SIMONE. *The Need for Roots,* trans. Arthur Wills. New York: Harper & Row, 1971.

WEISGALL, HUGO. "The Music of Henry Cowell." *Musical Quarterly* 45 (1959), 484-507.

WEISSMAN, ADOLPH. "The Tyranny of the Absolute." *Musical Quarterly* 2 (1925), 17-20.

WEITZ, MORRIS. *Philosophy of the Arts.* New York: Russell & Russell, 1964.

WHITHORNE, EMERSON. "Where Do We Go from Here?" *Musical Quarterly* 4 (1927), 9-14.

WHITMAN, WILLSON. *Bread and Circus: A Study of the Federal Theatre.* New York: Oxford Univ. Press, 1937.

ZELOMEK, A. W. *A Changing America.* New York: Wiley, 1959.

Index